MINSKY'S BURLESQUE

• • • •

MINSKY'S BURLESQUE

Morton Minsky
and Milt Machlin

ARBOR HOUSE
NEW YORK

Manufactured in the United States of America

10 9 8 7 6 5 4 3 2 1

Library of Congress Cataloging in Publication Data
Minsky, Morton.
  Minsky's burlesque.
  Bibliography: p. 311
  1. Burlesque (Theater)—United States.
  2. Minsky, Morton.   3. Theatrical managers—United
States—Biography.   I. Machlin, Milt.   II. Title.
PN1948.U6M5   1986   792.7′0973   85-20137

ISBN: 0-87795-743-6

All photos are from the author's personal, private collections.

The lines from "National Winter Garden" from THE COMPLETE POEMS AND SELECTED LETTERS AND PROSE OF HART CRANE, edited by Brom Weber, are reprinted by permission of Liveright Publishing Corporation. Copyright 1933, © 1958, 1966 by Liveright Publishing Corporation.

THE LITTLE FLOWER © 1983 Lawrence Elliot. Reprinted courtesy of William Morrow.

To my dear, darling wife, Ruth, for her courage,
understanding, generosity, and unselfish love and devotion
MORTON MINSKY

CHAPTER

1

ETHEL DE VEAUX: Oh, I think I am in love with you! Yes, I am—take my eyes. Take my arms. Take my lips.

JOEY FAYE: Sure, the best parts you keep for yourself!

ETHEL (*with a rhythmic chant*): Well, you can meet me round the corner in a half an hour. Meet me round the corner in half an hour. (*Turns to Joey, grinding and bumping to a slow, rhythmic beat.*) M-e-e-t m-e r-o-u-n-d t-h-e c-o-r-n-e-r i-n a h-a-l-f a-n h-o-u-r! (*She bumps; Joey's hat flies off although he's fifty feet away from her.*)

JOEY (*as she exits*): Wind that up and set it for six o'clock!

I WAS ONLY fifteen and still wearing knickers when I got my first look at the bouncing, bawdy, and often stimulating world of burlesque—a branch of the theater in which my family name was to become a byword. Minsky's Burlesque had been operating in a sixth-floor theater known as the National Winter Garden, at Second Avenue and Houston Street, for a year when I got my first chance to see the show everybody was talking about.

The Winter Garden was in a building actually owned by my father, and his office was on the same floor as the burlesque show, but my father never set foot in the theater once it had become devoted to burlesque. He would walk stiffly past the row of pictures depicting the delectable lineaments of the Minsky chorus line, muttering to himself, *"Nofkes! Nofkes!"* If you didn't know, *nofkes* means "prostitutes" in Yiddish.

But he had never actually forbidden *me* to go into the theater. In fact, since he preferred not to talk to my brothers Herbert, Abe, and Billy about anything concerning burlesque, it turned out to be my job to run errands between my brothers and my father—carrying legal papers back and forth between the theater and the apartment building where we lived on 10th Street and Second Avenue, about ten blocks apart.

I suppose one reason that my father didn't actually forbid me to see a burlesque show was because he had faith in my virtue, and he was right about that. My virtue had not actually been put to a test as yet, and it remained pristine.

At this point I had yet to date a girl or even be alone in the company of one, other than my sisters. About the closest I got to the female anatomy was in the office of my friend Harold Frankel's father, who was a doctor. We spent hours in Dr. Frankel's library going through his medical textbooks trying to make head or tail (you should excuse the expression) out of the female anatomy, which was illustrated largely in the form of colored sketches complete with veins and arteries and various reproductive organs, but hardly the sort of artwork that would turn even so eager a student of anatomy as I was into a tower of lust. Harold, who claimed to know something about it, assured me that the real thing was much more exciting than the pictures in his father's anatomy texts.

On this particular spring evening in 1917, my father had sent me over after dinner to pick up something from his office. I got to the sixth floor at about 8:00 P.M. I'd never been to the sixth floor that late in the evening. It was very different from the daytime. The show hadn't yet started, and the men were still filing into the theater. The empty lobby that I was used to seeing had been transformed by their excited voices and masculine anticipation.

Trying to look as grown-up as I could in my Brooks Brothers' knicker suit, I sidled past the straggling ticket holders into my brothers' office. It was a large room, with a huge safe in the center, in which the box-office receipts were kept overnight. Billy kept his good Scotch in the vault too. He said it aged better in the presence of money.

The secretary who worked there during the day, a pretty young girl with theatrical ambitions, had left at 5:30 P.M. Herbert was alone in the office with his typewriter, behind his big mahogany desk, going through a pile of contracts. It was usually Herbert who stayed in the office taking care of the paperwork involved in running the business. He had been to Columbia University and had a law degree, and this seemed suitable. My brothers Billy and Abe seemed to be more involved with the actual theater end of things, going to agents, scouting talent, and arranging for the acquisition of material.

Herbert was deeply immersed in his paperwork that night—evidently too busy even for a chat with me. He looked up, temporarily distracted by my presence.

"Here for father?" he asked me.

I nodded.

"Finished?"

I nodded again.

"Then why don't you go in and catch the show? You're right on time; they're just starting now, and I'm going to be busy here for at least another hour or so. We can walk home together afterward."

Herbert was actually in the Army Corps of Engineers at Bush Terminal, Brooklyn, at that time, but he was on temporary leave, so that he was living at home sharing a bedroom with me. I didn't mind it at all. He had decorated the room just like a theater, with colored spotlights that the theater electrician set up for him with an impressive array of cords and switches. Sometimes when we were together in the room he would put on a sound and light show for me, singing a popular song of the time, something like "Because," as he turned the room every color of the rainbow.

But that bedroom show was just an appetizer. The real thing had something that Herbert could not supply—sex.

"Would you like to see the show?"

"Sure," I said, trying not to show my excitement. I'd been hearing vague stories about what went on in the theater for over a year from my classmates at Stuyvesant High School. Now I would have a chance to see what my father disapproved of so severely and made the others smile lewdly at the mention of the name "Minsky."

I slipped into the theater and took an aisle seat as unobtrusively as possible as the lights were going down. The air was redolent with the smell of pipes, cigars, and cigarettes, for smoking was still permitted in theaters in those days. The walls of the theater were concrete, so there was no fire hazard, and the floors were of multicolored tile. Intermixed with the tobacco smells was the sweet and heady aroma of talcum powder, perfume, and greasepaint drifting from behind the closed curtains. On the walls were mural paintings of dramatic scenes from Shakespeare, mainly *Othello*. Those parts of the walls that had no murals were painted a dark, brooding red and adorned with silk drapes in various shades that complemented the colors of the tiles on the floor. The seats, brown wood, were very uncomfortable, but no one cared. On stage the first curtain was a red velvet traveler. Red was the predominant color of the auditorium. As far as my brothers were concerned, there was something exciting about the color that symbolized the feelings they wanted to express—drama, romance, mystery, and, well, *sex.*

Herbert had been very involved with the psychology of color. Blue, he told me once, was cool and remote. Green, soothing. Yellow, cheerful. But red or magenta—that was the color for Minsky.

Originally he had tried using red gels on the lights too, but he decided that it made the place look too much like a brothel, so he modified the color to magenta, which flattered the flesh tones of the women in the show. My brothers had only recently spent the money on power cables for that stage lighting—at least a couple of thousand dollars. Billy, I remember, complained about the expense; but before that the stage had been quite dark. The only lights came from a footlight trough that gave an eerie look to the performers, illuminating the bottoms but not the tops of their legs, their chins, and sometimes their double chins—although Billy had determined that all the girls working for Minsky's would have to conform to a slimmer image.

As the magenta lights focused on the still-closed curtain, there was an aura of murmuring expectancy in the house, and I began to get a tingling in my feet and hands in anticipation of the entertainment to come.

The fourteen men in the orchestra pit were still tuning up, and even those cacophonous sounds were adding to my excitement. The conductor approached the podium to scattered applause, more for what was to come than for his music, and raised his baton. The audience was not exactly made up of music critics, but they manifested considerable impatience with the musical introduction.

The red curtains finally rose into the flies, and here was a chorus of eighteen girls in what I can only call abbreviated costumes. In fact, they were wearing short red tutus over their leotards and black lace garter belts, and they were wrapped in masses of feathers, also red. They looked exactly as I imagined the French chorus girls did in all those places that my brother Abe was always talking about when he went to Paris. A larger and more toothsome display of female flesh than I had ever seen in my life. I'd never even seen *one* girl in such a sketchy outfit let alone eighteen. They were singing and dancing to some number that had nothing to do with any story line. I couldn't catch many of the words, but their song had something to do with everybody getting together and having a wonderful time. The men in the audience were certainly having a wonderful time. They leaned over the railing in the loges. Whistles and catcalls punctuated the music. One of them, a bit tipsy, in a big black top hat, almost fell into the orchestra, and was just saved at the last minute by another playboy, who wasn't much soberer than he was. To tell you the truth, their singing was not exactly from the Metropolitan Opera or even the *Ziegfeld Follies,* but when the girls started dancing and kicking their legs in unison, I found myself becoming stimulated in a way that I had never been when I was reading Dr. Frankel's anatomy books. Keep in mind this was in preflapper days, when skirts were down to the ankles and calves, knees and thighs simply not seen in public. I felt my face flushing with excitement, and little beads of sweat popped out on my brow.

God knows how excited I might have become if the brief chorus number had not ended, to be succeeded by the comic turn. The audience laughed and hooted as soon as the comic half of the team came out. After all, he had a big putty nose and baggy pants. The straight man was dapper in his striped suit, vest, and straw hat, and it always seemed that he would try and victimize poor, old baggy pants. The lines were certainly "straight," sometimes as simple as "hello," but it all had to do with the *way* in which those lines were delivered. The rolling of the eyes and the exaggerated double takes gave a significant change to the lines that in my youth I didn't always understand. For instance, at that time, I did not quite get the bit where the straight man gazed into the widely gaping waistband of the tramp comic, took off his hat, and held it delicately over his heart as though in mourning for something that had died. At that point in my life what was assumed to have died somewhere down in the baggy depths of the comic's pants had not yet *lived* for me, let alone died. But the gags came quick and fast, and even though I didn't understand half of them, the audience's laughter was so infectious that I found myself roaring in appreciation. I was also probably laughing with relief after the prurient tension engendered by the legs and thighs of the opening dance act.

Next came a woman elegantly but completely clothed who had a very nice soprano voice and sang "Un bel di" by Puccini, a number that was probably inserted at the suggestion of my brother Herbert, an opera fan, as a means to elevate the cultural level of the rowdy audience.

The next act was, I suppose, meant to be a reversion to some of the sexually stimulating material for which Minsky's had become known. It was the Cooch dancer, a lady of uncertain age but enough to have gained vast experience, who went through a series of amazing contortions and gyrations. The audience applauded wildly when she was finished and seemed very appreciative of what she had done. By now, after seeing the much younger and more shapely legs and body parts of the chorus, I could not find the contortionist all that exciting, but the rest of the audience wasn't that critical.

Then came a dramatic sketch, of all things—a serious one. There would be a slight story line that always wound up in tragedy and tears. It reminded me much of the pattern of the plays that were showing in the Yiddish theater downstairs in the same building. Frankly, my entire attention was not upon it—I was still thinking of the feathers and the garter belts.

Anyway, the sketch dealt with a young man who leaves his family and goes to the city. As might be expected, he falls in with the wrong companions and ends up breaking his poor old mother's heart. He feels so bad about this that he shoots himself. The audience seems almost as concerned about the fate of this *schlemiel* as they were excited by the bouncing legs and fannies of the chorus. A long sigh is heard from the crowd when the profligate son's old mother, looking just like Whistler's Mother, is shown in the last scene walking back and forth in front of her parlor window, waiting for the son who would never return.

Of course, I recognized the poor, old mother. She was Mother Annie Elms, the stage mother who was supposed to look after the girls and see that they minded their morals. I'd seen her in the office, and she always patted me on the head and offered me sweets in dirty paper from the pockets of her old cardigan sweaters. Since I always turned them down, I'm not sure it isn't the same candy that she'd been offering me since I was little. But she didn't seem to mind. Mother Elms never seemed to mind anything. Of course, at the time what I did not know was that ninety percent of the time she was filled to the eyeballs with gin.

Then came another chorus number, and I was in blue heaven. Although the girls weren't very good as dancers or singers, they were certainly young and pretty. I was still in a state of euphoria when the next act came on—a very young and extremely attractive girl, the *soubrette* (every burlesque company had one). The soubrette was the youngest of the featured women and often in training for a more active part in the program. In this case, she sang a couple of popular songs and danced around fetchingly, giving an occasional flash of her legs. It was all pretty tame stuff, I suppose—those were the days before the striptease or anything like that, but it was enough to get my blood churning. This time in earnest. I thought that this *soubrette*—her name was Ethel De Veaux—was the most beautiful creature I had ever seen in my life. Since she was the youngest one in the company—probably in her teens—it was easy for me to imagine myself possibly actually speaking to her. I might even ask her out for a soda or a walk. After all, the theater did belong to my brothers. But no . . . I wouldn't let myself think of that—yet. Actually, from the time Ethel appeared my mind clouded over. There was another comedy scene involving a woman, a comic, and a straight man and another chorus number, and then just before closing, a troop of acrobats from vaudeville and at last, the finale—but by this time my mind was awash in dreams of Miss De Veaux.

The entire company assembled on stage with the chorus, and they sang a finale number with a reprise of some of the songs in the first half. This was followed by the intermission. Everybody got out of the seats to walk to the back.

As yet, there was no candy butcher to hawk the virtues of postcards from Paris or books that revealed lubricious secrets when held up to the light. I'll tell you all about that later. But at that time there was a stand in the back where they sold hot dogs, soda water, and popcorn. I went back and had some strawberry syrup diluted with seltzer—we called it a *shpritz.*

The second half of the show was much like the first half—comedy acts, dancers, and so on, but a bit shorter. As I recall, there was a big classroom comedy scene, with three or four of the comics and several of the women featured who played in the skits and were called talking ladies. The whole thing didn't end until about a quarter to eleven. It was the latest I'd ever been out at night alone.

I was still dreaming about my sight of Ethel De Veaux in the second half of the show. It was true that she didn't have bare legs, but her stockings were so tight that you could imagine very well what was underneath them. The red and black coloring of her abbreviated dress covered with spangles and sequins gave her the unreal beauty of a fairy-tale princess. I found her very, very attractive. I constructed an instant plan of how to meet her in person.

CHAPTER

2

ANN CORIO (*as customer in sporting goods store*): I'll take that baseball.

MAX FURMAN: One baseball!

CORIO: I'll take that glove and mask.

FURMAN: Glove and mask coming up! (*Puts them on the counter.*)

CORIO: And give me a bat.

FURMAN (*doing a take*): Yes, madam. What size?

CORIO: A nice big one!

FURMAN (*holding up bat*): Like *this?*

CORIO (*Checking out bat*): Just the right size.

FURMAN: Tell me, madam, are you sure this is all you want?

CORIO: Why, yes. My boss said that if I played ball with him he'd give me a raise tonight!

BEFORE THE TIME the final curtain came down and I had to meet Herbert to go home, I shoved my way toward the steps of the stage, battling against the tide of overstimulated men leaving the theater. At the stage steps my legs were actually shivering with excitement. I had to see Ethel. This was it. I was in love. I wasn't sure what I would say or do when I met her, but I figured I would deal with that later. I knew one thing. I had to have one more look at that beautiful face before I left the theater.

9

I tried to sneak past the electrician, who was standing at stage right in front of his board, but, of course, he noticed me out of the corner of his eye.

"Hey, boy! Nobody allowed . . . Oh, it's you, kid. What're you doing here, Morton?"

We were old friends. I had met him during the many nights he spent in my bedroom wiring up Herbert's magic lights.

"Gotta see my brother," I mumbled, my eyes downcast.

"Oh yeah." He waved his hand absently toward the backstage and turned back to his buttons and switches.

Backstage was pandemonium. Movement everywhere as stage-hands rushed around seemingly with no special purpose. Some were moving pieces of scenery from one side of the stage to the other. The propman was standing at his table making sure that everything was accounted for—the bladders for the comics with which they hit one another, the whiskey bottles, the funny hats, the seltzer bottle . . . they've all got to be ready for the next show. He didn't even give me a look. You realize that, although I had met some of the people, I'd never been backstage before.

I wandered around wondering where the women's dressing rooms were. My face must have been as hot and bright as a magenta spot. I noticed a stairway going down to my left and started toward it. A young fellow came bounding up the stairs as I reached the top and grinned at me.

"Here to pay your respects?"

The question was cheerful, and the young man vanished. I figured if he'd been down there, it must be okay, and I started down the stairs. But all I found down there was a large, open room filled with a bunch of tables and mirrors and clothing racks. A few men were removing their makeup. I recognized some of them as comics and some of them as straight men. It was obvious that Ethel was not there. I climbed up again before anyone could say anything to me, full of guilt. But nobody really seemed to be paying attention. Then I found myself looking into the kindly but snozzled face of Annie Elms.

"What're you doing here, boy?" Her tone was severe. But then she recognized me. "Oh, it's little Mr. Morton, is it?"

"I'm looking for my brother!"

My voice was quick and breathless, and even though it was true that I was sort of looking for Herbert, I felt as though I was being caught in a lie.

"Well, isn't he in his office, then?" Annie Elms said, smelling a rat.

I was certain that she had read my mind and turned, if possible, even redder than before. But before I could come up with an explanation, a door opened at one side of the stage and two girls appeared. I was struck speechless because one of the girls was *Ethel!* Without her makeup she looked even prettier than I thought she looked onstage. My tongue stuck to the roof of my mouth, which fell open as I gaped at her with soulful yearning. But she brushed past me without even a glance. She and her girl friend were talking and laughing in low, excited tones. I had to realize even in my confused state that it was not likely that she would stop and chat with a kid in a pepper and salt Brooks Brothers' suit complete with knee pants.

By the time Ethel was out of sight, Annie was involved with a problem with one of the other Minsky Rosebuds, as we called the girls. I took the opportunity to escape, and ran down the stage steps almost into the arms of my brother Herbert, who had come down the aisle looking for me.

He put his arm around my shoulder and smiled at me benevolently. "Well, did you like the show?"

"Who is Ethel De Veaux?" I asked, my heart thumping.

Herbert's smile grew broader. "She's a very nice, sweet girl. But she's a little bit older than you, and I don't think she's the type that Momma and Poppa would be pleased to have you meet."

I turned as red as the theater curtains and stammered, "I . . . I . . . I didn't mean . . . I mean, I was just curious."

Herbert patted me on the back as we walked the few blocks to the Minsky apartment on 10th Street.

"Listen, kid. I don't blame you. She's very beautiful. But we're owners and we can't allow ourselves to become involved with the theatrical help. It wouldn't be right. You know what I mean?"

I *knew* what he meant. Ironically, Herbert was the one who would ultimately violate that rule.

"You've been backstage?" he asked, apparently seeing nothing wrong with that. "Someday, when I have a little more time, I'll take you around and introduce you to everyone . . . the girls and the comics."

Oh, dream of dreams! To be presented as the youngest Minsky brother. I was sure that Ethel would have to pay some attention to me then. By that time maybe I'd be able to get some long pants. But I thought that the best thing was to say nothing to Herbert at that moment about my high ambitions. We walked home in companionable silence, with me muttering Ethel De Veaux's name under my breath practically every step of the way. Although Herbert was the closest to me of all my brothers in age—he was eleven years older—I decided that I wouldn't tell him my new secret, romantic ideal. He had already indicated that he didn't approve of mingling with the theatrical personnel. How could *he* understand my longing for Ethel?

CHAPTER 3

COSTELLO: I need a lotta money right away!
ABBOTT: I'll get you a loan in the bank.
COSTELLO: Who wants to be alone with you in a bank?
ABBOTT: I'm trying to tell you, you can get a lien against your house.
COSTELLO: Lean against the house? Whatsa matter with the joint? Is it going to fall down?

YOU MIGHT SAY it all began in a church. Not that my father had anything to do with churches as such. He came from a long line of very devout Orthodox Jews. My great-grandfather, in fact, in the old country was one of the most learned men in the area, and after he went blind from the years of rabbinical studies, he became quite famous as the Blind *Magid* from Grodno.

My grandfather, Aaron Selzer, didn't follow the Great Magid into the rabbinate but instead became a feed merchant. Meanwhile, the persecution of the Jews in Russia and Poland continued fiercely, and almost every Jew who could get the money had hopes of going to the Golden Land—America. Aaron decided that his second son, Aryeh Lev, should be the first in his family to go.

Following the custom of the time, Aryeh Lev took on a new name for his immigration. I'm not sure how it came about that he chose the name "Louis," but "Minsky" was adopted from the city of Minsk, which was the nearest metropolis to the *shtetl* in which my

13

family lived. That was how my father, now Louis Minsky, came to Manhattan's Lower East Side in 1883. He had married my mother, Esther Litski, in Russia in 1881. My oldest brother, called Avram when he was born but renamed Abe when he became Americanized, was actually born in Russia in 1882. As was frequently the custom in those days, my father came on ahead to try to build a nest egg so he could bring his wife and child over at a later date. He got his start as many of the Jewish newcomers did, as a peddler with a pack on his back, and he was some terrific salesman.

Just two years after he'd sold the first book of pins out of his pack, Louis had saved up enough to open a store—Minsky Wholesale Dry Goods and Notions, L. Minsky, Prop. Downstairs were the warehouse, the showroom, and the office, and upstairs in the Orchard Street brownstone was my father's apartment. When his business needed more space, he moved to Forsythe Street. The business dealt mostly with supplying pushcart peddlers with the goods they needed. My father was one of the few who would give credit to any Jew as long as he had an "honest face" and went to *shul* regularly.

By 1890 the whole population of the Lower East Side had doubled; the old brownstones that had been the principal buildings in the area were torn down and replaced by tall tenements.

This spelled the end of the era of the foot peddler, who was my father's best customer. New shops and department stores became the places where the new citizens went to buy their goods. My father decided to get out of the peddler trade and open a general dry-goods store.

In a way this might have been our family's first contact with show business, because for his new store Pop bought the biggest building on Grand Street, which was called the Grand Museum. It was a downtown version of the Eden Musée, a famous, old waxworks and freak show on 23rd Street.

By the time my father bought the building, there was a theater on the ground floor, which played a one-act drama called *The Honest Hebrew*. Between shows there were four rounds of boxing. On the second floor were a magic act and an illusionist. The third floor contained a curio hall, which included a ventriloquist, an armless wonder, a fat woman, and Herman the Strong Man. The top floor had an act called the Irish Exiles, which was a banjo quartet, and a minstrel company. As the new landlord, my father's first job, which he didn't mind at all, was to throw them all out.

Now that he had a dry-goods store he competed with a lot of the older establishments on the street, such as Arnold Constable, Lord & Taylor, and Milgrim's. Being a newcomer, he felt that the only way to win away their customers was with clever stunts and promotion, many of which were then new to retailing.

For instance, he put a soda fountain in the entranceway, figuring that shoppers struggling to the area by trolley or ferry from Brooklyn or rumbling in on the sweaty cars of the Manhattan el, might arrive in the area parched with thirst. For two cents he would give them a glass of seltzer or for a nickel, a sarsparilla. There the seltzer or sarsparilla would be, all ready at the door at *Minsky's.* Another gimmick introduced by my father was to pass out free *matzoh* at Passover. I believe he also originated the throwaway newspaper and the advertising "spectacular." He published a newspaper called the Minsky *News,* much like today's "shoppers." Between the full-page and half-page store ads he included morsels of neighborhood news and gossip. As for the advertising "spectacular," he sewed together a number of bedsheets and with a magic lantern projected slides on them with old proverbs and jokes of the day.

The new store became an enormous success owing to my father's innovative schemes as well as a place of employment for his far-flung family. I must admit that not all of the family made ideal employees. In fact, some of them were stealing Pop blind.

There's an old family story about my father walking home with one of his friends, a lawyer. They passed the home in which one of my father's cousins lived. He'd held a job for some time with him as a floor manager in the store.

"How can you stand it?" his friend, the lawyer, said. "Look in those windows—the velvet drapes, the crystal chandelier. How can a man live like that if he isn't stealing you blind? Even from here I can hear his little girl practicing on a grand piano. There's no way on earth that he could have earned all that money on what you're paying him. Why don't you fire him?"

"It's like this," my father explained, falling back on his Talmudic logic. *"If* I fire him, I'll have to hire a new man. This *schmendrick* has stolen so much already that he doesn't need any more. But if I hire a new man, he'll have to start robbing me from scratch. I'll lose twice as much!"

My father was becoming rapidly Americanized, but he still remained at heart the son of a rabbi. He wouldn't allow any artwork to be hung on his walls, considering this all too frivolous, although we had Oriental rugs and fancy mahogany furniture. He never went to a concert and never saw a theatrical performance in his life. In his free time he continued to study the Talmud. Yet, as he got richer, he spent quite a large amount on clothes. I don't think he ever had less than twenty hand-tailored suits in his wardrobe, and he always wore a diamond stickpin and carried an expensive, silver-topped cane.

By 1895 my father had so much clout that Big Tim Sullivan, the Tammany Hall boss in the area, asked him to run for alderman, figuring that Louis Minsky could definitely deliver the Jewish vote in a ward where eighty percent of the voters were Jewish. My father was honored. And he used the same promotion and publicity tricks in his campaign—lantern slides, leaflets, and the rest—that he used in building up his business.

My father won his district by a landslide, and Tammany, by fair means or foul—and many of their practices could be called at least questionable—was again in control.

Living on the Lower East Side at that time was scarcely a picnic. In Russia the Jews were subjected to pogroms, but at least they had fresh air. The Lower East Side was described at that time by Jacob Riis, the famous sociologist, as the location of the most ferocious streets in the nation. Tuberculosis abounded. Prostitutes came naturally out of the poverty. There were at least 2,000 people to an acre. Fire, murder, suicide, and theft were all common in this largely Jewish warren. The houses in which the refugees from persecution lived had wooden stairs, dark, unlighted halls, outside privies, and shrieking babies. Some said that Tammany, which had been instrumental in getting my father elected alderman, was responsible for much of the vice in these slums. There was some truth to that, but at least my father, in his position, was able to see that the Jews in his ward got their share of the 10,000 pounds of turkey given away for Christmas, the 6,000 pairs of shoes, and the 800 tons of coal that Tammany gave to its supporters. And some said that my father was the only really conscientious member of the board of aldermen, and he fought hard for the Sixth Ward.

As I recall my childhood on the Lower East Side and later, it was basically a happy one, but there were tragedies in the family. The first occurred when my brother Benjamin drowned in the Hudson River in Nyack, New York, at the age of nineteen. He was then attending City College, and he was with my brother Herbert, who was at Columbia at the time. They were out in a rowboat. I was only about eight or nine years old then, but I still remember the call from the river and the screams of my mother sitting up on the patio of the hotel overlooking the river.

Then, only eleven months later, my brother Irving, who was a graduate attorney and was already practicing law, died of a spinal ailment. These were shattering experiences for my parents, although they're dim in my own memory. I also remember in those early days taking rides with my father in his luxurious car, a Winton Six, one of the very first on Second Avenue. It was chauffeur-driven, and we went to a very famous restaurant, the Petit Trianon at Lake Ronkonkoma. My sister Isabel and I would sit on the jump seats, and my mother and dad would sit facing us, and we'd drive down to Long Island, sometimes to the Hotel Nassau in Long Beach or Reisenweber's in Brighton Beach. They didn't serve kosher food there, but my father would sometimes relax his orthodoxy on such occasions. I recall staying at a hotel called the Ricadonna at the end of Ocean Parkway at Coney Island.

Motion pictures were often being filmed right in that area—the old silent comedians John Bunny and Marie Dressler and sometimes even Charlie Chaplin shooting one-reelers.

The Minsky family could be said to have gotten its start in show business in 1908, when my oldest brother, Abe, discovered that when the earlier immigrants—Germans and Scandinavians—left the area, they had left behind a big Lutheran church on Houston Street.

A friend of Abe's suggested to him that if they could raise the money to take over the building, they could take a stab at a new wrinkle in the entertainment business—the nickelodeon—which was named for the five-cent peice required as admission. Motion pictures were new and exciting, and even the exorbitant charge of five cents and the lack of comfort—the building still had the hard, Protestant pews—couldn't keep customers out. My father wasn't exactly sure what sort of films were being shown by Abe and his partner in the theater, which they named the Houston Street Hippodrome, but the nickelodeon was a success from the start. Abe never even had to put money into redecorating or refurbishing the old church, and the customers found that the racks that once held hymnals were marvelous storage bins for the bagels, salamis, and other eatables they brought with them for nourishment through the long program. As for New Testament murals that remained on the walls, they could hardly be seen in the darkness.

Between reels of films like *The Butler and the Upstairs Maid* Abe had a lanternman project slides in Yiddish and English warning people against spitting, noise-making, reading titles aloud, and pickpockets.

Of course, my father knew something about slides, since he had used them in his store and for his political campaigns, so he assumed that nothing wrong was going on in the old church, and things went along swimmingly for Abe for at least three years.

Somewhere in that third year, however, my father got wind of the spicy goings-on in the Hippodrome and put his foot down. No son of Louis Minsky was going to make his living showing dirty movies. He ordered Abe to sell the theater and get into the real-estate and construction business with him. His new business was, in fact, thriving. But Abe, who was always thought of as the playboy of our family, was restless, even though he managed to make some money selling and building houses.

Abe was part of the new generation of Jews who were learning liberal, Yankee ways. A man named Saul Birns opened a piano and gramophone shop right across the street from our house. A neighborhood kid named George Gershwin lived upstairs, and Birns allowed him to wind his phonograph and play records.

Meanwhile, my brother Billy was becoming even more involved in affairs outside the Lower East Side. When he was still in his teens, he talked his way into a job on Park Row as a society reporter for the New York *World*.

Billy did not exactly have what you would call a formal education. He went to grammar school and stayed in high school for six months. He always told people he had a G.E. degree, by which he meant a "gutter education." He started as a messenger boy for a Wall Street firm, then he was a telephone boy on the New York Stock Exchange, and it was just after that that he got his job on the *World*. He was sharp, bright, and scrappy and had considerable charm. As a reporter he interviewed J. P. Morgan and was the only newspaperman present at the Count Szechenyi and Gladys Vanderbilt wedding. He got in by dressing in his old messenger-boy clothes. For this coup he was rewarded with the assignment of society re-

porter, of all things. From then on Billy patrolled the society hang-
outs in an entirely different kind of uniform, a tuxedo. Billy's first involvement with the theater had to do with my father's new project.
With Max D. Steuer, Pop had decided to erect the National Theater
on Houston Street to present Jewish plays, which were then very
popular on the Lower East Side. Originally, a producer had con-
tracted to put the shows on, but once the theater was built, the operators backed out of the deal.

This was in the summer of 1912. Earlier that year Billy had,
through a gambler acquaintance of his named Beansie Rosenthal,
been tipped off to evidence concerning the corrupt activities of New
York's most notorious crooked cop, Police Lieutenant Charles
Becker, the number one shakedown artist and strong-arm man of
the whole Midtown area. To collect his graft Becker had a group of
bagmen who could have stepped out of a chamber of horrors. These
included a man named Billiard Ball Jack because he had a head like
Kojak's, Big Jake Zelig, a mad-dog killer from our own ghetto, and
Gyp the Blood, whose real name was Harry Horowitz. These thugs
were helping Becker to apply muscle to all of the prostitution and
gambling places in mid-Manhattan. Billy began to turn up facts in-
dicating the extent of Becker's crookedness and his collusion with
the underworld and his stories were given a big play in the *World*.
But Becker, who thought he could get away with anything, and
practically did at that time, wasn't one to take this sort of press exposure sitting down. Meanwhile, Billy's stories, which were by-lined,
had already resulted in the jailing of a good many of Becker's racke-
teer associates. The stories were excellent ones, and Billy found himself shining in the spotlight of local heroism. Unfortunately for Billy,
one of the gamblers who had been put away as a result of his ex-
posés, was let out on probation in 1912 and decided it was time to
get even with my brother.

Billy was coming home after a late night's work at the *World*,
climbing the steps of our Manhattan brownstone when he heard
someone shout his name. He turned and found himself looking right
at the barrel of a loaded revolver. Reacting with a nimbleness
learned from dodging rocks and other missiles in the ghetto, Billy
dropped to the pavement and the gambler's shot passed over his
head. Lying there on a Manhattan pavement, his usually immacu-
late tuxedo grimy with street dust, Billy was suddenly taken by the

conviction that crime didn't pay either for the perpetrator or for the reporter.

Next day he called my father with a new thought.

"Listen, Pop," Billy said, "you know that deal you've been talking to Abe about, showing movies on the National Theatre roof? Well, I think I'm interested in it after all. I think I've just about had it with the newspaper business."

He started to give details of his night's experience, then thought of the reaction my father would have to it, and decided to keep the information to himself.

After his initial arrangement with the acting company had fallen through, my father leased the ground-floor theater to a Yiddish acting company. There was a magnificent stage, and the actors were the great stars of Yiddish theater in the days when it *was* theater— the famous Boris Thomashefsky, Jacob Adler (the father of Stella and Luther Adler), and David Kessler.

(Every time I hear Thomashefsky's name I think of the joke they used to tell about him. Thomashefsky became one of the most successful actors in the history of the American Yiddish stage, and one of the most wealthy. But he was also noted for his stinginess, as well as for his roving eye for women. One of the stories they told was how a woman had come to Thomashefsky in his dressing room and offered herself to him for amorous purposes. When Thomashefsky had finished availing himself of the lovely lady's charms, he reached into his vest pocket and proudly presented her with two passes to the evening's performance.

"You are a charming woman. Now take these passes and enjoy yourself. They are the best seats in the house."

The young woman threw herself on her knees, clasping Thomashefsky about the legs. "I don't need theater tickets. I am starving. I must have bread or I will starve."

Thomashefsky looked down on her with a sad smile. "If you want bread, make love to a baker. From Thomashefsky you get theater tickets.")

Above the Yiddish theater there was a second auditorium, a portion of the top three floors. The sixth floor was the orchestra level, and the theater extended up through the eighth floor. In the rest of the space there were meeting rooms, which my father also rented out, but Billy always called it the roof. In those days roof-garden theaters were extremely fashionable. Thomashefsky, Adler, and company had a twenty-one-year lease for the ground-floor theater, and Billy Minsky, although he recognized that several theaters were operating successfully as roof gardens, was not thrilled at trying to run a theater that required a sixth-floor elevator ride—even when the elevators worked, which was not always a certainty.

My brother Irving, who died at the age of twenty-one, was engaged to an attractive woman named Rae Kaufman. Rae had a gorgeous, tall red-haired sister named Mary. Billy had always been very attracted to her. When Irving died, they naturally spent a lot of time together, mourning his death, and this developed into a romance that lasted the rest of their lives. Billy married Mary in 1913, and shortly afterward they had a son, Robert. Rae eventually married Irwin Steingut, who became an important political leader in New York State. Billy and Mary lived on Eastern Parkway, close to the Brooklyn Museum at first, but as Billy became more successful, he also acquired a home in the elegant private resort of Seagate on the shore not far from Coney Island.

The marriage went very well and Billy was great friends with Mary's father, Dr. I. Kaufman, an astronomer and mathematician. I remember that his pet name for her was Lovey, and she called him Ookey. It was a bit sickening.

As long as Billy's end of show business was exhibiting movies, everything was hunky-dory between them. Later, however, there would be some problems.

So now that Billy was out of the newspaper business, he joined Abe in managing the building, and between them they agreed to go into the movie business in the sixth-floor theater. My father really wasn't thrilled by this, but Abe showed him the books of his old Hippodrome Nickelodeon and convinced him that films were sure-fire money-makers. Besides, Abe promised Pop this was not going to be just a cheap nickelodeon. He would not feature the spicy back-stairs romps of butlers and maids but the great dramas of the day, which were now being made in film. So, reluctantly, my father agreed, and he was now the owner of two theaters—in the top and bottom of the Houston Street building. But despite the fact that he was a theatrical entrepreneur, he still never basically approved of such frivolity and to my knowledge never actually set foot in the theater.

Somehow, even though the roof garden was very poorly designed as a theater, requiring all sorts of zigzagging and detouring to get to the orchestra seats, it prospered. In fact, from the beginning it made more money than the more prestigious National Theatre did downstairs. It made so much money, in fact, that Abe and Billy between them decided that they would stop working in my father's real-estate business and devote themselves full time to the movie house. Taking a look at the books, my father couldn't disagree.

Nickelodeons were growing at an enormous rate. In 1904 there was not a single five-cent theater devoted to moving pictures in the country. By 1907 there were 5,000 nickelodeons. About 1908 the "pick-vaud" combination really became hot, with storefront nickelodeons replacing the old museum variety combination. There were over 200 of these store shows in New York City alone at that time, showing movies and vaudeville for five cents in the afternoon and ten cents at night.

The movie house was making a good profit, such a good profit that when Billy and Abe retired from the real-estate business, my father raised their rent.

My father was secretly pleased too to see Abe doing well in business. His early history had been something that could well have been featured as the plot of one of his own nickelodeon films. Gambling, women, a disastrous first marriage, which was about as long as the ceremony. Abe had cut a wide swath through the wild life of the world and had not exactly paid much attention to the advice of my father, or my mother either for that matter. In fact, it was my mother who kept him financially afloat by surreptitiously lending him money whenever he ran out. When he got out of high school, Abe had gone into the dry-goods business with my father on Grand Street. That store was doing so well that after my father was elected alderman, he decided that he ought to open a branch in the growing state of Texas, and he sent Abe down to Houston to take charge.

That was a big mistake. Abe spent half the time shooting craps and half the time chasing the wild Western women. In short order the Texas branch went bankrupt and Abe returned sheepishly to New York. By the time my father set him up in the Hippodrome, he had spent at least ten years in various business ventures—all of them unsuccessful.

What Abe and Billy were telling my father was true. Films were

now becoming longer and more complicated, and a whole generation of film stars was being born. Billy and Abe got their hands on as
many of the new five-reel specials as they could. By 1915 they were
running such epics as D. W. Griffith's *The Birth of a Nation* and
Thomas Ince's *Civilization,* as well as J. Stuart Blackton's *The Life of
Moses.* With the longer films came elaborate musical scores requiring
twelve- or fourteen-piece orchestras. The roof-top theater was really
one of the most glamorous spots in the somewhat intellectually un-
derprivileged Lower East Side, and people from the neighborhood
flocked to Billy and Abe's picture house in droves.

In 1914 my brother Herbert graduated from Columbia Law
School and joined my two brothers in the business. Things went
along well. Herbert is the brother closest to me in age . . . if you can
call an eleven-year difference close. But we were close in other respects too because we shared a bedroom when Herbert was staying
at home in my father's house.

Anyway, Herbert fit in very well with Abe and Billy, contributing
not only his legal talents but many theatrical ideas on lights and
music as well. It was Herbert, in fact, who convinced my brothers
about the magenta spotlights.

During the war years, the steady run of successful box-office takes
began to decline. Movie chains emerged and began bidding against
my brothers for the major pictures. Keith-Proctor built the 14th
Street Jefferson Theater which was in direct competition with the
National Winter Garden. Loew's opened the Avenue B and the De-
lancey, both on the Lower East Side. It was the early days of the big
studios—Vitagraph and Biograph—originally based in Brooklyn
and New Jersey. But these companies were just starting, and there
still weren't many films to choose from. Without first-run showings,
my brothers suddenly found themselves in serious trouble, and even
Billy's charm couldn't talk the distributors into supplying him films
that they didn't have. During this time, Abe and Billy not only lost
their product, they almost lost Herbert too.

Herbert had been working at developing an advertising campaign
for the National Winter Garden, hoping this would improve business. For instance, he tried to use reverse psychology to attract
crowds to those few films the Minskys could line up. "Minsky Bros.
National Winter Garden," his posters challenged. *"Try* to get in!"
Unfortunately, not enough people did try. Herbert was discouraged

and felt there was no future in show business. The Kaiser, according to the newspapers, was practically knocking at our front door, so he might as well enlist.

However, his dreams of great adventures and gay Paree with the AEF (American Expeditionary Force) were thwarted. My mother burst into tears when she heard of Herbert's rash decision. Billy, who was very involved in politics, took a chagrined younger brother Herbert by the hand and led him to a train and whisked him to Washington, D.C.

Only Billy would have tried to wheedle the United States Army out of its newest recruit. The clerk at the War Office was stunned when Billy, assured and elegantly dressed, swept into his office and demanded to see someone in charge. From there he went to the next in line and the next in line and the next in line until he got to somebody who could do something about Herbert. By the time the afternoon was over Herbert was assigned to a Corps of Army Engineers stationed at Bush Terminal, Brooklyn. Good-bye Gay Paree!

If Herbert wasn't comfortable on an army cot, he could always go home to sleep. And what's more, he could keep working at the theater, which was what Billy had in mind all along. Billy felt that when things got big for the Minsky brothers, as it inevitably would, a lawyer in the family would come in handy.

After taking care of the Herbert problem, Billy went back to try to salvage his floundering movie palace. Maybe Billy wasn't even that bothered that the movie business was rotten. It was Abe who had always loved the movies. But Billy, who had seen a lot of Broadway in his days as a reporter, was not impressed. As far as he was concerned, movies were a passing fad. They'd never last. What interested Billy was theater—live entertainment. Broadway shows. Vaudeville. Maybe . . . even . . . *Burlesque*!

CHAPTER

4

DR. KRONKITE: How old are you?
PATIENT: Forty-nine years.
DR. KRONKITE: How long have you been out of work?
PATIENT: Forty-nine years!
DR. KRONKITE: What's your father's name?
PATIENT: Ben.
DR. KRONKITE: What's your mother's name?
PATIENT: Anna!
DR. KRONKITE: What's *your* name?
PATIENT: Ben-Anna!
DR. KRONKITE: Do you have a fairy godmother?
PATIENT: No, but we've got an uncle we're not sure about!

LIVE ENTERTAINMENT WAS not exactly a new idea for the Minskys. Even during their one-reel days, Abe and Billy had involved themselves with vaudeville. The films in those early days had been very short, and even the big five-reelers ran only about forty minutes. So it became a custom in most of the film palaces to follow each film with five or six acts of vaudeville. As a result, Billy knew all of the booking agents. In fact, he had to curry favor with these agents because vaudeville was becoming more and more popular and it was tough to book the hottest acts. But Billy's gift of gab could work wonders. He managed to get comedians like George Price and Clark and Verdi, an Italian duo who did dialect comedy. There was Belle Baker, who was the original Yiddish mama and very popular on the Lower East Side. He booked troupes that did dramatic sketches with as many as seven actors and lasting ten to twelve minutes. And, very popular on the Lower East Side, because you didn't have to know English, were what they called the sight acts: tumblers, jugglers, gymnasts, and animal acts, as well as tap and ballroom dancers.

This was what Billy liked. Films were boring. How could you talk to a piece of film? How could you influence it to do things in a certain way—in a way that you had dreamed up in your own head? With movies you couldn't wheedle, or cajole, or negotiate. What Billy liked was working with people, and he loved the idea of a theater full of excitable, sweaty, temperamental performers.

But bucking the major vaudeville houses, like the Palace, Proctor's Fifth Avenue, the Riverside, and the Alhambra, was hopeless. It was the same problem that they had in competing with the bigger film houses. The Minskys simply didn't have the money to outbid these larger outfits.

But, burlesque. Aha! This could be a different matter.

What actually *was* burlesque? Some people called it the poor man's *Follies*. It was a popular and inexpensive form of entertainment whose basic ingredients were girls, gags, and music. The girls showed as much of themselves as the law and what passed for local option allowed. The gags were broad and topical and were often takeoffs on the Broadway shows uptown. The music was popular. Theatrical historians have told me that American burlesque sprang from everywhere and from nowhere. Like vaudeville, it owed much to the circus, the circus sideshow with its Cooch dancers, beer, and dance-hall honky-tonk. It always had girls. In the early days they usually wore one-piece union suits. Later they began to derive a lot of the material from Broadway revues, like the *Ziegfeld Follies* and *George White's Scandals*. It was these shows, by the way, that first introduced nudity to the Great White Way.

I'll have to admit that burlesque certainly frequently skirted the fringes of the law and had problems with the local bluenoses. But in the early days it might just as often have been the humor of the skits and the gags by the baggy-pants comics that drew the attention of the law as the increasing nudity.

In those days burlesque shows were supplied to theaters by organizations that were called wheels. There was The Columbia Wheel,
The Mutual Wheel, and The American Wheel. The American
Wheel, for instance, in a typical year took seventy-three shows on
tour to eighty-one theaters and cities stretching from New York to
Omaha, playing to about 700,000 people. The entrepreneurs of the
wheels would supply a different road show every week—everything—costumes, scenery, comedy, music. All the theater owner had
to do was to open the doors, sell tickets, and sweep out after the
show.

Billy figured that the Minsky brothers could do a heck of a lot
better with this sort of an operation than they were doing with the
movies. But the first show booked from The American Wheel proved
to be a disaster.

On the day before the road show was scheduled to open at the
National Winter Garden, everything arrived. Costumes, scenery,
and performers. But Billy and Abe discovered there was a slight
problem in their plans. The sixth-floor theater, which had been designed for a nickelodeon, had no provisions for getting in stage sets.
Even if the elevators had been big enough, there would have been
no way to get the scenery into that side of the building. Billy called
piano movers and tried to haul the scenery up via the roof, but all
they succeeded in doing was in smashing a very heavy and expensive
flat. It appeared that the Minskys' plans to enter the world of burlesque and their hopes of making a fortune in live theater was also
flat at that moment.

With his perennial optimism, Billy proposed that they close for
the summer, announce that they were reopening in the fall with a
live burlesque policy, and figure out a way to get around the problem of mounting the show.

CHAPTER

COMIC: I'm named after my parents. My dad's name
   was Ferdinand. My mother's name was Liza.
STRAIGHT MAN: What's *your* name?
COMIC: Ferdiliza!

THERE SEEMED TO be really only one solution to this problem of
having a theater into which the burlesque scenery couldn't fit. My
brothers decided that the answer was to build their own scenery
right there in the theater. Once they went to this expense, Billy argued it would also be cheaper to put together the shows themselves
than it was to rent the shows from any of the three wheels, since the
wheel shows included the costs of the sets.

According to my brother Herbert, it was in the summer of 1916
that it became evident who was going to be the top man among the
Minsky brothers of the burlesque era. Herbert spent the summer
learning to drive on Long Island and reading up on classical theater
comedy. Abe decided that if he wanted to see Paris, he'd better
hurry and do so before the Germans captured it. But Billy spent
every minute traveling around the Eastern states and watching
every burlesque show he could find. By fall he was an expert and
ready to go ahead and produce and direct his own shows. I wasn't
yet on the scene so I'll let Herbert describe the way he saw it: "We
prospered at once, and largely due to Billy's genius we kept on pros-

pering. It took genius too. The public was accustomed to burlesque shows that were musical comedies with complete books and original music. That was made possible by the wheels, which enabled each show to be set up as a road unit that could play the same show an entire year, traveling from town to town. But we had our own stock company, which had to play one show and rehearse the next simultaneously. There was no time to write books or to learn roles. All we could do was slap together a vaudeville show using the specialties of our performers over and over and hope the public wouldn't notice.

"Billy had enough imagination or whatever to keep the shows looking fresh. One week our 'first banana,' Jack Shargel, couldn't come up with a new sketch. Billy took him out with a movie camera one day and improvised a six-minute comedy film sequence starting with Jack's hooking a piece of fruit from an Orchard Street pushcart and being chased up the street and right up the fire escape of the National Winter Garden building. The film ended with Shargel dashing on the stage, live, from the wings. As it came to a close, Jack went into his comedy routine onstage. His entrance was so spectacular that hardly anybody noticed that he was still doing the same comedy routine he'd done the week before.

As a matter of fact, our shows were stimulating enough to attract a good many of the uptown intelligentsia. Otto Kahn used to put in a regular appearance once a week, driving up to the front of the theater in his huge Minerva limousine, always faultlessly dressed in evening clothes and with a beautiful girl on his arm.

What was the appeal of burlesque to these high-brows? Let me tell you the way George Jean Nathan, erudite critic and one of the earliest fans of Minsky's saw it:

> Burlesque remains true to its first principles and devotes itself to pure, unadulterated and heart-warming, old knock 'em down and drag 'em down comedy. From the gashouse quartet to the hootchie dames, from the venerable money-changing act to the flossy with the red tie, from the show curtain with the chewing gum advertisements to the boy who sells boxes of candy on the aisle—twenty-five cents—a quarter—and a prize in every box. The good old smell of stale cigars and cigarettes, of cheap hair tonic and Third Avenue drug store perfumery, of the hospitably near, frankly unabashed and doorless 'gents walk' . . . it's all very gay and just a bit sad.

To Nathan there was a wistful appeal to its "memorable fram-

ing of rears, and its cracking of bladders on pates, in its spacious
pants and red-lingeries and crepe whiskers and pink wigs.

But the classier the people who came to see us, and the more attention we drew with shows that we thought were vastly superior to
the wheel shows, the more we attracted the *other* kind of attention.
The kind we didn't want. The bluenoses, who saw something dirty
in every smile, move, or inch of skin. The aggravation we had from
these self-appointed moralists started almost at the beginning of our
burlesque experience and haunted us to the very end. *Was* it dirty?
Let's give you an idea of what went on, on the stage, and you can
judge for yourself.

CHAPTER

STRAIGHT MAN: So your wife ran away with your best
  friend. Who was he?
COMIC: Search me! I never met the guy!

OF COURSE, IN this epoch, during World War I and just afterward, I
was still in school and not an active part of the Minsky brothers' organization; but from my brother Herbert, to whom I was very close,
I got an idea what happened. Here's how he told it to me: "Billy was
a driving director. He kept the shows moving fast and the performances spontaneous. We were all in a perpetual frenzy of creation of
material. Joke books, we found, weren't much use in creating comedy. The material wasn't basic enough. But when we went back to
Aristophanes, there was endless stuff that made comedy scenes that
are still in use today. This stuff, of course, was often racier than anything permitted on the stage at that time or even later on. But the
shows we developed went. The first year we didn't have any big sen-
sations and there was rarely a sellout. Still we showed a good, steady
profit.

"As the weeks went by, however, we saw that the business wasn't
going to last forever. The audiences were getting used to our comedy
formulas and half the time they shouted out the punch lines to the
jokes before the comedians. They were getting more interested in

31

bringing oranges, pastrami sandwiches, and knishes than in what was happening on the stage.

"We all knew the answer. *Girls!* The only trouble was that the girls were in the show to be looked at, and there wasn't really enough light on the stage to see them as the audience wanted to see them. The theater had never been wired for stage lighting, since it was designed to be used to show films. To bring enough power cables at this point was going to cost several thousand dollars, which was a lot of money at that time. At first we just did without the lights and consequently without the 'living pictures' that were so popular then. This would be a tableau of girls sometimes posed in the style of a famous painting, like a Watteau or a Rubens. All right, not *too* much like them. But still, there was a resemblance, and the law seemed to feel that as long as the girls didn't move or jiggle, a considerable amount of nudity was tolerable, just as it was in the art galleries.

"We couldn't even back our *soubrette* with a chorus line. To back the *soubrette* with a chorus the girls would have to come right up to the footlight trough to be seen at all and then, where would their leader have taken her position?

"We were going over the problem together one evening over a couple of drinks when Abe, who had just returned from Paris, began talking about his trip. When he got to Paris, Abe had been diligent in his research. He went to as many performances of the *Folies Bergère* and shows at the Moulin Rouge as he could attend. He also learned a lot about black leotards, red garter belts, and cootch dancers. This influenced the somewhat Gallic-American flavor of Minsky's shows later on.

"We listened to Abe's every word, for he indeed was the traveler and *bon vivant* among us. Suddenly he remarked, 'Ya know, if we could only get lights somehow, there's quite a stunt they pulled at the *Folies Bergère* in Paris. They paraded girls on a runway—'

" 'Runway? What kind of runway?' Billy pounced on the remark like a cat.

"Abe explained that there was a raised platform coming down from stage right into the theater. 'The audience went crazy when they paraded down in spotlights. If we could manage a few spots—'

" 'Spots, hell!' Billy said. 'If it's in the house, we'll use the house lights. They may not be glamorous, but they'll be able to see the girls. For the moment we can do without the glamour or at least until we have some more money for spots.'

"The following Sunday, when we were closed, we called in a crew of carpenters who worked all day. The runway they built ran from the orchestra pit up the center of the house to a point just under the rim of the balcony. This meant losing forty-eight orchestra seats, but it was worth it. When we opened the new show on Monday, the National Winter Garden featured the first runway parade in American theater history. And what a parade! We had six girls, none under thirty. Under the yellow house lights their makeup looked terrible, and their neck-to-toe pink tights were ghastly. But they *were* girls, and the audience, mostly male, could look right up their legs. You must remember that in those days before the flapper era, women wore skirts down to their ankles, and the sight of a leg, even if covered with tights, was extremely stimulating. (Picture the reaction of modern young men to a wet T-shirt plastered against a young lady's breasts. The shape is what counts.) Our audience howled. That whole week was a sellout. We all agreed. The way to sell out the house was to show plenty of girls and light them as well as possible."

With the publicity that resulted from the use of the runway, admission to Minsky's was raised from ninety cents to a dollar and later on to a $2.20 top for the seats nearest the girls.

Out on the runway illuminated by brother Herbert's sexy magenta lights, Maisie Harris's cheerful and seductive troupe was able to get so close to the audience that they could actually smell their perfume and hear their heavy breathing. It was sensational! Never before had an audience been able to get so close to the performers.

"As soon as there was time to do so we hired some really good-looking girls for our chorus and stole a first-class *soubrette* named Mae Dix from Ben Kahn, who ran the Union Square Theatre. Mae was a red-haired beauty with a gorgeous figure and a great way of putting over a comedy song. She used to do all the old Anna Held numbers, and believe me that was all we asked her to do. She was a great performer who was starred at Minsky's before the 1916 through 1917 season was over. (This was the time that Herbert was shuttling back and forth from his Army post to the theater.)

"It was toward the end of that season that Mae had her lucky accident. On a stifling hot night she was working in a black short-skirt dress with a detachable white collar and cuffs. They were detachable so that they could be laundered daily, but Mae liked to save a little money and make them do for two days. As she went off at the end of her number, she pulled off the collar, trying to save it as much as she could. The audience saw her do it, and some gagster started applauding for an encore. Mae came back without the collar, raising a storm of applause, bowed, and pulled off the cuffs as she left the stage for what she thought was the last time.

"But they wouldn't let her go. They clapped like crazy, this being a time when a woman on the stage was allowed to show no flesh at all. Between the heat and the applause, Mae lost her head, went back for a short chorus, and unbuttoned her bodice as she left the stage again.

"Nick Elliott, our house manager, ran backstage to bawl out Mae and fine her ten dollars, since showing more than the script called for was a punishable offense. Then he ordered the house lights up, to quiet the audience, which was going crazy, and went out on the stage to bawl out the customers. The Minsky brothers, Nick told them, ran a decent theater. There was going to be no more of that, and if they didn't like it, they were free to leave.

"Nick was one of our most loyal employees, but it took a lot of guts to try and calm down that audience. Once Mae's accident had happened and the effect of what was one of the first stripteases had been discovered, nothing could have held the audience back. Anyway, we didn't try. What, were we crazy?

"Billy gave back the money that Mae had paid as her fine and gave her a ten-dollar raise on top of it, provided that she repeated the same 'accident' every night. When Nick protested that the police would stop the act, Billy said, 'If people want it, we'll give it to them. When a court finds that I've broken some law, I'll stop. Until then, we'll sell tickets.' "

You'll hear a million stories about how the striptease started. Some people will tell you it was Hinda Wassau. Hinda was a tall, pale-skinned golden blonde who was a big star in the early phases of burlesque. There was a rumor that it was Hinda who really started the strip. There were also stories about a restaurant in St. Louis that featured strippers in addition to their rare meat. All I know is this is how it started at Minsky's.

Herbert was the theater manager when all this happened, and the trouble that Nick had predicted came soon enough. A couple of weeks after the strip act started a horse-drawn paddy wagon pulled up to Second Avenue and Houston Street, and the officers hand-cuffed Herbert inside the theater and took him "downtown" for a talk with Inspector McCaullaugh at the precinct station.

If the inspector hadn't been an honest man, he probably could have become mayor. He had the most fluent tongue and potent speech ever heard. He shouted and ranted at Herbert for an hour and a half, condemning his indecency and moral influence on the community.

"I have never before or since," Herbert told me, "felt quite so mean and worthless."

When McCaullaugh was through with him, Herbert shook his hand contritely. "Have your men drop in any time," Herbert told the officer. "They'll never see anything off-color at Minsky's."

But if Herbert's promise was kept to the letter, there might not be anything off-color onstage but there would only be one color in the company's books and that would be red ink. To ward off further troubles, Herbert installed red, white, and blue lights in the center of the footlight trough and wired them to the ticket-taker's booth, where he was stationed every night. As soon as he spotted a cop, he would press the button that turned on the red light, which was the warning. The cast would immediately switch into what they called the Boston version of whatever they were doing. So in a sense, Herbert kept his promise, since the police never did see anything off-color, if the Minskys could help it.

By 1918 the Minsky-type of burlesque had caught on so well that we had two rivals, the Star and the Empire, both in Brooklyn. To tell the truth, burlesque was on its way to becoming nothing more than a legal way of selling the illusion of sex to the public. And while people flocked to pay admission, in their private lives they had nothing but scorn for those who made their living in burlesque, in-cluding the owners and managers.

There was no place in which this feeling was deeper than in my own family. Certainly my father was humiliated that his sons were in such an enterprise. So, when Herbert became interested in one of the girls in the chorus, my parents were utterly shocked. A girl in show business? And she wasn't even Jewish! Not to be prejudiced, I'll let Herbert give his version of it: "Her name was Juanita Dixon. A pretty kid of about twenty, she had already been married and divorced. She might have become tough and bitter and she might have been a lot better off in burlesque if she had. But she wasn't that way at all. A soft little kitten of a girl, she was only in our show because she could make a living wage that way, twenty-two dollars a week, whereas she couldn't have made more than twelve at any other job, which wasn't enough even then for a girl living on her own.

"I became interested in Juanita when she came to me with the story that another girl in the chorus was getting in trouble with a married man, and asked me to do something to prevent it. The kid was on the point of tears over the sin that was being committed and over what she finally fondly believed would be the unending remorse of the other girl."

Backstage morals were a recurring problem for us anyway. Abe finally decided that the best thing to do about it was to hire a stage mother who could advise the girls and try to keep them straight. He found a seventy-year-old double for Whistler's Mother named Mrs. Annie Elms. She was an old show girl herself, but central casting could have sent her for the role she played for us. The fact that she constantly had recourse to the flat pint of gin in her reticule had nothing to do with her efficacy as a backstage mother. Mother Elms was with us for ten years and really did a lot of good among the girls. They all felt that she really was a mother to them and brought her all their problems. Mother Elms was just what we needed to improve our image with the public.

Before we got Mother Elms, backstage was a pretty rough place. Herbert was disturbed to think of a fresh, young girl like Juanita exposed to that influence. So he made her a cashier at the same salary and put her in the box office, where she could work in her clothes. But that cut no ice with the family.

"What about that Dixon kid? Are you sleeping with her?" Abe the playboy asked.

Herbert told him that he would love to sleep with Juanita but she just wasn't that sort.

"Well," said the worldly-wise Abe, "just see that you don't lose your head and marry her."

Abe's opinion was that of the entire family. Maybe Juanita was playing hard to get, but as far as the family was concerned, she was still basically a chorus tramp and someone to be wary of. But Herbert ignored all this and took Juanita out on a number of dates. Now the warnings from the family became continual.

"Rather than fight with the family," Herbert told me, "I let Billy's wife, Mary, introduce me to some 'nice girls.' "

Meanwhile, the Minsky business was getting into a peculiar predicament. We had a reputation for dirty shows. The Minsky boys were considered a disreputable clan who didn't care what kind of raw stuff they pulled as long as they made money. It would have been fine if it were only true. But the fact was that our shows were getting more and more disappointing to our patrons because they were mere Sunday school stuff compared to what was going on uptown in the respectable productions of legitimate theaters. Florenz Ziegfeld in his *Follies* productions was parading naked girls all over the stage, hanging them from the drapes, and swinging them on the chandeliers. George White and Earl Carroll had other fancy tricks, like displaying girls bathing in champagne. Not that they didn't get in trouble once in a while themselves. Earl Carroll in fact ultimately put in a short jail sentence for his exposure of a girl in a bathtub full of champagne—a transparent bathtub.

However, generally it was all classified as "art" and okayed by the police, I suppose because the girls wore very fancy, artistic headdresses. But we, meanwhile, weren't allowed to show an unclad leg on the stage. A man was able to see more skin in his daily paper that on the stage at Minsky's.

TALKING WOMAN (*as wife*): Scratch, when you came
home last night you told me you had been at the
Biltmore with Wilson. Mrs. Wilson just called and
said that you were both at the Trocadero. Why did
you say you were at the Biltmore?
SCRATCH: When I came home last night, I couldn't *say*
Trocadero!

AT SIXTEEN I began to lose my innocence—at least intellectually.
   Although it was a long time before I ever got to meet Ethel De
Veaux personally, I still carried her image in the warmest part of my
heart and her picture in my breast pocket. The very sight of her even
from the back of the orchestra could set my pulse racing and cause
my face to turn candy-apple red. But it was hard for me to retain my
image of her virginal innocence when I saw some of the roles she had
to play in the comedy skits.
   For instance, Ethel comes on in a short and daring black dress slit
to the thigh.

ETHEL: Oh, my, oh, my! Boo-hoo-hoo!
COMIC: (*dressed in baggy pants, a checked vest, a ragged derby, and carry-
ing a long, black cigar that he flicks suggestively at every opportunity*):
What's the problem, my dear?

ETHEL: I'm so sad. My husband just died! What will I do, my husband just died!

COMIC: Come, come, you're a beautiful girl. You'll probably get a new husband tomorrow.

ETHEL: (*slowly starting that sinuous and highly suggestive movement called the grind*): But what am I going to do *tonight*? (*She finishes this with a big bump climaxing her initial grind.*)

COMIC: (*His hat flies off his head. He picks it up, brushes it off, and bows politely to Ethel.*) Well, look, I'm an out-of-work husband. What did your husband die of?

ETHEL: (*going into her grind*): He died of in ... (*bump*)flu ...(*bump*)enza! (*Bump!*)

COMIC: I'm a little hard of hearing. Would you mind repeating that?

ETHEL: (*going into her scene again*): He died of in ... (*bump*)flu ... (*bump*) ... (*bump*)enza. (*Bump!*)

COMIC: Your husband didn't die of influenza.

ETHEL: He didn't?

COMIC: No, you *bumped* him off!

Was this my innocent Ethel? Well, show business made strange bedfellows, or so I hoped.

As I spent more time in the theater, I began to get used to the girls and no longer got excited at the sight of their legs or other parts of their anatomy, but I never stopped being fascinated by the humor. It isn't always easy to explain burlesque gags in print; as they say today, "You had to be there." By that I mean that each line was accompanied by a leer, a bit of business with a prop like a billy stick or a cigar, a double take, which I believe was invented in burlesque, or a hit with a bladder. (These bladders, by the way, were actually animal bladders obtained from various slaughterhouses around town, dried and inflated, since rubber bladders would never stand up to all the pounding.) The purpose of the bladder was to be able to emphasize points with comic violence but without really hurting anybody, like the stick in a Punch and Judy show. In burlesque there were a lot of props that had standard functions that the audience got to know, so they would anticipate what would be their use in any given situation. A hotel was a place for naughty goings-on, a bed was for husbands to sleep in and lovers to hide under, a bucket had to get a foot trapped in it, a pie was a facial decoration, never a dessert. Seltzer water was a weapon and never a drink. Salamis, bananas, billy sticks, all symbolized the same Freudian thing. Of course, once into the classics, I realized this was not much different than Aristophanes' *Lysistrata*.

The cast of characters that appeared in the skits all had fairly clearly defined roles to play. Judges, doctors, and lawyers were incompetent nincompoops and good targets for bladder bouncing.

I will admit that usually Ethel's role as the *soubrette* did not require too much of that bumping and grinding, it was just that she was so *good* at it. Usually she would be the innocent girl who would cross the stage, approach the comic, and ask him, "Are you Mr. Myers? I've heard all about your lovemaking."

Myers the comic, shuffling his oversize shoe shyly on the stage floor and with modesty, would say, "Oh, it's nothing."

And Ethel would say, "That's what I heard!" And then exit.

This broke me up every time, and like a lot of burlesque humor, it was hard to put your finger on what about it was naughty, although obviously it was sexy in its intent. But some of the humor, which will be familiar to anybody who has seen enough amateur theatricals or television comics, had no sex in it at all.

For instance, the straight man is standing at a lectern and the comic comes from one side of the stage carrying a suitcase. He starts to cross to the other side of the stage passing before the straight man.

> STRAIGHT MAN: Hey, wait a minute. Where're ya going?
> COMIC: (*stopping and giving the straight man a take*): I'm an attorney and I'm taking my case to court. (*He exits.*)

The audience does not howl, but it snickers. The straight man continues his spiel. Maybe there's a gag in between with another comic, and then the attorney appears from the other side carrying the same case and a small stepladder, passing in front of the straight man again.

> STRAIGHT MAN: (*irritated*): Where're you going now?
> COMIC: I'm taking my case to a higher court! (*He exits.*)

After another bit of business, the comic attorney reappears with a sad look on his clown face, carrying an empty clothes hanger.

STRAIGHT MAN: Well, what is it now?
COMIC: I lost my suit! (*Bang, bang, bang on the head with the bladder.*)

All of these comic bits were going one, two, three, four, one gag after another. They remind me much of the current Benny Hill type of humor, in which the jokes come so fast and furious that you haven't got time to realize that some of them are not exactly the cream of wit.

For instance, the following was a typical bit that was practically a must in burlesque restaurant scenes.

WAITER: Would the lady like some tongue?
TALKING WOMAN: Sir, I'll have you understand that I never eat anything that comes out of an animal's mouth.
WAITER: Then how about a couple of eggs?

If the lady gives in and asks for eggs, he asks her how she wants them and she almost always says, "Fry one on one side and one on the other." Sometimes she might ask for soup.

WOMAN: Waiter, I want one order of chicken soup.
WAITER: (*calling to the kitchen help*): One order of chicken soup!
WOMAN: Listen, I changed my mind. Make that pea soup instead.
WAITER: Hold that chicken! Make it pea!

Granted, all these lines have a slightly stale aroma; but remember that they were already a little putrefied by the time I heard them, and that was around 1919. However, they did make a big hit around the school, and pretty soon I was bringing several of my classmates to the two-thirty matinee. In that era there were no PG performances and nobody asked you how old you were when you came in, although as I recall we were all over sixteen at the time. And what a time it was!

Just after the war America was treated to the unsettling phenomenon of Prohibition, which, by making almost every American a flaunter of the law at one time or another, changed the whole moral attitude of the era.

In those early Prohibition days, when women were just getting out of hobble skirts and into flapper gear, I entered New York University and had a happy social life with my fraternity, although we didn't get involved with the drinking and speakeasy crowd. We'd get together at the fraternity house for dances and teas, and on Sunday afternoon we'd go to a dance at the Hotel Pennsylvania or the McAlpin Grill or Roof with our girl friends. This was the era that seems in retrospect much like a John Held cartoon, with Stutz Bearcats and raccoon coats and the rest.

In those days, while I admired my brother Billy a great deal, it was Herbert, closest to me in age, with whom I spent most of my time. I began to see how Herbert would incorporate some of his cultural background into the shows, either including operatic arias or sometimes references to his classical education. I remember one number in which each of the girls appeared dressed in a costume representing a flower. Herbert wrote dialogue for the straight man and gave a classical allusion to each costume:

> STRAIGHT MAN: When the great Catullus told the gentle youth to press his blushing tulips to his Maytime bosom, could he, by any chance, have meant the *two lips* of our own Miss Andrea Delight?

It wasn't Herbert's fault the straight man put a heavy stress on the word "bosom."

Or else, he might include a reference to some of the great English poets:

> STRAIGHT MAN: The great poet Tennyson once said, "In the spring a livelier iris changes on the burnish'd dove;/In the spring a young man's fancy lightly turns to thoughts of love." The poet must have been referring to our own lovely iris, Miss Pepper Ross!

Or,

> STRAIGHT MAN: When John Keats wrote, "The blue bird spread its eternal bosom and made the morning precious," he could have been describing our own precious glory of the morning, Miss Mitzi Malone.

Although Herbert injected a lot of "culture" into the show, I noticed that he did manage to find lines that stressed the word "bosom" quite frequently, although at this time the striptease had not gained its preeminence as a part of burlesque and a bosom was essentially concealed artillery.

As far as I could see from my inside position, business went very well at first, and my brothers did an excellent job of mining the current Broadway hits of George White, Earl Carroll, and Florenz Ziegfeld to give laughs and stimulation to their own special audiences. If Ziegfeld did one of his elegant extravaganza-type spectacles, often directed by Ben Ali Haggin, he would bring out a completely nude girl on an elephant with her golden tresses hanging down. Then they would raise a magnificent curtain revealing twelve elegantly costumed ladies with their bosoms absolutely exposed. This was considered "art" because it was uptown. Billy figured that if it was permissible to expose the attractions of sixty gals at Ziegfeld's at $4.40, it was equally permissible to offer a dozen similarly clad girls at one-sixth the price. But Minsky's seemed to offend the Legion of Decency, while Ziegfeld didn't. Minsky's also seemed to offend the interests of George White, the Broadway producer, and Archie Selwyn, the owner of and producer at the Selwyn Theatre. So pressure was put on the authorities, and the Police Department would come down there every now and then and in their brusque way make comments about our supposedly racy dialogue. Remember, in those days even the words "hell" and "damn" were offensive. Perhaps you may recall the uproar made by the Broadway show *Tobacco Road*, which first brought such language to Broadway. People flocked to the theater for the titillation of hearing these words exposed so frankly to the public. But this early hassling by the courts was just the tip of the iceberg. By the time I got into the management of the theater itself in 1924, censorship had gotten much, much tougher.

Prohibition served as a great leveler of classes. When people went into a speakeasy, they would be associating with people they might never have met before the era of the great drought. The Lower East Side, where Minsky's was located, and where I grew up, was basically an area of foreigners newly arrived from Eastern Europe or the Orient. Somehow, the upper classes felt that with the arrival of Prohibition the thing to do was to go to places where they might not be seen by their other snooty friends. So shortly after this, slumming became the thing to do. Adventurous souls from the upper reaches of Park Avenue discovered the area and dared one another to go down there, though in fact in many ways it was one of the least corrupt neighborhoods in the city. But the thing that made them flock to the Lower East Side was the multitude of speakeasies, which sprang up like mushrooms.

In a sense, my friends from NYU were also slumming, since most of them had very little experience in that neighborhood. What added to the thrill for them, and to my popularity, was the fact that we all got in for nothing at least once a month. Up to that time I'd been regarded as the most innocent one in our crowd. Now I was regarded as something of a sophisticate. But in real life most of them bragged of experiences that were well beyond me. I had still never had any experiences with women, not even a chaste kiss. I think I would have been more embarrassed than proud if they had heard about my next encounter with Ethel De Veaux.

CHAPTER

I WAS PAINFULLY shy in those days, as most sixteen-year-olds are
with women, and particularly with the glamorous and highly visible
women employed by Minsky's. Nevertheless, using my family privi-
leges, I began to spend more and more time backstage, hoping to
bump into Ethel someday.

One day I ran into her accidentally in the lobby, where, in fact, I
had been waiting for her to come out after her performance. I was
all alone, and I asked her whether I could walk with her to the subway, which I knew she took to get home. Naturally she said, chewing
thoughtfully on her wad of Wrigley's Juicy Fruit, that she could see
no harm in letting me escort her. Harm! I was at least an inch
shorter than she was and not exactly King Kong in the physique department. Her station was at Union Square and 14th Street. We
walked up Third Avenue and into Cooper Square and finally to
14th Street. I gave a lot of thought to what I would do when we got
there. Perhaps I should ask her to have a cup of coffee or a soda or
something. Perhaps I could suggest riding home with her on the
subway. No, that would be too brash.

We got to the subway and I turned to her, manfully squaring my shoulders. "Miss De Veaux . . . Ethel, I mean . . . would you . . .?"

Ethel flashed a brilliant smile at me. She had some set of choppers!

"Would I what, Morton?"

She called me "Morton"! It was too much! I held out my hand stiffly and said, "Well, good-night!" Then I turned on my heel and practically fled downtown toward Cooper Square. What an idiot I felt like! I decided that I would have to wait a few more years before I was ready for someone like Ethel De Veaux.

Later I rationalized that probably it would be better for me not to get involved with anybody in the theater. I knew how my parents already felt about backstage involvements. No, it was better to stick to school and just see the shows from the audience. However, I would say that I never quite got over my crush on Ethel. Two years later she married Jack Diamond, a burlesque comic.

I told a lot of stories about Minsky's as a kid, but I never told *that* one at Stuyvesant High School.

Still, I was gradually growing closer to the business and to my brothers. Sometimes after the theater Billy would take me with him to spend the night at the Pennsylvania Hotel Turkish baths. When we did, Billy was sure to call his wife, Mary, who was as tall and beautiful and statuesque as any showgirl, to point out that if he was out all night, it was okay since I was with him. Billy had a sometimes-deserved reputation as a woman chaser, and he wanted to be sure he didn't get into trouble with his wife.

Meanwhile, it was quite an adult experience for me. We'd go through the routine of the baths, the steam room, the massage, and all of that and then sleep in a little room. Other times Herbert would take me to Proctor's Fifth Avenue, which was at 28th Street and Broadway in those days. They had seven acts with big-time vaudeville: Sophie Tucker, Belle Baker, Fink's Mules, whatever. It was always a thrill for me to go there with Herbert and then go to Child's after the show and have their famous griddle cakes and come home.

I didn't realize how much I would need the show business lore I was gathering backstage and at those vaudeville entertainments; but I soon would need every shred of the show biz knowledge I had assimilated in my salad days.

FIRST BANANA: Ginger ale, please.
SECOND BANANA: Pale?
FIRST BANANA: No, just a glass.

THE SHOWS WORKED up by my brothers were really quite different from the wheel shows that had dominated burlesque until our National Winter Garden opened.

Billy had been watching burlesque ever since he was a child and had picked up ideas from various vaudeville acts that he'd seen. Abe also had ideas from his theatrical career and his experience exhibiting movies. Herbert, who had some artistic talent, painted backdrops in the style of Aubrey Beardsley—certainly a novel touch in a burlesque theater. Maisie Harris, our zippy choreographer, developed a somewhat more earthy version of the Nutcracker Suite ballet, despite the fact that she had never actually seen it.

In the early days families were invited to bring their kids to the show, which was essentially wholesome. Probably the biggest kick the kids got was riding the elevator, an experience new to most of them. In fact, when people brought their kids, half the time they rode the elevators up and down throughout the show and never bothered going into the theater.

One of the earliest comedians we acquired, Jack Shargel, could not even speak English. So Billy decided that he would be strictly a pantomimist, and Shargel developed a fantastic Chaplinesque routine in which as a sad-faced comic in baggy pants he would woo a big, chesty chorus girl with a hopeless expression on his face, offering her a lovely long-stemmed rose that she disdained with a wiggle of her considerable hips. Finally, the sad-faced clown, discouraged at the hopelessness of his suit, would turn away from his curvaceous inamorata and in a mood of deep discouragement would throw the lovely rose at her feet, whereupon it shattered with the loud sounds of breaking glass. The surprise and the charm of this bit of business got the audience every time, family or not. Even though they frequently knew what was coming, it always brought down the house (e. e. cummings was a particular fan of Shargel's.)

Billy got himself and Maisie one of those little notebooks that school kids use. They went uptown and watched the shows, writing down all of the song lyrics, the blackout punch lines, and the details of the costumes and dance routines. After finding that it was the girls and the sex that brought the audience in and not the wholesome family routines, Abe and Billy had Herbert paint a new sign:

BURLESQUE AS YOU LIKE IT—THE POOR MAN'S FOLLIES!

Not a Family Show!

This certainly had a healthy effect at the box office, and the gate picked up considerably in the following months.

By the time Ziegfeld discovered that the Minskys were pirating his material and began to talk about a court injunction, my brothers had taken down their "Poor Man's Follies" sign and were working on a new show at the Garden. This one was a takeoff on one of the Shubert musicals; I don't remember which one, but, remember, Broadway had a lot more shows per season in those days than it does now. So now the Shuberts were alerted that the Minskys were doing a takeoff on them, and then Hammerstein, and then the rest. The screams and complaints of what we shall have to call the legit producers only attracted more attention to the Minskys, and oddly enough to the legit shows too. Pretty soon Ziegfeld told Billy's former paper, the *World,* that he intended to sue Billy Minsky for $100,000 for plagiarism. The next day the paper carried Billy's answer: MINSKY DISAPPOINTED ZIEGFELD DOESN'T SUE FOR A MILLION.

To keep things perking along at the National Winter Garden we would stage weeks in which we had a special event each night. For instance, Monday: Chorus Girls' Shimmy Contest. Tuesday: Perfect Form Contest. Wednesday: Chorus Girls' Black Bottom Contest. Thursday: Oriental Dance Contest. Friday: Living Picture Contest. And Saturday, our big day, would be topped off by a popularity contest for the entire company in which members of the audience participated enthusiastically.

All of this did no harm to the Minsky enterprise. Now we were really on the map. Billy relished the attention and publicity, and also the money, which was beginning to be pretty good. So now the real division of tasks between my three brothers began. (I was still just a wistful hanger-on who dropped by the theater and peeked at Miss De Veaux whenever the time was available between classes.) Billy handled the staging of the shows and the publicity. Abe took over the business office. Herbert, who was now being called H. K., handled the artistic side—lighting, stagecraft, and "culture." The Minskys were becoming personages on the entertainment scene. Billy acquired one of the first Stutz Bearcats and bought a splendid house in Seagate, to which he moved his elegant red-haired wife, Mary. The fact was, I suspected, although I never knew for sure, that Billy was not above having some splendid nights out himself, and preferred to have his wife safely stowed away in the dim reaches of the Borough Over The River. To Mary he always insisted that she would never like coming to the theater. Even though he didn't really see it as his own cup of tea, business was business. To Mary he referred to the burlesque company as his "other family," but Mary always retained a jealous attitude toward that "family" and time after time got Billy to promise that the minute he got the business really rolling, he would retire.

How do I know that Billy ran around? Well, he never talked about it to me, but one way or another it came to my attention. For example, Mary was always calling our house to check on Billy's whereabouts, so that in itself made us wonder.

But the time I remember best is when the whole family was up in the Catskills. I must have been about sixteen then, just about the time that Billy was always taking me to the Pennsylvania Hotel. The father of my friend Henry Hirsch was running one of those little boardinghouse places up there near Fleischmanns, and the whole family went up. We were having a marvelous time in the greenery of what was just then beginning to be called the Jewish Alps. (Don't think, however, that the Catskills were strictly confined to Jews. It depended on what part you went to. Other sections could have been called the Irish Alps or the Italian Alps.) Anyway, we were all up there—my mother, my father, my sisters—and who shows up on a weekend in his fancy three-door Stutz Bearcat but Billy, with some show girl.

My mother froze with disapproval. I don't remember who the girl was, but I must admit she was very attractive. I can't imagine what made Billy do such a thing. As for my mother, I'd never seen her act so chilly. Billy had some kind of explanation. I think he said the girl lived upstate and he was just giving her a ride to the city. A likely story. Of course, my mother or father didn't believe it. But to some extent they had gotten used to Billy's scandalous behavior. If you could accept the National Winter Garden, you could accept a blond show girl, I suppose.

Meanwhile, perhaps sobered by his new preeminence as an impresario, Abe decided that *he* would retire from being the family bachelor playboy. In the spring of 1921 the family *bon vivant* decided to join the bourgeoisie and get married. He put his striped blazer in moth balls and burned all of his little black books. The object of this inspiration was an attractive widow named Molly Unger, the mother of two small children. It took some time before Abe could actually win this independent lady over. But in time she yielded.

Her family, which was in the dairy business, was not ecstatic about the liaison. All they knew about the Minskys was that their name appeared above a theater in which parts of women not usually on display could be viewed in intriguing motion.

As far as they were concerned, a person with such a name could be nothing but unsuitable for their Molly, either as a husband or a father to little Sylvia and Harold.

My mother put on her best new dress, got into the family limousine, which was the second biggest car on Second Avenue (the biggest was a Pierce Arrow belonging to Thomashefsky, the Yiddish actor), and made a social call on the future in-laws.

The Ungers were dazzled and impressed by her visit. My mother made it clear to them that the Minskys were not only wealthy but important figures in the community and synagogue, as well as in the political world. The Ungers gave in with relief. Molly and Abe were married. Abe seemed determined to stick to his reformed life. He paraded his new family all over Second Avenue and introduced them to everybody as "my little corporation." In time this became more than a family joke, since Molly ultimately took a very active part in Abe's business affairs.

As the shows became gamier and less family entertainment and as Prohibition led to people carrying hip flasks and sometimes getting a bit boisterous in the audience, my brothers hired Albert and Walter, two beefy, retired Pinkerton operatives whom they called The Specials. They wore rented policelike uniforms with impressive-looking badges from the prop department and carried billies that could also make a deep impression when properly wielded. Albert and Walter patrolled the lobby, orchestra, and balcony during the show and afterward threw out the sleepers, who might be inclined to stay until the next day's matinee.

It was also about this time that my brothers hired Tom Bundy, a vaudeville comedian, as a combination company manager and master of ceremonies. It was then, too, to keep the peace backstage, that they hired Mother Annie Elms.

Once the runway was established, it led by natural steps to a growing dynasty of "exotic," "Oriental," or even "classical" dancers who wiggled, jiggled, and bumped in a way that was new to theatergoers. There was no question that the cooch dance had come to burlesque to stay. The girls might be gross at times, but the gross at the box office compensated well for that. It was on a Minsky runway that New York first saw the tassel dance, originated by the immortal burlesque queen Carrie Finnell and passed along to her protégé Fern Perry. Carrie's special talent was to make the tassels attached to her breasts twirl singly or together or even in opposite directions by the unusual development of her remarkable pectoral muscles.

Of course, the prima donnas who sang the operatic numbers, the tenor who did the interludes, and the straight man had nothing to do with the runway. Neither did the comics, except for one unfortunate attempt by Jack Shargel to use this new means of communicating with the audience.

The problem was that neither my brother Billy nor Shargel appreciated the fact that the audience took very slowly to innovations or new material. Far from resenting the fact that all of the gags, routines, and skits tended to be repetitions of or takeoffs on one another, the audience looked forward with anticipation to familiar material and were very uncomfortable with anything that was really new. So this technique of stealing bits of comedy from one another was an honored tradition in burlesque. It is like any of the traditional forms of comedy, or even drama. If you go to a Western, you know that in the end the good guy is going to shoot the bad guy one way or another. If you try to give it a different ending, the audience is liable to throw rocks at the screen. So in the world of burlesque comedy, ritual was ingrained. If a fat comedian bent over to tie his shoelace, it was not because it had become undone but because he was about to be a target for the straight man's toe. If a pretty show girl wiggled across the stage, it wasn't simply because she wanted to get to the other side; it was so that the drummer could blow his wolf whistle and bang the bass drum and the comic could do a google-eyed double take, or skull, as it was called in burlesque jargon.

This would be followed up by a straight man who would come across the stage, sidle up to the comic, and say, "You see that beautiful girl, how would you like a date with her?"

Things had to be done that way, as I explained a little earlier, and there wasn't much consideration for oppressed minorities. Homosexuals were frequent targets, and the mentally ill were considered just one more opportunity for loony humor. In fact, there were really two kinds of burlesque comics. Some of them could have been called technicians. These were actors who figured out every single move and bit of business until you could set them with a stopwatch. The others, the more talented group, were the naturals, whose goofy and inspired humor could seldom be described. It's like trying to write down the routines of someone like Jimmy Durante, who was not in burlesque but who easily could have been, with his indescribable character humor. There are also different categories of comedians. There was the rube, or country comic, the tramp, the dialectitian, who could work in any of a number of accents—Hebrew, Dutch, French—and the silent or sad or dancing comic, like Jack Shargel.

Probably the tramp and boob comics were the top of the line. They included stars like Bert Lahr, Sliding Billy Watson, Bozo Snyder, and Snuffy the Cabman from the old days of the wheel. Others included Stinky Fields, Boob McManus, and Spit-in-the-Hat Kelly.

We, ourselves, produced quite a few comedians who really developed and became well known as performers at Minsky's. Besides Shargel, there was Walter Brown (who was known as Schultz the Butcher), Scratch Wallace, Joe Rose, and Steve Mills. Some people said Shargel was a Chaplin in a time when there was no place except in burlesque for another Chaplin. Other Minsky star comics included Eddie "Nuts" Kaplan and Pigmeat Markham.

Later on, in the 1930s, Minsky's was a jumping-off point for such well-known comics as Phil Silvers, Joey Faye, Red Marshall, Eddie Green, Jack Diamond, Rags Ragland, Abbott and Costello, and Red Buttons.

Unfortunately, the people who never achieved real fame and were often unknown to the audience were the straight men, without whom the comedy couldn't happen. At Minsky's we had two of the best—Raymond Paine and Al Golden, Jr.

So, what does a straight man do? Isn't the comic the one who gets the laughs? Most comics would be the first to admit that to be a great straight man requires exceptional talent, timing, and a vast knowledge of all the sketches out of which burlesque routines are constructed. Often the skit or sketch would be put together by a comic and a straight man in a few minutes, before they actually appeared on stage with just a few brief references: "You know the Dr. Kronkite bit? Okay, we'll do that and we'll end up with the Gazeeka Box."

Sometimes the comic didn't even know what burlesque bit was coming up until he was actually onstage and the straight man would drop a line giving him a cue.

Okay, I'll admit that the comedy wasn't always as clean and pure as I'm presenting it here. Otherwise, would we have had all the grief we did from the Legion of Decency? But it's my story, and I'll tell it the way it was. To be honest, I'll have to give you a glimpse at some of the more . . . earthy . . . bits too.

CHAPTER

10

TALKING WOMAN: Your Honor, he hit me in the nose, he
   hit me in the eye, he punched me in the head, he—
STEVE MILLS: Don't pay any attention to *her,* Judge.
   She's punch drunk!

THOSE YEARS THAT were formative for Minsky's Burlesque were
also my own developing years. After I got out of Stuyvesant High
School I went to New York University, where I took a combination
of courses at Commerce and Washington Square College. By this
time I had met my darling Ruth, and this put all thoughts of ever
having a friendship with another Miss De Veaux out of my mind.
Ruth was the first and only girl I ever really loved. Still is. Her father was then a very successful merchant—more than a merchant.
He was one of the operators of a very well-known retail furniture
store on the Bowery south of Grand Street, called Cohan and Goldstein. That was the place to go if you were part of the Lower East
Side elite—in other words, if you wanted the finest crafted furniture
and could afford to pay in cash. Cohan and Goldstein never sold on
credit or even installments. They were proud of that.

From the beginning I became very much attached to Ruth. We
seemed to have an instant understanding. We met at a party at the
home of a mutual friend, Henry Hirsch. The Hirsches had a brownstone in Harlem. Henry asked me there, probably to meet one of his

four or five sisters. But anyway, they invited some girls and Ruth was one of them. I think it was his sister Susie that asked her. We met that night and she instantly made me feel more comfortable than any woman I had yet met. Of course, I wasn't exactly experienced, but I knew what "good" was. It turned out that our fathers knew each other—they had gone to the same yeshiva in Russia. At last—a girl that both I and my family could appreciate! We were going steady by the time of graduation and very serious about each other. This made me think about what I was going to do in life. I first thought maybe I'd go into the furniture business with Ruth's father. After all, my college courses were all business-oriented. But her father was a partner with his brothers in the business and they were getting ready to retire. There was a chance that there would be no business by the time I could really get established as a furniture person. Although it was boom times then under Coolidge, a person starting out as a married man still had to have some idea of what kind of work he was out of.

Meantime, the burlesque theater was going so well that my brothers decided to open another—the Park Theatre on Columbus Circle. The building in which they set up the Park had been owned by William Randolph Hearst, who had called it the Marion Davies Cosmopolitan Theatre, after his beautiful blond mistress. My brothers took a lease there and opened with a policy called "Burlesques ... the *S* makes the difference!" This was supposed to be a pun. If you'll say it aloud, you'll get the meaning. But it was a very elegant show, with twenty musicians in the orchestra pit alone. One of the stars was a comedian named Tom Howard, who later became famous in vaudeville as part of the team of Howard and Shelton and then was a big radio star on *It Pays to Be Ignorant*.

The show was not only more elegant but cleaner than the show down on Houston Street—not that I'm admitting there was anything dirty about *that*—but after all, this was uptown, and uptown had to be classier than downtown. Certainly the New York *Telegraph* recognized the show for what we wanted it to be: "The new *Burlesques* revealed in all its pristine glory at the Park is like a composite picture of the best bits from all the best musical shows you've ever seen or ever hope to see." That's a review! And it was what Billy had in mind.

Charles Darnton in Billy's old paper, the *World,* said of the women: "Six of the girls danced well and all of them kicked themselves so free of clothing that it was almost impossible to believe this statement in the program.

" 'Stockings, tights and union suits by Nat Lewis.' "

This was typical stuff. It was the best review Minsky's or perhaps any burlesque had gotten up to that date. It was also a pretty important occasion in my life. After hanging around the theater since I was in knickers, I was finally asked to play an official part. Billy was supervising the production at the Park, and he asked me to come up and help out at the box office while Abe and H.K. took care of things downtown. At the time, I was working for a mail-order educational institution called the Alexander Hamilton Institute selling courses in education by mail. It wasn't too hard to make up my mind that a switch to the family might be in my interest, and then there was Ruth waiting for me to get my start.

CHAPTER

11

ABBOTT: You don't know where you are! I'll bet you twenty dollars you're not here, and I'll prove it!

COSTELLO: All right, go ahead. Here's my twenty.

ABBOTT: You're not in St. Louis.

COSTELLO: Right, I'm not in St. Louis.

ABBOTT: And you're not in Chicago?

COSTELLO: No, I'm not in Chicago.

ABBOTT: Well, if you're not in St. Louis or Chicago, you must be someplace else. And if you're someplace else, you can't be here. (*Costello snatches the money.*) Hey! I didn't lose! Give me my money!

COSTELLO: Waddaya mean?

ABBOTT: You took the money right out of my hand.

COSTELLO: I did not.

ABBOTT: You did.

COSTELLO: Look. You said I wasn't here—I was someplace else. And if I was someplace else, I couldn't be here. If I couldn't be here, how could I take your twenty dollars?

BILLY HAD ME working the outside box office. At that time we had *two* box offices. One was the regular one inside the lobby, and the other on wheels was moved out to the sidewalk, where the choice tickets were sold and additional payments were allowed to be made so that the viewer could be up front and get a better-than-average view of the comedy, or the girls, or whatever he had come to see. For this they paid a premium. In other words, we were scalping our own tickets. This was why a member of the family had to be appointed to work in the portable box office. Since there was no cash register and the amounts of money paid for the scalped tickets tended to vary quite a bit, it was necessary to have someone absolutely trustworthy in the job. Who better than the youngest brother, Morton?

I'd like to say that my entry into the theater, and my participation in the most elegant enterprise yet attempted in Minsky's Burlesque, led to eventual financial and theatrical acclaim. But unfortunately this wasn't true. Burlesque audiences wanted to see the same old thing that they were used to. They were not enthusiastic about innovations or adding style to the formula. Just give them the same old bladder, pie in the kisser, and seltzer in the pants and they would be happy. This made Billy very sad, and I didn't like it much either. But eventually we had to scale down our box office from $1.60 to $1.00. People were staying away in droves.

Billy tried very hard to make the thing work. He planted publicity items and had stilt walkers distributing the first twofers ever seen on Broadway. It was Billy's invention—giving two tickets for the price of one. But still nobody came. Billy estimated that part of it was competition from the Columbia Theatre Burlesque, which was at 47th Street and Broadway, and from Hurtig and Seamon's Burlesque, which was at 125th Street. The Park show stayed open nearly six months, and lost a fortune. There was nothing to do but close it down at the end of the six-month lease.

By then my brothers had taken a lease on the "Little Apollo" Theatre on 125th Street. Nobody held me responsible for the failure of the Park, and in fact, my brothers were pleased with my work there, so they asked me to come up to the Apollo.

"You can pitch in there and make it your permanent work," Billy said to me. I was thrilled, naturally. A promotion on my first job. All right, it was in the family. Still, it was a promotion.

Of course, they had a house manager up there and they had a complete staff too, but I was sent to sort of watch over the box-office treasurers and the manager and to keep my eye open as the resident Minsky. However, they also gave me a chance to handle the advertising and work out some of the copy.

Working at the Little Apollo was not exactly like the Alexander Hamilton Institute. In the first place, I walked in there knowing that everybody would have to welcome me, because I was the kid brother. And it was very nice. Everybody was glad to have me. I would work some at the box office before the show, then I'd go home for dinner, and I'd come back at eleven at night to look at the books and review the financial statements from the day before and help out with the payroll, details on insurance claims if somebody got hurt, the compensation report, things of that nature.

I worked in an office behind the seats on the balcony floor, and Billy would be there all the time to supervise the new project, while Abe and Herbert remained downtown.

So now at last I seemed to be settled in a career. The family burlesque business. It seemed the right time to get married, and Ruth was more than willing. My brothers didn't pay me exorbitantly, but it was a living wage, and Ruth and I had waited a long time.

The wedding was an elegant one at the Hotel Commodore, all formal and strictly kosher. The guests were family, friends of the family, and political connections. Nobody from burlesque was invited, unless you count Joe Weinstock, who was connected financially with the Minsky enterprises. The ceremony was performed by Rabbi Elias Solomon. It must have been a very well-made wedding, because it has lasted until this day.

My work in the theater included the count-up. This was when we would check the number of stubs in the ticket box and reconcile it with the number that was indicated in the statement. When the count-up was finished, I'd pop into the theater, have a couple of laughs at the show, and go home. The count-up was again a matter in which it was best to have a family member involved. In one case we actually found there was collusion between the doorman and the treasurer. They were taking money without turning in the stubs. But we didn't prosecute them, and even though they were bonded, we didn't press charges. However, we fired them.

On my days off I used to go to the Broadway theaters, especially to the revues, the Earl Carroll, George White, and Oscar Hammerstein shows, and pretty soon I was contributing bits that finally appeared on the stage. When I came back from a show, I would tell about a certain scene that I found amusing, and before you knew it, they would send in an assistant manager to steal the scene.

After his experience on Broadway, Billy was anxious to make sure that the new Apollo got started with a bang and didn't flop the way the Park had. On the same block Hurtig and Seamon, one of our major competitors, had built themselves a brand-new theater, called Hurtig and Seamon's. They were veteran showmen and very stiff competition for anyone. Billy decided that he had to give a much less classic and much hotter show than he had given downtown. He really wasn't afraid of police raids at the time; in fact, I think he would have welcomed an arrest to make a test of the issue.

He decided to do a broad burlesque of the "artistic" way the Broadway theaters were handling nudity. He called in Mae Dix, who was not only captain of the girls' chorus but a great comedienne as well. Did she have any ideas? She sure did! The Broadway revues in 1924 were featuring girls dressed in flowers who wound up their parade by tearing off their costumes, flower by flower, and throwing them to the audience. Mae suggested we should use a banana costume. Singing an old Anna Held number, "Take a Look at This," she snapped bananas off her bosom and hips, leaving one dangling in front of her crotch, which she broke off just as she went into the wings.

Josephine Baker, the famous black dancer, appropriated this banana gag and included it in her act with which she wowed the audiences at the *Folies Bergère*. It was sort of turn-around being fair play. After all, we got our runway idea from the *Folies*.

Mae's number was a sensation. In fact, it was so sensational that the show was promptly raided. Billy was delighted. It was good publicity and it gave him a chance to go into court, indignantly demanding to know why Ziegfeld's girls' flowers were more artistic than Mae's bananas. The court couldn't come up with an answer, so the charges were dismissed, and the audience flocked to the Apollo box office.

Once we actually won that court case we could go ahead and produce shows that were much closer to the kind of thing that was then being done on Broadway. And we began slowly to introduce the striptease, which still had not come to dominate burlesque as it later did. Two strip acts in every show were becoming standard. But at that time they were done as much for comedy as for titillation and were not the highly glamourized display of nudity that stripping later became.

Around this time a couple of comics came to audition for the show: Joey Faye and Maxie Furman. They were both pretty funny young men, and their act was fresh as far as burlesque material went. Billy asked Faye, "You got any more material?"

"I got a lot of material," Faye replied, "but it's all stolen . . . most of it anyway."

"Stolen?" Billy started to smile.

"From the *First Little Show*, from the *Second Little Show*, *George White's Scandals, Ziegfeld's Follies*, the Palace Theatre, the *Greenwich Village Follies* . . . all the shows around." Faye shrugged sheepishly.

"Well, let me see some of the stuff," Billy demanded. His smile was getting bigger.

Faye and Furman ran through a few of their routines, and Billy laughed heartily.

"Can you put one of these on for Friday?" he asked. It was already Wednesday.

"Sure," Faye said.

"Well, for every sketch you put on, I'll give you twenty-five extra bucks in addition to your salary."

"I can give you five by tomorrow," Faye said, getting excited.

Billy laughed. "I can only use one a week."

Faye looked concerned. "Won't you get sued? After all, it's not our material."

But Billy had been working this gimmick for years. "How can I get sued?" He raised his eyebrows innocently. "We open on a Friday. We do the show Saturday and Sunday. They can't sue me until Monday. Tuesday I go to my lawyer. By Wednesday, we answer the suit, Thursday the show is finished, and Friday we put on a new one. No show, no suit. So don't bang my teakettle." Which in Yiddish is "don't hock me a chinik," which in turn means something like "don't talk nonsense."

The Little Apollo was a big success from the start. For four years it showed a profit of $20,000 every week. Within two years we bought out Hurtig and Seamon and took over the Hurtig and Seamon Apollo, one block away.

But it was during that time that we had a little family trouble. Just when things are going great, something happens to throw a monkey wrench into the machinery.

The family was still pretty upset about Herbert's wandering eye.

It was obvious that he still had a crush on Juanita Dixon, who still worked in the box office. So they dug up a friend of Mary's named Charlotte. She was quite a girl, a real beauty, a college graduate, and she had something in common with Herbert—an interest in good music.

Meanwhile, Herbert would stop to chat with Juanita practically every day, and every time he passed the box office, she followed him with her eyes. It was obvious that she was still in love with him and he with her. But the family kept telling Herbert about what a great match this Charlotte would be, what a fine family she came from, and what a wonderful mother she would make.

There was no question that she was the kind of girl a person would be proud to escort to a restaurant or a concert. Finally, Herbert, somewhat bullied by the family pressure, decided to make everybody happy by getting engaged to Charlotte, but this was before Charlotte had any real idea of how Herbert made his living. She just pictured him being in some terribly romantic theatrical venture. Once she got a look at the show at the National Winter Garden, she all but fainted. She explained to Herbert that she couldn't have any real feelings for a man who made his living in that gross fashion.

Herbert, who had never actually been in love with Charlotte, meanwhile did a little checking around and found out that she had a boyfriend on the side. He confronted her with it and she laughed at him. So as far as Herbert was concerned, that was that. Remembering that time, Herbert told me how it was with him: "Juanita, sweet kid that she was, felt real sorry for me. She gave me a lot of sympathy, which I realized I didn't need. I was glad the engagement was broken. I wanted to marry Juanita all along, so I proposed, and I was the happiest guy in the world when she accepted."

The next day (they didn't have blood tests then) Herbert married Juanita in Greenwich, Connecticut. He had invited a few family friends to attend the ceremony, but except for Ruth and me, no family members were there. He spent his honeymoon at a tourist cabin in Westchester, and we had the adjoining room. I tried to make Herbert feel accepted by pulling some of the old newlywed stunts— rocks in the bed and a squeaker in the mattress. I think it cheered him up. Meanwhile, the family, although disappointed, avoided an outright break with Herbert, but there is no doubt that his marriage created a family problem.

Herbert might have been happy (and that didn't last forever either), but the family was really upset by the marriage. Juanita was not Jewish, a divorcée to boot, with a child of her own. Maybe if they had found a better friend of Mary's than Charlotte, things would have been different. But things only got worse.

HARRY CONLEY (*In diatribe against much put-upon wife*):
You walk down the street. Everybody's looking at
you! Everybody's laughing. Making a fool of yourself, and me too. You and your . . . ingrown knees!
You walk like you've got a diaper rash! I tried to help
you. I got you a good job down at the winery stomping grapes with your feet. And you got *fired!* Sitting
down on the job!

MAYBE THINGS WERE not so perfect in the family during that time,
but at the Apollo and the National Winter Garden they were just
fine, thank you. We went from two shows a day to four shows a day
and were still packing them in. It seemed to me that practically
every few months there was some new innovation to keep things
lively. It was certainly a lot more interesting than going to New York
University had been.

One of our innovations was to move the candy butcher from the
back of the house to the front to make his pitch during the intermission. We thought that between the boring movies—old Andy Clyde
comedies and moldy travelogues—the real seat warmers would go.
It was hard to get more people in if the ones that were there insisted
on staying through several shows. So, we talked to Markowich.
Oscar Markowich was the tsar of the candy butchers. He had his

concessions in every theater and ultimately became one of the big financiers of a good many burlesque shows. Of course, concessionaires have always been a part of burlesque. They were a holdover from the carnivals, in which many of them started. The candy butchers actually had two purposes: They filled in a certain amount of time so that we didn't have to use that time for our paid talent and, of course, they served to clear out the house of those hangers-on we called the lodgers before the start of the next show.

Thus, after the starring strip act went out and the curtains closed, the candy butcher would come down front in the auditorium, just in front of the orchestra pit, and the spotlight would hit him, as though *he* were now a star. I'll give you an idea of his spiel. It went something like this:

"My friends tonight I shall speak to you frankly, sincerely, and without camouflage. In this theater we call a spade a spade, and if sometimes there's a little dirt sticking to it, I think you'll forgive us for that, because I know and I'm certain that you're all men and women of the world or else you would not be in this particular place of entertainment. Am I right? I can see by your faces that I am right.

"If I could, I would come down there and go up into the balcony to shake hands with each and every one of you and look you in the eye, man to man, to tell you how sincerely I believe in the offer I'm about to present, an opportunity that knocks once in a lifetime.

"I must make the best of the time so graciously offered to me by the Minsky brothers and be concise and brief. There is only time for me to describe but once this offer I am about to present, and then there will be time for me to get to the point with no more beating about the bush. Nobody's going to pull the wool over anybody's eyes, so why should I try to deceive anybody in this particular place of entertainment?

"I'm holding up a box. You all see it? In each and every box that I'm holding up is an exotic assortment of genuine, imported chocolate bonbons especially made for this exacting Minsky audience at this famous theater.

"You will ask how can they sell an assortment like this for the ridiculous sum of twenty-five cents a box? The answer, my friends, is we are not selling these delectable confections, we are giving them to you absolutely free, *gratis*. Now, you may ask what are you paying for? I will tell you, my friends, what you are paying for. When I have finished describing what you will soon purchase for the measly sum of one quarter of a dollar, I insist you tell me man to man and eye to eye if this is not the most fabulous buy for twenty-five cents that you've ever been offered.

"What's that, sir? What? You ask if there's not a valuable prize in certain boxes of bonbons? I beg your pardon, sir, but you're wrong. There is a valuable prize in *each* and *every* box. You, sir, you raise your hand? You wish to speak? I see. Look at this. On this gentleman's wrist down here is a genuine seventeen-jewel Elgin wristwatch with a fourteen-carat solid gold case." At this point a shill, or sometimes nobody at all, would raise his hand and everybody would crane their necks to see where the lucky recipient of the watch was, but by now the candy butcher was going on with his spiel.

"Thank you. I merely asked you to look at it. Look at the evidence and decide for yourselves whether I'm telling the truth when I say there is a valuable prize in each and every package. Thank you, sir, for your kind and unsolicited testimonial." (Still no sign of the watch holder.) "Thank you, sir."

"How many others are proud recipients of brand-new wristwatches and genuine alligator wallets? How many of genuine onyx rings? Raise your hands, please. Look at that show of hands!" (Where? Where?)

I can assure you that the candy man and his boss, Oscar Markowich, did not go broke from giving away all these items to the not-too-eager patrons. But they made a nice buck, and we got a certain share for the concession. The funny thing is that as time went on, people who would come to the theater began to see the pitchmen as entertainers and comedians as much as the people in the show itself. Some of them, in fact, did go into theater management or into other businesses. The experience they gained in sales at Minsky's and the other burlesque houses did them a lot of good in their later lives. For example, Sid Stone became famous for doing a similar pitch on Ed Wynn's Texaco television show.

As for the spicy contents of the literature and photos being given away, they were reprints of girlie cartoons or de Maupassant stories.*

So important a part of burlesque did the candy butchers become that they formed an organization called the Theater Candy Conces-

* See Appendix H for the pitchman's spiel.

sionaires Association (later called the Theatrical Concessionaire Managers Association), which held dances and socials for the members, during which they got a chance to talk without having to sell anything at all.

Unfortunately, however, many of the burlesque owners ultimately became bound over hand and foot to Oscar Markowich and frequently it was his money alone that kept the theater open. I always understood that it was Markowich who had supplied the money to Hurtig and Seamon to open their Apollo on 125th Street, a definite thorn in our side.

Meanwhile, after working in the theater for a while and talking with Billy, I began to get some ideas myself. One of my big inspirations when I went back to work at the National Winter Garden was the annual birthday party for Mother Elms. We would send invitations to the press to come down to see this dignified old ex-chorus girl. They were hand-written invitations on the bottom of a photograph in which Mother would write, "Won't you come and help me celebrate?" All the local press came—even Brooks Atkinson of the New York *Times*.

Mother's presence in the company simply emphasized the way we saw our operation. The fact is that there *was* something special about Minsky's. A warmth and intimacy and a feeling that we were working as a team. This came essentially from the fact that we had a regular company working together week after week. People got to know one another like a family, and that's the way I saw the Minsky troup, as a regular family. Mother Elms, for instance, knew each girl by name, she knew all of their peculiarities and their vices, but she didn't talk much about that. Besides, she had been far from an angel herself in her theatrical past. In the same bag Mother kept her gin she had an assortment of cosmetics, razor blades, powder puffs, and even condoms that she sold to members of the cast for a modest profit. And don't forget the candy she always offered me as a child. It wasn't a bad life for a seventy-nine-year-old former hoofer, and I know that she appreciated it.

CHAPTER

13

JOEY FAYE: My brother's in the hospital. He got run over by a streetcar.
CONNIE RYAN: I'll bet you feel badly.
JOEY FAYE: I would feel badly, if he was my *real* brother.
CONNIE RYAN: Don't be silly! Isn't he your real brother?
JOEY FAYE: No. Since he's been run over by the streetcar, he's only my *half* brother!

AS WE PROGRESSED into the Prohibition era there were a lot of changes on Second Avenue. For one thing, our audiences became different. Uptowners would come to one of the best speakeasies in the city, Manny Wolf's, only a few hundred yards from our front door, take a few drinks to get themselves in a relaxed mood, and show up at our sixth-floor theater in a very mellow and tolerant state of mind. This crowd, along with those who had started coming on passes that I gave away when I was in college, more or less elevated the level of the audience, so that besides the locals, we were also attracting people from all parts of the city and getting a lot of attention in the press not only from the daily reporters, but also from some of the most prestigious drama critics and commentators in the city. Brooks Atkinson was a great fan, as was Robert Garland, the Broadway columnist who practically adopted the National Winter

Garden. Garland wrote about the Second Avenue Minsky theater in the New York *Telegram* in 1927:

". . . a jolly evening. In the East Side's revue there's no smirk, no art for art's sake, no double-entendre. A spade's a spade, especially when there's dirt sticking to it. Which I suspect is why the National Winter Garden has grown from a joke to a national institution."

Brooks Atkinson generally gave us a pretty good plug. Once he said, "What the *Folies Bergères* is to Paris the Minsky shows are to a lucky New York."

There is no question that as the youngest Minsky I was having the time of my life working backstage and being part of show biz, as they call it now.

And, although show business could be fun, there were plenty of problems being the front of the house manager and occasionally poking my head backstage.

Here are some of the things that might happen in one of my better days:

- The cashier doesn't arrive on time to open up. A dozen people walk away because the box office is closed.
- Two of the usherettes are out sick.
- Business at the first show is lousy.
- The box office is short on the third hour's checkup.
- Three bulbs go out at the same time under the marquee. I finally manage to locate the house electrician, but find out that he has no bulbs.
- The theater is too hot. People are complaining. So I turn down the heat. Backstage the chorus and principals are yelling it is too cold. I turn up the heat.
- It looks cloudy, so I pray for good weather for that weekend. I get good weather. Business is lousy.
- The next weekend we have a snow storm and surprise—we sell out!
- We have a terrific show. Great comedy, terrific girls. What happens? No business. The next week we have a show that I think stinks on ice, and we can't handle the crowd.
- When business is poor, we try to think what we can blame it on. Maybe there's too much competition. Maybe it's the fights. Maybe it's wrestling. In the summer or late spring we might have competition from baseball.

- I have to straighten out the state tax, the federal tax, the new social security tax, the city tax, and frankly, a few payments to representatives of the police department and other law-enforcement agencies who come in to watch the show and stop by the manager's office for their little present.
- We get an SOS from backstage. The toilet is stopped up again. Where am I going to get a plumber at ten-thirty at night?

Probably the most dramatic incident I remember while running the front of the house was when one of the customers came running to me one night and told me that there was a guy sitting up in the loge fondling a gun—the loges were in the front part of the balcony. From time to time, according to my excited informant, the loge sitter would point a pistol at the stage. I notified Nick Elliott, the manager, who was after all an ex-cop, and he ran up and grabbed the man. As he struggled in Nick's brawny grasp the customer kept twisting around to point his gun back at the stage, yelling, "I'm gonna kill that comic! I'm gonna kill him!"

Who knows what the comic had said to set off this lunatic? But it sure added a certain amount of spice to an evening that already had more excitement than I could use.

You're beginning to get the picture? Life at Minsky's was not always a basket of rosebuds.

Meanwhile, we would use a million exploitation gimmicks to get audiences into the theaters. Billy sent out thousands of subtly perfumed notes with pictures of the strippers to a posh list of male New Yorkers. The notes were written in a very frilly, feminine hand in red: "When will I see you, honey? Same place, same time—corner of Houston Street and Christie! Your sweetie, Madam Lazonga" . . . or whoever. The passes were books of coupons, and each was good for one free admission for bearer "unless accompanied by wife." We sprinkled several judicious dollops of Woolworth's best Nuit de Passion before slipping them into their plain wrappers. The perfumed passes were sent to a list composed of members of the 40 and 8 Club of the American Legion—all former officers, Dunhill's private-blend tobacco customers, a list that we got from the Duveen and Wildenstein art galleries of some of the most important buyers of French Impressionist paintings, regular customers at Sweet's Seafood Restaurant near the Fulton Fish Market, and every third physician listed in the classified directory.

Billy also circulated around the Harvard and Yale clubs, the University Club, the Racquet Club, and the Union League Club, where he left the girls' calling cards on the bulletin boards. Nobody seemed to complain that he was not a member.

If you didn't belong to a club you could still pick up twofers on the street. They were in the form of a season pass. You would have to fill in your name, and when you came to the box office, you would have to pay a service charge. It could be fifty cents at night or twenty-five cents for a matinee. For the price of the matinee you would get a $1.10 seat; in the evenings you'd get a $2.20 seat. We even had a man on our payroll who was nicknamed Twofer and wandered all over town wearing a sandwich board plugging the National Winter Garden and carrying a handful of two-for-one passes.

Then every year we'd run a popularity election for the Queen of the Winter Garden. We'd give out buttons to the audience during the campaign: "Curls Mason for Queen," "Vote for Lola," "Chubby Is the Choice." We'd paper the lobby with electioneering posters, just like a regular election, and the girls recited their campaign pledges during the first-act-curtain production number.

Here was Maisie's campaign speech: "Up with Maisie, down with Prohibition, and off with union suits!" (Loud cheers.) Ballots were handed out and marked as collected.

These promotional bits really paid off. Our company played to full houses, twice a day, six days a week, forty-two weeks a year, and the money rolled in. When we upped our prices to a $2.20 top, scalpers on Second Avenue were getting $7.00 and $7.50 each. Those were boom days. Who cared for money! As I said, we were getting a pretty classy clientele. Regulars at that time included the publishers Condé Nast and Frank Crowninshield, the writers John Erskine and John Dos Passos, the columnists Walter Winchell and Mark Hellinger. Such distinguished commentators as Robert Benchley, Irvin S. Cobb, and George Jean Nathan were loyal attenders, as was a shy poet named Hart Crane, who wrote this poem in our honor:

National Winter Garden

Outspoken buttocks in pink beads
Invite the necessary cloudy clinch
The world's one flagrant sweaty cinch.
And while legs waken salads in the brain

You pick your blonde out neatly through the smoke.
Always you wait for someone else though, always—
(Then rush the nearest exit through the smoke).

That's a poem, right? But while "legs were wakening salads" in Hart Crane's brain, the women backstage were even more earthy than the poet's visions of them.

But be that as it may, the new type of burlesque girls, slimmer, saucier, and unquestionably nuder than they had been in the past, were filling the Minsky theater seats. So well did business seem to be going that in 1931, in the depth of the Depression, the Minsky brothers decided it was time to take another stab at Broadway.

CHAPTER

14

DR. KRONKITE: Are you taking the medicine I gave you
regularly?
FIRST BANANA: I tasted it and decided I'd rather have
the cough!

TO PEOPLE OF the postburlesque generation, *The Night They Raided
Minsky's* was a revelation. Many of them had heard the name
"Minsky" and had a vague idea of what burlesque was. But Rowland Barber's masterful book (published in 1967) presented a vivid
and generally colorful picture of the burlesque scene. Frequently, it
was quite accurate. Barber, as a writer of what he called "a fanciful
expedition to the lost Atlantis of show business," constructed a brilliant, fictional plot around the real-life background of the National
Winter Garden in 1925. Of course, he got most of the material for
the historic background from me and such relics of the old days who
were still around, and later I served as technical adviser of the successful film that was made from the book. I was delighted to see the
name "Minsky" alive and well in the context of burlesque, even
though for only a brief moment on the screen.

As for April 20, 1925, the day that the raid on which the book was
based took place, it was hardly epochal in the history of burlesque,
but it did turn out to be a prelude to much greater troubles. Barber
built his story around Mademoiselle Fifi of Paree, who was, as I re-

73

call, a woman named Mary Dawson from the mountains of Pennsylvania. In Barber's book she was named Betty Buzby, the daughter of a Pennsylvania cop who was a Quaker no less. Personally, I never heard of a Quaker cop, but since the cops are supposed to be keepers of the peace, it may be possible. Certainly, Mademoiselle Fifi was real and a big draw on Second Avenue at the time. She had a fabulous figure, a genuine ball-bearing movement, a generous bust and hips, and a lovely thin waist. She also had a crush on my brother Billy, which I do not believe he returned in kind, or if he did, he kept it under his Homburg. Remember, Billy had a pretty hard time getting a night out to himself with ever-suspicious Mary always keeping an eye on him.

Rowland Barber had a lot of fun with the concept Mademoiselle Fifi. But when the book came out, Mademoiselle Fifi came out of the woodwork, which in this case was Juno Beach, Florida, and figuratively blew the whistle on Barber. Of course, I knew who she was all along, but there was no sense in crabbing Barber's act, especially since the whole thing was largely fictionalized.

Of course, her character, Mademoiselle Fifi, was fictionalized even when she was working for us. I remember when Billy conducted full-scale press conferences he would always have the questions addressed to him and then whisper them to "Mademoiselle Fifi," and have her whisper her answer in his ear.

"Mademoiselle Fifi," he would explain, "does not speak so good the English. So I will be her spokesman." I'm not sure that the newsmen ever believed this either, but Billy had the charm to make them go along with his publicity conceits.

Mary Dawson, who was in actuality Mademoiselle Fifi, was not a stripper in the first place. She was an "exotic" dancer—a cooch dancer. Mary in an interview years later said, "I never did anything risqué, although I worked with a lot of strippers." That was largely true in the sense that Mary never showed any forbidden parts of her shapely body, but she created a dance that was extremely popular with the audiences.

Her father, I learned later, really was a police officer and a straightlaced Quaker, but he never came to New York City and certainly never led a raid to shut down one of our burlesque houses.

Anyway, the raid story was fun, but the raid itself was simply one of dozens to which we had become accustomed. Certainly no crisis.

The year 1925 was the beginning of the period when sex was to be the dominant factor in burlesque, but not yet in the form of a fully developed striptease. Girls would take off a garment here and there and flash an extra bit of anatomy, but the highly developed art of striptease, which emerged in the next few years, was still in its formative stages.

That day in 1925 was a balmy spring day. But we brothers might have seen less joy in the buds of spring let alone our own Minsky Rosebuds if we had had access to the letter written to our father at his realty office by John Sumner, secretary of the New York Society for the Suppression of Vice. Sumner had ascertained that my father owned the premises of the National Winter Garden and had somehow decided that he was responsible for the performances with which we entertained the neighborhood and the hoi polloi. In those days, censors and self-appointed critics like Sumner were not so much interested in nudity, of which there was not a great deal, as in the sometimes racy material in the sketches. At that time we were doing two such sketches, which I am proud to say I titled myself, one being "Anatomy and Cleopatra." (Sumner did not even get the joke and in his letter to my father called it "*Antony* and Cleopatra.") And "Desire Under the El," a put-on of Eugene O'Neill's *Desire Under the Elms*, which was playing on Broadway at the time.

In his letter to my father, Sumner pointed out that he had seen the show on the Monday before, and despite the big sign in front of the theater that said "Burlesque As You Like It," Sumner did *not* like it. He found the two sketches to be "lewd, obscene, contributory to immoral conduct, and in gross violation of Section 1140 A of the Penal Law." Sumner wrote to my father that he intended to buy a ticket to the National Winter Garden on April 20, and if he found that the comedy sketches were still in violation of the law and public taste he would not hesitate to call the police and have the theater served with a complaint. Apparently Sumner saw nothing wrong with the ladies of the chorus, who comported themselves, he said, "with great zest and jollity, with no resort to unseemly actions." He even said that he enjoyed Mademoiselle Fifi's "Oriental shimmy ballet" as "an exemplary model of popular entertainment."

My father was startled to get this communication but not actually surprised. In the first place, although he had never attended a performance, he was well aware what was involved in a burlesque theater. Furthermore, he had never been entirely happy about our operation. So he put the letter in his pocket without bothering to inform Mr. Sumner that he had absolutely nothing to do with the theater. As far as he was concerned, his wayward sons could face the music or the police, and perhaps the pressure by the authorities might induce them to leave the shameful business in which they were engaged and return to the honorable business of real estate.

But if he was hoping that we would get caught with our pants down, so to speak, on this particular night, he was mistaken. It's true that we had touted the opening of the show, which featured the return of Mademoiselle Fifi from parts unknown, as the hottest thing since the cremation of Dan McGrew. But it was also true that Billy's gorgeous wife, Mary, had for reasons of her own, informed him that she intended to be present at the first show, and Billy, who had always assured her that the goings-on at Minsky's were purer than a Chattauqua tent tour, was not anxious to be proven a liar. So word had gone out for that night to stick with the Boston version.

The show opened with a chorus of Rosebuds, featuring Billy Carson in a shimmy and modified strip, followed by a sketch called "A Quiet Game of Cards," which featured our star straight man Raymond Paine; Scratch Wallace, one of our lead comics; and comic Jack Shutta. This was a standard old burlesque bit, featuring huge rolls of stage money, knives, hatchets, cudgels, pistols, slapsticks, bladders, seltzer bottles, and even a cannon once in a while. It featured such racy gags as the following:

> PAINE: My friend, that's a terrible cold you have there, terrible! Didn't you say you always slept in a nice, warm bed? How come you caught a cold?
> WALLACE: Last night her husband showed up and I had to get up out of the nice, warm bed and go home.

Nothing there that Mr. Sumner could complain about. Finally, after a lot of dancing, wiggling, and kicking, we got to Mr. Sumner's "naughty" sketch, "Desire Under the El," with Raymond Paine, Scratch Wallace, and two talking women, Chubby Drisdale and Holly Dean.

Scratch enters alone and delivers his classic line, which I'm sure you've all heard repeated in a million contexts: "Dis mus' be de blace!" He looks all around desperately. "But where's *Ray-mund*? Oh, *Ray-mund*! I hope nothing's happened to him. This is a dangerous neighborhood. Oh, my golly!" He notices something lying in the street and picks it up. It is a prop leg. "That looks like Ray-mund's leg! And this looks like Ray-mund's other *leg!*" Now he picks up another leg. "*This* looks like Ray-mund's arm!" He picks up prop arm. "And *this* looks like his *other* arm!" Scratch finally reaches the head. He picks it up, shakes it and looks it in the eye. "Ray-mund! Ray-mund! Are you all right?" (This always got a big laugh, and certainly wouldn't be enough to raise Sumner's hackles.)

Now, the sexy part. Chubby enters as a fast-talking flapper, and Holly, as a sweet, young thing. There is a certain amount of heavily loaded give and take as the well-endowed Chubby, whose bosom comes about up to Raymond's nose, does a bit of business trying to seduce him while Raymond tries to show Scratch "the art of Casanova," but the boys get nowhere.

> RAYMOND (*discouraged*): We gotta change our approach! We gotta play hard to get.
> WALLACE: But are we going to vamp them?
> PAINE: No, first we let 'em *scrutinize* and *then* we *vamp* 'em.
> WALLACE: "Scrutinize 'em! *That's* playing hard to get?"

This was the essence of humor in many burlesque bits. Words like "scrutinize" dragged out lasciviously could almost always be milked for a laugh. But it was still doubtful that Sumner could make much out of that.

Then came another girl number:

A MINSKY'S DOZEN—THIRTEEN LUSCIOUS PEACHES
ON THE ILLUMINATED RUNWAY OF JOY!
Spotlighting
Eva LaMonte and Her Union-Suit Teasers!

Eva's solo went like this:

> A gentleman came to my flat last night.
> He said, "Are you ready to do it? Then don't waste time
> with idle chatter—I'll take it out and let's go to it!"
>
> *Chorus*
> *Oh, save a little ray of golden sunshine for a*
> *rainy, rainy day!"*

The first way was standing up, then he said, "Let's try
the couch—your legs up here, your head down there.
Great!" he said, and I said, "Ouch!"

Chorus
It will come in mighty handy when the skies are
gray!

Oh, we tried it on the pedestal, we tried it in the
Morris chair,
on the carpet, on the table, against the wall and on the
stair . . .
We tried it with the lights all on, and by the yellow
candles' blink;
He made me try it everywhere excepting the kitchen
sink!

Chorus
Oh, save a little ray of golden sunshine for a
rainy, rainy day . . .

"At last," he cried, "I'm satisfied! I hope I haven't
done you wrong."
"Oh, not at all—don't fear," I said,
"I could do it all night long! . . ."

A few more verses and she was getting near the punch line.

When he wiped it off and put it away,
We laughed and laughed and laughed—
At the funny positions a girl must get in,
To have herself pho-to-graphed.

So we went on with the usual show—a chorus number, a shimmy,
a comedy number—and we got to "Anatomy and Cleopatra, or
Shakespeare Shimmies in His Grave." This one starred Paine as
Caesar, Wallace as Marc Antony, and Chubby Drisdale as Cleopatra; it also featured Jack Shutta, Tom Bundy, Holly Deane, and Eva
LaMonte. They went through the familiar routine, which ends with
a stagehand running down the runway, after the curtain call and
the death of Raymond Paine as Caesar, with a chair:

PAINE: What's that chair for?
STAGEHAND: For rigor mortis to set in! (*The curtains come together.*)

Much of the suggestiveness in these sketches was conveyed in the double takes, the leers, and the positions of the actors, something hard to establish for someone like Sumner, who was trying to copy down the lines in his notebook in the balcony.

Now, Barber tells this all in great and highly imaginative detail. Of course, I was in the front of the house counting the take. Billy was in the back of the house when who should come in but Joe Weinstock, Billy's principal money backer, who had been talking very seriously about featuring Fifi in the Park uptown. Billy didn't know what to do now, since Mary was sitting there catching the show, and I had had a feeling for some time that Billy's interest in Mademoiselle Fifi was more than platonic. But business was business. And if Weinstock saw the tamed-down show, he'd never come up with the money. So Billy went backstage and whispered in Fifi's ear. Who knows what he said? Maybe Barber had a tape recorder backstage. I personally don't know. But I know the results. Whatever he said to Fifi persuaded her into wiggling her substantial and curvaceous form into the wildest and sexiest exhibition seen at the National Winter Garden to date.

Although Sumner had previously seen nothing wrong with Fifi's act, he now realized that this was the moment that he had come for. He had taken the precaution of alerting detectives who were stationed through various parts of the house. When Fifi flashed that magnificent chest, he blew an urgent whistle. The detectives were standing by, and on the signal they lumbered up the aisles, blowing whistles and yelling to beat the band. One detective ran for the telephone and called headquarters to send a uniformed squad and plenty of paddy wagons. The infamous raid was on and there was plenty of action to come!

CHAPTER
15

TOM BUNDY: How can you lie like that, and look me in the face?
STEVE MILLS: I'm getting used to your face.

THERE WERE DETECTIVES all over the place trying without being too indecent to put the pinch on the girls in their various states of undress. Two of the cops tried to pull the curtain closed, but they got no help from the stagehands and neither of them knew how to do it. Meanwhile, the audience, after watching to make sure they were missing none of the spicier action, headed in disorder for the lobby, the elevators, and even the seldom-used staircases. In the end the cops filled three paddy wagons with various members of the cast and staff, including Raymond Paine, Scratch Wallace, Tom Bundy, all of the chorus girls, the featured women, the talking women, and even a few of the stagehands. In the end, by the time the people of the state of New York actually moved on the complaint, the only ones who were named were Billy, Mademoiselle Fifi, Paine, Wallace, Holly Deane, Eva LaMonte, Chubby Drisdale and Jack Shutta and Tom Bundy.

Weinstock was there, delighted with the whole deal. Although the show in general had been tame, Fifi's finale and the sure publicity that would follow the raid would ensure full houses at the soon-to-be-opened theater uptown. It was Weinstock, in fact, who put up bail at the arraignment.

The trial that followed was longer and probably funnier than any show that had played at Minsky's to date. It ran for seven weeks.

You have to realize that the complaint that Sumner filed was not a police complaint but more or less a citizen's arrest. Remember this was 1925, still the days when Jimmy Walker, the suave man about town, was mayor of New York and when Billy knew most of the political figures through his newspaper connections or our father; even the magistrate in charge was a family friend. Nobody was actually panicked at the accusations, and the publicity didn't do any harm at the box office. The court sessions ran only from ten-thirty in the morning until twelve-thirty, so that the performers could get back to the theater for the matinee. The first surprise of the trial was the state's Exhibit A—a carbon copy of the letter Sumner had sent to my father. This was introduced to show that Sumner had given us a fair warning.

I was at the theater when all this was going on and got my reports from Billy and the press. All of us were astonished because it was the first any of us had heard or seen about Sumner's letter. Only our father knew about it. Paul Weintraub, who represented us in this case, had the letter thrown out as evidence. The judge at the same time managed to get in a zinger at Sumner. "I must chide the State's Attorney for inadequate preparation in this case," the judge said, "and I must express dismay over the underhanded conduct of Complainant, in that he must address his letters of warning to names he finds on cornerstones. Or should I say not 'underhanded' but 'pussyfooted.'"

The truth was that Sumner had a very slight case against Minsky. The judge directed the state to drop its case against Wallace, Paine, Chubby Drisdale, Holly Deane, Eva LaMonte, Jack Shutta, and Tom Bundy. Among the performers, this left only Fifi. But before those charges were dropped, the comics put on a performance of "Anatomy and Cleopatra" in the courtroom using no costumes or props except a fire-extinguisher hose that Chubby requisitioned for use as the "as-ip." Despite the lack of props, the skit done against the unusual background of the courtroom still brought down the house.

Finally, they got down to the two points of Sumner's argument. One was that "the defendant, Miss Fifi's pelvic contortions during the dance programmed as 'The Shame of La Bohème' were such as to be lewdly suggestive, of lascivious import, and therefore indecent and immoral." The judge, barely able to restrain himself from breaking out into laughter at the concept, asked Sumner to explain what he meant by "pelvic contortions." Did you ever try to describe a wiggle or a bump or a grind in plain English? Sumner wiggled around verbally but couldn't define what he meant by pelvic contortions to the judge's satisfaction.

"I said pelvic contortions such as what? If you lack the powers of speech to deliver a clear answer to my question, I suggest that you call upon your powers of locomotion."

"Meaning what, Your Honor?"

"Meaning, Mr. Secretary, that you step down here, before the bench, and demonstrate with your own anatomy exactly what you saw the defendant perform on the night of April 20, 1925, and which did so offend your sensibilities that you drew up a complaint of violation of Section 1140 A of the Penal Law. That's what I mean."

Sumner protested vainly that he couldn't really do a good job of it without musical accompaniment. The judge asked for volunteers among the cast who could possibly sing the music that accompanied the dance. Raymond, Tom, Holly, and Chubby all knew it. The judge ordered them to sing while Sumner danced. And Sumner, red-faced, did his best to give an interpretation of the movements of the sinuous Fifi. Needless to say it was hardly "lascivious," to put it mildly.

"Mr. Minsky," the judge asked, "would you as proprietor of the National Winter Garden hire this dancer for your show?"

"Your Honor," my brother said, "I wouldn't wish this dancer to waltz on the grave of my worst enemy."

So point one was effectively blunted. But it took some time to get the convulsed court into order again. Now all that was left was the second point of the prosecution, which was that Fifi, of her own free will and with the knowledge and consent of Mr. Minsky, "during the aforesaid performance did bare her breasts and cause them to move indecently." Now Weintraub got a crack at Sumner again. He asked him if Fifi was "devoid of any clothing from the region of her navel to the top of her head." Sumner averred that she was "nude from the waist up, in the parlance of the theater." Weintraub seemed taken by the expression. "In the parlance of the theater? Which theater are you talking about? The National Winter Garden, is that the theater that you speak of?" Sumner said he wasn't specifically referring to the National Winter Garden but speaking in general.

"Is it the general practice in theaters of this city to display young ladies 'nude from the waist up'?" Heatedly, Sumner denied this.

"Is it done in any theater in this city to your best knowledge, Mr. Sumner?" Sumner *phumphered*, looked to the state's attorney for help, and finally made a croaking noise. The judge directed him to answer more intelligently, and bit by bit Weintraub elicited his answer.

"Have you ever been to shows produced by Earl Carroll or the Shubert brothers?"

"Yes," Sumner admitted miserably, "I have."

"And in such shows have you not seen women 'nude from the waist up'?"

"Yes," Sumner mumbled almost inaudibly.

"But you never charged Earl Carroll or the Shubert brothers with putting on an indecent performance? Why didn't you ask the police to halt the *Vanities* or *Artists and Models*?"

"Because I did not see anything in them of an immoral nature."

"Not even half-naked young women?"

"Correct."

"Could you explain why exposed breasts are decent north of Fourteenth Street but indecent south of it?"

"Well . . . yes. You see, the difference is the movement. On Broadway unadorned female figures are used to artistic advantage in tableaux. They do not move. But Mademoiselle Fifi on the night of April 20 was nude from the waist up and she *did* move."

"Did she assume a still position, immediately on removing her upper garment?" Weintraub asked. He threw his arms up in a position resembling a classical statuette. "Like this?"

"Well, yes. That was approximately her position."

Weintraub went to the defense table and took two illustrations, which he established had been taken from an authoritative book of art history. In one there was a detail from a Greek temple in Sicily. The other showed a fragment of an Egyptian vase. He asked if Sumner could deny that Fifi's pose after disrobing at the National Winter Garden was exactly that of the Egyptian sunworshiper or the goddess Aphrodite in the art-book illustration. Sumner caved in. What could he say? He couldn't deny it. But then he couldn't confirm it either. Finally, after much prodding he admitted that Fifi's pose could possibly be construed as artistic.

"Of aesthetic appeal?"

"I suppose so," Sumner said.

"But how could Mademoiselle Fifi's appeal be aesthetic—and at the same time, as you charge, indecent and immoral? Do you, sir, equate the ancient and classical arts, the handiwork of the proud Egyptian and the noble Greek, with a dirty peep show?" Now Sumner seemed to change his stand. He said he had "no objection to the so-called artistic pose assumed by the defendant."

"So what do you object to then?" asked Weintraub.

"Well . . . to what the defendant did following her . . . her *tableau.*"

Weintraub asked what that was.

"She moved. She moved in a heated . . . I might say passionate . . . fashion."

To everybody's surprise, Weintraub dismissed the witness. But he didn't rest the case. He now asked the defendant, Mademoiselle Fifi, to be recalled. When he had her on the stand, he asked her if she had heard and understood everything said in the court this morning. Fifi nodded that she had.

"Tell the court if you please," Weintraub said, "what you did on the night in question following your 'tableau,' as we shall call it."

"You mean after I made a pose like this?" Fifi said, demonstrating the approximate position.

"Yes. Following that, what did you do?"

"I moved."

"How would you describe your movement?"

"Well, I was pretty worked up, I can tell you that."

"Would you say that you moved in a heated or passionate fashion?"

"Do you mean passionate like 'all hot and bothered'?"

"Yes."

"Then that's how I moved, Mr. Weintraub, I mean the kind of fashion I moved in you could describe it as 'passionate.' "

"Why did you move in such a fashion?"

"Why? Well, *golly,* Mr. Weintraub, you'd move in such a fashion too if two big gumshoes were chasing you down the runway!"

It took a while to get the court into order after that. It was by now the end of the seventh week of the trial. The judge asked Weintraub if he was ready to move for a dismissal of the complaint. Billy smiled placidly. He had little doubt of what the outcome would be. The judge looked over Weintraub's document very carefully, held it up to the light, put it down on his bench, and whacked his gavel.

"Complaint, dismissed!"

Relieved, everybody from the Minsky contingent went out into the hot summer air and drifted into Manny Wolf's cool speakeasy for a drink.

It was a serious defeat, but Sumner wasn't through with the Minskys by a long shot.

16

SCRATCH WALLACE: I've been misbehaving and my
conscience is bothering me.
RAYMOND PAINE: I see, and since I'm a psychiatrist, you
want something to strengthen your willpower?
SCRATCH WALLACE: No, something to weaken my conscience!

THERE WAS A poignant sidebar to the story of the raid. During the
previous week, Billy had hired a petite pony dancer named Thelma
"Giggles" Leonard. Since I was in the front of the house, I saw her
infrequently, but she was kind of cute, to my taste—slim and flap-
perish, and not as beefy as many of the principals then working for
Minsky's.

She had, as I remember, a thatch of badly dyed henna-red hair
that a modern punk rocker would envy. But there was something
cute and wistful about her. She had a certain innocent quality.
Later I heard that Giggles claimed to be Jewish on her father's side.
Of course, according to Hebrew law in order to be Jewish you're
supposed to be Jewish on your mother's side. I heard a rumor
around the theater that one of my college crowd who had been
coming regularly to the National Winter Garden since I had graduated from NYU had a serious crush on her, but I never meddled in
the private lives of the girls backstage. Anyway, Giggles was one of
the girls gathered up in Sumner's inglorious raid, but since she had

nothing to do with nudity, and wasn't even a talking woman, they could pin nothing on her and dismissed the complaint against her on the very night of the arraignment. But while she was being questioned, one of the police sergeants on the scene asked her to step aside so that he could talk to her about another matter. During the excitement of the evening the members of the cast lost track of her, but they became concerned when she didn't show up for the show the next day. Just as Maisie was about to replace her in the pony chorus, Giggles appeared in the dressing room, looking pale and shaken and out of breath. This was because she had ignored the elevator and run six flights up the fire escape at the back of the theater. Meanwhile, my friend from college had come around to the front office concerned about Giggles and asked if I could carry a message to her. So I went backstage and told her that there was a young man asking very urgently to see her. Giggles, to my eyes, was hardly in any shape to see anyone. She looked completely shaken, about the experience in the police station I thought at that time.

From what I heard, Giggles was far from her charming self that night as she ran through the various pony numbers: from the "Luscious Peach" to the not-so-modest maiden of the "Persian Garden of Mademoiselle Poupique" and the "Ain't We Got Fun Girl" to the courtesan of the "Court of King Louis" to, finally, her role as a risqué "Minsky Model." But when the finale came, Giggles wasn't to be found. At first the other girls thought she had gone home early, but her coat and street clothes were still in the dressing room. The mystery of her disappearance was solved when the stage manager opened the double doors to the rear fire escape as he always did to air out the theater after the show.

Giggles was found lying on the fire escape platform. She had drunk a half bottle of silver shoe dye. The poison had apparently killed her instantly. She was wearing her "Fun Girl" union suit, decorated with blue banjos and orange musical notes. The cast was utterly shattered. Back in the dressing room one of the girls produced a late edition of a newspaper item that explained the whole thing. She had been holding it back in order not to embarrass her friend.

GIGGLES HAS LAST LAUGH

Also held for questioning, but not in connection with Sumner's complaint of indecent performance, was Thelma "Giggles" Leonard, twenty-four, dancer in the chorus line. Miss Leonard was or-

dered held after Sergeant Davies recognized her as the wife of
Marvin "Bang-Bang" Spangler, who is presently serving a
twenty-year sentence in Sing Sing. Early in 1919 Spangler and
Thelma Leonard, then his bride of three days, were nabbed at the
scene of a warehouse robbery in Long Island City. Spangler was
convicted on second offense of grand larceny and Mrs. Spangler
was placed on indefinite probation.

At the precinct station last night Thelma Spangler—oops, pardon us! Giggles Leonard—was presumably questioned by detectives regarding the whereabouts of members of Spangler's gang
who were still at large. Giggles had the last laugh on the cops
when she was able to prove she had been in the Minskys' steady
employ since the fall of 1919.

Nobody turned up to claim Thelma's body and finally the cast
chipped in and arranged a funeral service for her—a *Jewish* funeral
service in honor of her claim to be partially, at least, of that religion.
Of course, except for the Giggles Leonard item, the publicity was
all to the good and boosted the Minsky stock around town enor-
mously.

I wouldn't want to tell you that the raid was the biggest event that
ever took place in Minsky history, but it furnished amusement for a
while and business picked up. Meanwhile, Billy took the opportunity to make good on a promise he had made to his wife long before—he took her on a long holiday. Fifi went into vaudeville with
her own act and became a star touring all over Europe. Billy went
uptown and operated the Little Apollo in Harlem. Mae Dix, the
saucy, former *soubrette,* now graduated to a feature shimmy dancer.
Herbert, Abe, and I were in charge of the National Winter Garden
for the opening of the 1925–1926 season. Herbert produced the show
and I handled the front end. I'm still not sure what Abe did. On
opening night I got a big seven-foot floral horseshoe and stood in
front of it and shook hands with every customer as he entered.

Even before Billy's return, however, the Little Apollo had opened
its 1926 season with financial help from Weinstock, and up there
they worked a lot rougher than we did down on Houston Street.
Mae Dix regularly danced with an entire bare-bosomed chorus line
to an old song called "Take A Look At This." The Apollo even used
Herbert's old publicity line "Try To Get In!" But this time things
were more successful than in the early days, and mobs were actually

turned away. Billy came back, and with the money pouring into the new uptown theater, he bought Mary a yellow Packard touring car that had been custom-built for Babe Ruth. But it was so garish that Mary never actually rode in it.

It was now the Roaring Twenties in earnest. Prosperity everywhere. Billy began to play the stock market heavily. He plowed profits back into the market, and the money doubled and tripled. With enough of it he could buy a theater of his own, and maybe become a legitimate producer. Meanwhile, Abe was drifting further and further from Herbert and me. He still resented Herbert's involvement with Juanita Dixon perhaps. But also his wife was urging him to get her son, Harold, whom Abe had adopted and who was now named Harold Minsky, into the business, and none of us were inclined to make a place for him. Whatever, at that point there was a certain amount of bad feeling, which grew in the years to come into a family split.

The twenties were a sexy decade, not only for burlesque but for the country at large. Skirts swooped up from ankle length to knee length; Freud introduced the idea that sex could be talked about openly at parties and lectured on in schools. People had complexes and libidos, and sex was the answer. Sex was also the question—how far, how much, with whom, when, where? Rich Episcopal ladies, like Mrs. J. Pierpont Morgan and Mrs. Borden Harriman, got together to discuss ways to prevent "improper ways of dancing" and "excess of nudity"—and they weren't even talking about burlesque.

A bunch of ministers down in Philadelphia got together and designed what they called the moral gown, loose-fitting, with long sleeves and a skirt that was exactly seven and one-half inches off the floor. Needless to say it was not a big hit in New York, especially in our theaters. In Utah they were fining women with skirts "higher than three inches above the ankle." In Virginia they were passing laws against dresses showing "more than three inches of throat." In Ohio the limit was two inches.

Well, they could yell as much as they wanted, but sex was here to stay and we were making plenty out of it. We opened the Werba in Brooklyn, and pretty soon we were spreading out all over the country. More often than not I was sent out of town to get these theaters started. We had become a burlesque wheel of our own, after declining to join the Columbia or Eastern wheels in the beginning.

Meanwhile, other theatrical events were attracting the attention of Sumner and his self-appointed censors. Mae West had the nerve to open up in a show called simply *Sex*. Of course, the morals of the time would not let the New York *Times* accept an ad for the play with that indiscreet name, so they listed it only as "Mae West in that Certain Play." Mae's show packed them in at the Cort Theatre on 63rd Street. But it didn't take anything away from our box offices. The country was simply changing.

Sumner was as hot on Mae's tail as he was on ours and even sent a note warning Mayor Jimmy Walker that if Mae's next play, *The Drag*, opened in New York, he would interpret it as an invitation to invoke censorship. "Drag" by the way, meant the same thing then as it does now, and the open parading of transvestite males did nothing to take the heat off Mae. At Minsky's we had a few people that would occasionally show up for comic purposes as cross-dressers, but we never had any real drag queens as such. I really doubt that they would have made much of a hit with our audience. We were relatively clear of trouble in our theaters until 1927, when we had a police raid in which eleven of our dancers were arrested and Abe, of all things, was pinched for smoking a cigar in a no-smoking area.

During this time we were trying every gimmick we could think of at the National Winter Garden to keep people coming in. I ordered three-sheet and four-sheet posters to advertise our shows and finally even went to the twenty-four sheet ones, which are those big posters that you see on the rooftops. We hired top artists, like Carlos Fornaro, to design these posters, and John Wenger to design scenery. We had different contests each night. One night we'd run an amateur night, which was a big hit, and another night, a strip contest. Then, we might have a country store or an auction or a giveaway of gifts based on a raffle.

But the main thing that kept them coming in was that everybody always had a hearty laugh, and there was something intimate about the shows. The runway that Abe had introduced to our theater helped to give our audience that close relationship with our cast. They were always just out of reach. Sometimes there was even a certain amount of playful contact. For example, in one number the girls would come out with fishing rods and dangle pretzels beneath the noses of the spectators. In another they carried powder puffs suspended on long sticks and while doing this sang the song "Powder My Back." Members of the audience were invited to participate.

The girls could keep the customers aroused without really showing that much. Each star stripper had the talent and charm to make
every member of the audience feel that she was looking at him while
he was looking at her. It was a psychological rapport. A gal would
strip because she felt she was appealing to a particular individual in
the audience who may have appealed to her, and this would give a
special sexual quality to her actions. It's a theory that makes some
sense. So, sometimes the girls would play to their particular favor-
ites. The men, and sometimes the women, in the audience would vie
for their attention. They would shout remarks or encouragement
and the girls would answer back. This interplay gave a unique quality to burlesque that didn't exist in the legitimate theater.

The difference between us and our competition was expressed by
our good friend Edmund Wilson in an article he wrote in the *American Mercury* on the subject:

> The great thing about the National Winter Garden Show is
> that, although admittedly as vulgar as possible, it has nothing of
> the peculiar smartness and hardness that one is accustomed to
> elsewhere in New York . . . though more ribald, it is more honest
> and less self-conscious than the ordinary risqué farce and though
> crude, on the whole more attractive than more of the hideous
> comic-supplement humor of uptown revue and vaudeville. Nor is
> it to be confounded with the uptown burlesque shows of the type
> of Columbia, . . . the National Winter Garden has a tradition and
> vein of its own.

On the other hand *Variety* took a gloomy view of the general situation concerning exploitation of sex in burlesque only a few months
after our spectacular 1925 raid: "The current year in burlesque has
witnessed a distinct set-back for 'clean burlesque' and a proportion-
ate increase in the grosses of the Mutual Burlesque Circuit operated
upon the opposite theory."

On the Columbia Circuit, also very competitive, house managers
were instructed to go the limit "in the matter of showing scantily
clad choruses and principals."

But we were still in the Jimmy Walker era, and official censorship
was rare. I remember a woman named Mrs. McCarthy or Mrs. Sullivan or something like that, a policewoman. She would come into
the theater and sit in the back row, and every once in a while she
would put her hand to her mouth to cover her laughter when a

comic said something. I could tell she was having fun, but in the intermission she felt she had to come into my office and say that we had to cut out a "hell" or a "damn" or some word that could be construed as offensive. But I could tell that her heart wasn't in it. Besides, there was never really any enforcement of these requests, and we had a good connection with the police and politicians.

Although the *Times* was turning down ads for Mae West's *Sex, The New Yorker* was cheerfully publishing our ads every week, and Harold Ross, the publisher, was a frequent attendee, as was *New Yorker* writer A. J. Liebling. *The New Yorker* ads (which I usually wrote) made no attempt to disguise the type of show we were offering. One ad read, for instance, "Watch them agitate their anatomies! See burlesque—as *is* burlesque!"

In another ad, citing a possibly fictitious statistic, I wrote, "You be Columbus. Everyone knows that 72.6% of the Broadway revue stars were discovered in burlesque. You can discover tomorrow's stars yourself at National Winter Garden Burlesque. Join the I-knew-her-when club!"

Burlesque was changing though. Sex was becoming the dominant part of the show, and we were forced, if we wanted to fill the house, to feature some of the women principals who were beginning to develop techniques of stripping that were a new element in our theaters. What was being added now was the element of "tease" to the strip. There was not actually any more nudity than before, but the undressing was in many cases more artfully done. Also, the comedians were becoming if not more sophisticated, more natural in their makeup. There was a tendency toward clean-faced comics who didn't depend so much on putty noses and exaggerated clown makeup for their humor. One of the best of these was a former candy butcher from the Columbia Wheel, Steve Mills, who was hired by my brother Billy in the early 1920s.

So things were going splendidly through the 1920s for the Minskys, with Billy making a big hit uptown (where I was still learning the trade) and our theater on Second Avenue still packing them in.

I had continued at the Little Apollo until one day Abe, who was furious with Herbert over his marriage to Juanita, threw him out of the theater and asked me to come down and work at the National Winter Garden for more money than I was getting uptown, and more responsibility. I was fed up working with Weinstock, who was vulgar and overbearing, so I went down to replace Herbert while Billy continued managing the uptown theaters.

Then, in 1928, my mother, who had been ailing for some ten years, became seriously ill, and both my father and I were greatly upset. She required a lot of care in those final months. I was shattered when she died. We had all been so close. After my mother's death my father lived with my older sister for a while, but he was very unhappy and decided to live by himself at the Hotel Adams.

Even now, over fifty years later, I can hear my mother's wise old sayings ringing in my ears: "If you beat a dog enough, you can make him eat pickles." Or, "If God wills it, a broom can dance in the air." I particularly remember one saying that I was always having to quote to Billy, the brashest of the Minsky clan. "Remember what Mama says, Billy," I would warn him, "a wise man does not put his head into a tiger's mouth to prove the tiger roars."

But Billy was not one for moderation. He was riding high and loving it, and so to a lesser degree were all of us. Billy was still plowing his money into Wall Street, looking forward to the day he could open his own theater and be a legitimate producer. Any day, he said as the 1920s drew to a close, he would sell his holdings out, make his killing, and start the theater. But on Tuesday, October 29, 1929, that dream was shattered. The stock market collapsed. *Variety* ran its classic headline WALL STREET LAYS AN EGG! and Billy was broke by the end of the week.

It seemed as though Billy's luck had finally run out.

CUSTOMER: Have you got a room for the night?
ROOM CLERK: Sure, do you want it for sleeping or for
jumping?

AS IT TURNED out, the Depression, although it meant the end of
Billy's personal fortune, was the beginning of the greatest era for the
Minskys. In the first place, people didn't have the money to pay
$5.50 for a ticket in the legitimate houses. In the second place, with
all the unemployment, they had plenty of time to go to the theater,
and the longer the show, the better. Uptown, Billy had been running the new, larger version of the Apollo Theatre with his backer
Joe Weinstock.

The Apollo, as I have said, worked much rougher than we did
downtown. Comedy acts were often taken out to be replaced by sexier girlie bits. I remember that after the success of Mae's famous
"Pick a Banana Tutti-Frutti" skit, Billy at Weinstock's urging had
her do a second number, "Let's Take a Trip." In this act Mae allowed the audience to talk her into taking off her entire touring outfit of cap, goggles, and duster until all she had on were three small
strategically placed signs, reading "Stop," "Go," and "Detour."

Billy had always been chagrined at our failure to succeed on
Broadway back in the days of the Park Theatre. Now he had his
wildest idea ever. When he read that Broadway's longest running

show, *Abie's Irish Rose,* was folding after six years, he talked Weinstock into buying the theater in which it had appeared, the Republic, and turning it into a burlesque house. (Ironically, the plot of *Abie's Irish Rose* had been snitched from an ancient burlesque bit going back to Billy Watson and his Beef Trust called "Krausmeyer's Alley.")

While Billy was getting the Republic on its feet, business was bad down at the National Winter Garden. Nevertheless, I was not thrilled when I was called to serve on jury duty downtown at the federal court. I tried to give every excuse I could, but they wouldn't release me. When I went down there, it turned out the case was the biggest thing in the local papers—the trial of the gangster Jack "Legs" Diamond for running a still in upstate New York. There was of course a remote connection between the Minskys and Diamond via Beansie Rosenthal and Arnold Rothstein, for whom Diamond had been a bodyguard. (Beansie, you may remember, was Billy's informant in the Becker case.

The trial was a long and complicated one and quite nerve-racking. Ruth started getting calls at home from people who presumably were Diamond's henchmen warning her to tell me that I better vote the right way. Other members of the jury were getting the calls too, so we told the judge and he had us sequestered for the entire trial at the McAlpin Hotel. There were good reasons for these fears.

According to the Broadway columnist Louie Sobol, Diamond walked into the Hotsy-Totsy Club, a Prohibition gin mill one night in the late 1920s with some aides. He left at least four people dead as far as anybody could determine, although there were a lot of people around there who didn't like to give their names dead or alive. Shortly after the bloodbath, driving along with his girl friend at the time, Legs told her all the witnesses were dead—no one could point a finger at him. Whereupon the girl was supposed to have murmured, "But, Jack, darling, *I* saw what happened—you wouldn't, darling, kill me too?" And Diamond, so the story goes, said, "I'm afraid I'll have to." And he did! So it shows you the kind of guy that they were asking me to send to jail.

The young assistant district attorney prosecuting Diamond, by the way, later came to some prominence in New York State politics. He was Thomas E. Dewey.

A short time after Diamond lost his girl friend he focused his affections on the tall, beautiful ex–show girl Marian Strassnik, known professionally as Kiki Roberts. Wherever Diamond went, bullets were flying one way or another, usually at him, but also often at people he had become peeved at or estranged from for some reason. Only the year before, gunmen had invaded a cozy love nest that Diamond shared with Kiki Roberts in the Monticello Hotel in the Catskills. It was Dutch Schultz's mob combined with some of Waxy Gordon's men who pumped four bullets into his body and left him for dead. But he lived. When he got out of the hospital, he went to his country home at Acra in Greene County farther upstate. He had been there only a few weeks when he was shot again, as he was leaving the Aratoga Inn in Cairo. This time a shotgun was used. One slug got him in the right lung, another punctured his liver, still another one struck him in the back as he spun and fell, and the fourth one lodged in his arm. This time they were certain he was as good as dead, but he recovered again in time to go to trial in federal court. Governor Roosevelt was fed up with Diamond's attempts to dominate upstate New York. That was supposed to be Roosevelt's stomping grounds. From what I learned—and I heard a lot about Diamond during that trial—he had also been shot at in 1924 and in 1927.

Up to the point when he stood trial before my jury, for all his criminal activities Diamond had lost only two battles with the courts. One was in 1914, when he was sent to the reformatory for attempted burglary, and again in 1919, when he went to Leavenworth for desertion from the Army and stealing from his fellow soldiers. Other than that, he had beaten twenty-two other charges in the past, including five of homicide. The New York *Times,* reviewing his career, said of him that he had had a good chance to jump into commanding position in the underworld when Rothstein died, but he muffed it. He had money, he had a strong organization of men and hoodlums to do his bidding, and he knew the inside of the "racket."

But he drank too much, and when he was drunk, he lost all control of himself. He loved publicity, and his craze for public attention brought him so much to the notice of the police and the public that the smarter racketeers and bootleggers began to avoid him. He was bringing trouble upon them as well as himself.

Anyway, after sitting in the jury room for one night, the jury was unanimous, if slightly terrified, in finding Diamond guilty. The judge sentenced him to four years in jail, but his attorney had him released almost immediately on bail. He never put in a day in jail. But he was destined to cross my life at least one more time, this time in connection with Minsky's Burlesque.

Billy's new Broadway neighbors practically *plotzed* when they heard that a Minsky burlesque show was about to open on 42nd Street. They petitioned Mayor Walker and his theater license commissioner, James Geraghty, to find some way of ruling against the opening of burlesque on Broadway, but Billy still had friends in high places in city politics. Next thing, the Broadway producers sat around telling one another that the Republic was a rotten house for burlesque. There wasn't a big enough balcony, and it was too narrow for a runway. Billy heard about this and put in *two* runways! Actually, the Republic, as I remember it, had an orchestra and two balconies, with 1,100 seats.

By this time there was no question that the way to sell tickets in burlesque was with sex. Comics were what people loved once they were in the theater, but it was sex on the marquee that pulled them in. For the first time in burlesque, women were given billing over comics and the first one at the Republic to receive this billing was a long-legged, cool job from Seattle that Billy had discovered working in a burlesque joint in Philadelphia. Her name was Gypsy Rose Lee—real name, Rose Louise Hovick. The remarkable thing about her—and Billy appreciated this from the beginning—was that she had a very slim figure, and a flat bust, but she had mastered the art of the tease to such an extent that nobody minded. Her costumes were suggestive and seductive rather than the flowery, pseudo-virginal frocks assumed by the less imaginative. She used black silk stockings, lace panties, red garters, and mesh netting. In a manner new to burlesque, she turned her essentially shy feelings about disrobing on stage into a mocking, spoofing jest. She removed the pins on her trick costumes one by one. Each missing pin revealed just a bit more. As she stripped she would toss the pins into the audience. Each pin could be turned into the box office for a free admission.

While other strippers were scared to death at the thought of speaking words of more than two syllables, Gypsy, in her expertise, let her erudite, insinuating chatter seduce the audience into a state of near-hypnosis. After four or five minutes of strolling around she would consent to disrobe a bit more intimately, and then after all this hocus-pocus, mumbo-jumbo of suggestiveness and promise, there would be the quick flash of a breast and a bare hip bone as she slid off chuckling into the wings. Billy said of her, "Seven minutes of sheer art."

She was a tall girl, almost five feet ten, and weighed 132 well-distributed pounds. It was said of her that she suggested a ripe peach. Gypsy was an intelligent woman, and she and Billy both understood from the beginning the value of the big buildup he gave her debut at the Republic.

Back at the Houston Street theater we could only watch with amazement as Billy showed what he could do in turning on major publicity for the Republic. He hired a guy on stilts about seventeen feet high with an illuminated shirtfront to walk up and down Broadway announcing the coming of Gypsy Rose Lee to the new Republic Theatre. Later, he had a plane flying overhead, which was a big deal in those days, trailing her name behind it. Before Billy came in with the Republic, burlesque shows in the Broadway area had been conceived and advertised as miniature musical comedies, but since they didn't have the talent of musical comedies or the earthy quality of burlesque, they had all been miserable failures, including our own earlier venture at the Park.

Billy used reverse psychology when he opened the Republic, switching the angle. Instead of claiming that his show was good, clean fun, he said it was even saucier than it was. Even the title of his first show, *Fanny Fortsin From France,* was pretty racy for Broadway.

But Billy always went with class. When he opened on February 12, 1931, it was to a black-tie audience. Though the stress was on girls, Billy hadn't spared the dollar when it came to comics. There were four of them. Hap Hyatt was the fattest comedian in burlesque. When nothing else would work, he would bump his huge belly against the tummy or fanny of the nearest girl. The other three comics were masters at milking laughs also: Harry Clexx, Burt Carr, and Harry Seymour. Al Golden, a distinguished-looking smoothie, was the straight man. The prima donna was Ina Hayword. Gypsy, of course, was the star, but there was a pulchritudinous bevy of strippers and shimmy dancers to back her up. If they were not already famous, Billy gave them such tantalizing names as Hazel Nutt from Brazil, Betty Blushes from Peking, Lita Butt from Havana,

Etta Herring from Bismark, or Mademoiselle Sprouts from Brussels.

The people who came to the Republic were, according to one critic, "a sophisticated, knowing audience, middle-aged seemingly well-to-do men who duly tipped the pretty usherettes who led them to their reserved seats in the orchestra." But the critics were not so hot for the show, although they gave it some grudging praise. "The costumes and scenery are splendiferous," wrote Elias Sugarman of *The Billboard*, looking at the bright side. Brooks Atkinson, always a fan, said that the dancing and comedy were "the bawdiest this neighborhood has seen for years." That didn't hurt. But Sime Silverman of *Variety*, who was by now very down on burlesque, absolutely blasted it. He called the show "The Killer of Burlesque!" The subhead read: "Minsky's mess at Republic contains everything that ruined burlesque business in U.S.—cheapest dirt, dirtiest coochers and no talent."

Silverman proved to be a flop both as a critic and as a prophet. The combination of sex and comedy as presented by Billy was apparently exactly what the Depression public wanted. He made it fashionable to attend burlesque on Broadway. And shows were always kept lively and topical. When Earl Carroll presented a new edition of *Vanities* entitled *Murder at the Vanities*, a two-story banner appeared over the Republic across the street: "Slaughter at Minsky's."

At the same time that the Republic was thriving, the wheels were dying. In March 1930 the New York Columbia played its last show, starring appropriately enough one of its early headliners, Sliding Billy Watson. And the Mutual Wheel was not doing so well either. In 1931 the last wheel ceased to turn, just as Billy brought his special brand of burlesque to Broadway.

The year 1931 was one of those good-news, bad-news years for us. The grosses at the Republic looked terrific, but on Second Avenue we were definitely not too hot. Maybe it was the proximity of all those down-and-outers lolling around in the plazas at Allen Street and Second Avenue. Some people thought we were getting competition from other cheap forms of entertainment, such as radio, which was becoming very popular, and motion pictures, which were winging along very well since the advent of talkies. But that didn't seem to bother them on Broadway, where they were in more direct competition with the expensive girlie follies-type shows.

In 1931 and early 1932 we had acquired undoubtedly the best

strippers in the business, many of whom we had discovered or developed ourselves. The top stars of that time were Gypsy Rose Lee, Georgia Sothern, Ann Corio, and Margie Hart. The problem was that we were in constant competition with Max Wilner, who ran the Apollo across the street, for the talent. Once in a while he would manage to outbid us. I wouldn't say that loyalty was one of the qualities of these strippers, but then again, they were in business to make a buck just like all of us.

As if we didn't have enough trouble, one of Weinstock's kids, Harold, apparently got into a quarrel with Harry Rose, a burlesque comic, and beat him up horribly backstage. Through the intervention of the Burlesque Artists' Association, Harry Rose was prevented from filing a charge of criminal assault against Harold. Weinstock stepped in with his checkbook, and Rose made a settlement after his departure from Flower and Fifth Avenue Hospital. We didn't have anything to do with that, but I understand, and *Variety* confirms this opinion, that Rose got a year's pay without having to perform for it. Oddly enough, the page in *Variety* announcing settlement of the Weinstock case carried an obit for Raymond Paine, who had been playing at the Hudson Theatre in Union City, New Jersey, in an independent wheel show called *Nightclub Girls*. He had been drinking heavily, perhaps even more than usual because of an unusual year of misfortune for him. Within the year before he died, he had lost his mother, a brother, and two sisters. I mourn for him. He was one of the most talented people in burlesque.

It must have been Minsky's week in *Variety* because on the same page they ran a review of one of our Supreme Wheel shows called *Shim-sham Shambles,* and aside from the review I felt that they had libeled us unfairly. "Requirements for show girls in Wheel shows at Minsky's Republic are that they be at least a head taller than the line girls and always wear a bored expression. Looks don't count." That's what the reviewer said. The review itself wasn't bad, but I resented those remarks. Our girls were the most beautiful in the business, and if they looked bored, it was only by accident, not because we asked them to. But it was true that we liked them to be tall.

The Republic started with a two-a-day policy, but with the public clamoring to get in, it soon went to a four-a-day including a matinee. Where else could the Depression-weary man in the street get four hours of entertainment with comics, sex, and a few movies thrown in for a quarter?

The instant success of the Republic angered the producers of legitimate shows along with Great White Way even more. So exasperated did George White become—his *Scandals* was showing just down the street at a $5.50 top and not exactly prospering at the box office—that one day walking along 42nd Street he actually popped Billy one on the nose. Billy just laughed it off. As far as he was concerned, this was just his initiation into the big time.

But the angry producers were even more enraged when other burlesque showmen seeing the success of the Republic on Broadway, also began to open theaters in the neighborhood. One month after the Republic opened, Max Rudnick, an operator of Brooklyn film houses, decided to get in while the pickings were good. He leased the Eltinge Theatre, a former legitimate playhouse on 42nd Street, at $40,000 a year, and furthermore he snitched Burt Carr from our show. But that was all right. There were plenty of top comics waiting in the wings to get into the Republic. A few months later Billy countered by joining forces with Izzy Herk, a former head of the Mutual Wheel, to open the Central Theatre at 48th and Broadway, leasing it from the Shuberts. Finally, business got so good uptown that it was decided to close the National Winter Garden and bring H.K. and me up to help with the operation of the Republic and the Central.

Now the owners of the estimated $70 million worth of theatrical real estate along 42nd Street charged that their property rights were being jeopardized by the presence of the Republic burlesque show. In April, License Commissioner Geraghty finally gave in to their pressure and called for a hearing before he would renew the Republic license.

With all the uproar going on about the licenses and the opening of the new theater, Billy still found time to avidly read newspapers, and I was a little surprised at how much attention he paid to the fatal shooting of Legs Diamond in December 1931, just before our show was to open. Billy, of course, as a former newspaperman, was familiar with all the goings-on in the gang aristocracy. It had long been known that Diamond had made an enemy of almost every one of the organized mobs and was walking around with more lead in his system than the composing room of the New York *Times*.

I was also quite relieved by Diamond's demise since I had sat on the jury that convicted him of federal charges, for which he was out on appeal.

Diamond was finally through after having absorbed a total of fourteen hostile bullets in his short career. But Billy was already thinking ahead: "That Kiki Roberts, she's gorgeous, I met her a couple of times hanging around the clubs. I wonder if we could line her up. She'd be a lot better than Peaches Browning. She can even sing and dance a little." Around the same time, the newspapers were occupied with the murder trial involving the killing of the gambler Arnold Rothstein at the Park Central Hotel following what seemed to be a very questionable poker game. The cops thought the killer was another gambler and a former friend of Rothstein's named George McManus, who was supposed to have held IOUs from Rothstein in the amount of several hundred thousand dollars. Rothstein had a lot of names along Broadway. He was Mr. Big, Mr. A, the Brain, the Man Uptown, the Man-to-See, and had a big bankroll. In fact, in recent years he had been taking some of his gambling earnings to Broadway, investing in various shows along with his current partner in the bootlegging business, Irving Wexler, more famous as Waxy Gordon.

Waxy, who was friendly with Fanny Brice, once paid a fledgling impresario, Billy Rose, $5,000 for two skits to be used in a new musical that Waxy was sponsoring. When the show flopped in spite of the skits, Waxy sent for Rose and asked for his money back. Rose told the gangster that he would tell his wife, Fanny Brice, that the great Waxy Gordon was a cheapskate who wouldn't keep a bargain. Rather than chancing the loss of Fanny's respect, Waxy let Rose keep the money. Waxy was also the sponsor of the Club Dover, which introduced a great new comic, Jimmy Durante. When a battle royal broke out in the Club Dover, champagne bottles flew through the air and four innocent bystanders were knocked out cold. Durante, cool in the shadow of his nose, finished his routine and kept the crowd from panicking. Impressed by Jimmy's nonchalance, Waxy opened a new club just for the "Schnozz" named the Club Durant.

Rothstein, among other things, was a financier of the performer Texas Guinan at the famous El Fey Club, and ironically he had also loaned $25,000 to Anne Nichols so that she could keep her play, *Abie's Irish Rose,* running just a little bit longer in the theater that had now become the Republic Burlesque.

But it wasn't Rothstein's involvement in show business that interested my brother Billy. It was the fact that Rothstein himself had been the protégé in his early years of Beansie Rosenthal. Oddly, Rosenthal had been finally shot down at the Café Metropole, a gamblers' haunt on West 43rd Street, only a block from the Republic.

However, these headlines were only a minor distraction to Billy, who was thrilled with his final success on Broadway.

CHAPTER

18

BUD ABBOTT (*in schoolroom*): Hey teach! Want to come to
dinner tonight? I've got a canary that eats beans!
TEACHER: Why beans?
ABBOTT: Wants to be a thunderbird!
LOU COSTELLO: I *love* breans. Breans for breakfast,
breans for lunch—
TEACHER: Not *breans* . . . *beans.* Watch your diction.
"How now brown cow?"
LOU: Same way, black bull!

IN THE FOUR months following the opening of the Republic and
Billy's initiation into the ranks of Broadway producers via a punch
in the nose from George White, Billy had hired two press agents,
Mike Goldreyer and George Alabama Florida, or so he claimed his
name was, which I frankly never believed. The important thing
about these two men is that they are credited with inventing the
term "striptease" to describe certain actions that had been going on
on Minsky stages for some time.

With the enormous success of the Republic, the members of the
42nd Street Association, which included merchants, churches, *Follies, Vanities,* and *Scandals,* pushed John Sumner into a series of raids,
most of them unsuccessful or barely successful. Of course, Billy
again installed the John Law light, which could be signaled from
the box office whenever the police were en route.

Billy produced show after show whose titles often got him as much publicity as the new art of striptease: *Tillie Pipick from Peru, Countess Schmaltz from Capon, Ada Onion from Bermuda,* and *Carrie de Booze from Canada,* and some which I take some credit for having invented, such as *Mind Over Mattress, The Sway of all Flesh, Panties Inferno,* and *Dress Takes a Holiday.* In one of the shows we even featured a live horse on stage. When the horse ad-libbed a steaming pile on the stage, Steve Mills, who was working as second banana at the time, added this ad lib: "The horse wants to know if he can get his deposit back." Which brings us to the fact that the comics were not absolutely thrilled that the strippers were now getting top billing and going further than they ever had. "How can you follow a broad who takes her clothes off?" was what most of them were asking.

Meanwhile, a few of the Republic's customers were being siphoned off by a very attractive new stripper named Ann Corio working at the Eltinge across the street. In November 1931, while all the nonsense was going on on West 42nd Street, we finally played our last show at the National Winter Garden. The old burlesque family was breaking up.

Maybe all those impresarios of the 42nd Street Association were right to be frightened that Minsky would take away some of their customers. By May 1932, Sumner and the 42nd Street Association finally succeeded in dragging some of the Minsky people and also some from the Eltinge theater down before License Commissioner Geraghty. No less a publication than *The New Yorker* was calling that stretch of 42nd Street Minskyville. Here's how *The New Yorker* described it:

> Minskyville is conveniently located. It is near the hotel district and the railroad terminals and is accessible by subway and "El." It runs, roughly, from 52nd Street to 42nd Street on Broadway and from Sixth Avenue to Eighth Avenue on 42nd Street, taking in some of the side streets.
>
> The quarter takes its name from Billy Minsky, who with a half dozen closely related Minskys [only three, but maybe we seemed like more] . . . operates the Minsky burlesque chain. Hocus-pocus is taking place in Minskyville today. There is a conspiracy of rival interests to clean up Minskyville. The opposition has warmed up a forgotten official called the License Commissioner. Matters have come to such a point that Minsky has threatened to move away,

leaving Minskyville as dead as Virginia City or the ghost metropolises of the West.

As usual, the hearings at License Commissioner Geraghty's office produced many laughs for the audience, a field day for newspapers, and a big increase at the Republic box office. We couldn't have paid for such publicity—and such classy testimony. One of our theater managers, Edward W. Rowland, testified that he had managed theaters for the Shuberts and for Morris Gest and that the Republic played to audiences such as those that attended the Winter Garden shows "a few years ago" and to the same type of audience now seen at "the average musical show." (He wasn't talking about the *National* Winter Garden, but the *old* Winter Garden just up the street from us on West 42nd Street.

Mother Elms, the dipsy old darling, showed up also to speak on our behalf. She was ninety-three years old at the time, and she testified that she used to act in the old-time burlesque herself at Tony Pastor's and did not find the current 42nd Street burlesque objectionable. Watching the shows, she said, made her only wish that she were in them herself.

"Bad or narrow-minded people shouldn't go to any theater," she said. "I've seen the same dances and worse sketches in the big theaters. I go to church every day and I think I'm the best woman in America and I think there's nothing wrong in the burlesque theater. You don't have to put the wrong construction on the jokes you hear."

A reporter from the New York *American*, Louis W. Feher, told the commissioner that he went to the Republic thirty or forty times a year and he found the sketches and dialogue very similar to that in most Broadway revues.

The Members of the 42nd Street Property Owners and Merchants Association were going crazy. Furthermore, whenever they said how disgusting our shows were in their opinion, the commissioner struck the testimony from the record.

They pulled a low blow against us when they sent Samuel Marcus, an attorney, to the Republic undercover with Rabbi Alexander Lyons of the Eighth Avenue Temple in Brooklyn and Dr. J. C. Zipzer, president of the Men's Club of the Congregation Emanu-El. The idea of this trip was "to condemn the commercializing of filth and sex depravity by Jews." (Presumably, by a *goy* it was all right.) The idea, Marcus explained, was that Jews, without publicity, should try and induce the Minskys "to discontinue the display of filth." In his testimony he said he thought that the performances at the Republic were "improper." But Rowland counteracted this hysteria. Asked to name persons who had attended burlesque performances at the Republic, he answered, "Otto Kahn, Horace Liverwright, Maurice Chevalier, Gertrude Lawrence, and Clifton Webb and the entire cast of *Of Thee I Sing*." Under cross-examination Rowland admitted that pictures of "partly draped women were sold in the theater during intermission" and that "French postcards" were given free of charge with the purchases of candy.

Sophie Kelly, the chief woman usher at the Republic, told the commission that she had never been "annoyed" by patrons of the theater and that youths under eighteen years of age were not permitted to witness the performance.

In answer to the 42nd Street Merchants' claims that we were ruining the neighborhood, two cops, patrolmen Hubert F. Aherne and William Lustig of the 14th Precinct, said that passersby were no different from those frequenting the block before burlesque shows opened.

A restaurateur on the block went against the other merchants and testified that he was doing fifty to sixty-two percent better business since burlesque shows arrived on 42nd Street.

Reginald Marsh, the famous artist, said that etchings he'd made of burlesque actresses had been exhibited in the New York Museum of Modern Art, the Boston Museum, and the Brooklyn Museum. He said he thought burlesque was "a part of American life."

Another well-known artist, Cleon Throckmorton, said that patrons of modern burlesque shows were "hard-working men like plumbers and carpenters and as far as I can see they go there because they can't go to musical shows; all I can say is that it is simply a poor man's theater." Ferdinand Pecora, later a famous New York State justice, was counsel for the 42nd Street Property Owners. He asked Throckmorton whether some of the dialogue didn't have double meaning. Throckmorton answered, "If you throw a piece of pie at somebody, I don't know whether it would have a double meaning. If you know burlesque, you know only one meaning. It has a language of its own, like Shakespeare, if you know Shakespeare. There is a good hardy humor in a funny, human situation."

Then Pecora tried reading some of the bits that stenographers hired by the Property Owners had written down from our shows. Somehow they didn't come over with quite the same humor in the courthouse. Finally, when he was asked whether he thought that these jokes had a double meaning, Throckmorton said, "If a man comes up and hits you over the head with a barrel stave after you finish reading, I might laugh."

Our old friends at *The New Yorker* thought the hearing was ridiculous:

> Witnesses at the clean-up hearings before the License Commissioner testified that idlers along 42nd Street have been eating peanuts and commenting on passing women. It is a short step between that and whittling.
>
> The greatest shock to the burlesque profession was the testimony of the usually fair and accurate John S. Sumner of the New York Society for the Suppression of Vice. He said that the strip act or strip-tease act was not art, but was merely taking off clothes. This wounded a great many sensitive artists, for the fact is that stripping is the most difficult art in burlesque. The burlesque patrons are incredibily nice and exacting in their attitude toward strippers. The difference between a mediocre stripper and a great stripper is the difference between $35 and $400 a week. There is a virtuosity in unhooking, unzipping, and shedding; one conscientious stripper is suffered to leave the stage in silence, while another receives more curtain calls than the greatest opera star. When a stripper does not get her usual encores, it never occurs to her that she may be losing her genius; she accuses the orchestra leader, piano player, and first fiddler of having been bribed to ruin her by playing too slow or too fast for her strip rhythm. Terrible outbursts occurred in the wings before Minsky issued the order: "Anyone using slang behind the scenes will be fired immediately."

So another dreary attempt by bluenoses and self-seekers to shut down our show was defeated without adverse legal actions being taken against us. We got our license.

But what *The New Yorker* said about what were now called stripteasers was certainly true, and Billy was combing the hills, literally, for new talent. He discovered a fantastic new stripper delivering about a million ergs of energy at Izzy Hirst's Bijou Theatre in Philadelphia. Her name was Georgia Sothern and she was under contract to the Trocadero Theatre, which was a patron of the Mutual Circuit. But when Billy came to Philadelphia and saw her, he offered her fabulous money to come to New York and work at the Republic, bought out her contract, and brought her to New York. Georgia, herself, recalled it this way: "He started with the posters, plastering my name all over the city. Next thing I know he has this guy on stilts. His nose and shirt buttons and cigar all light up, and he's wearing a sandwich board, 'Georgia Sothern' walking back and forth around Times Square. . . . The way he advertised me I was a star in New York before I'd even opened."

So pretty soon we had the two most fabulous strippers in the history of burlesque up to that time—and afterward, for all that matters. As is usual with such talents—and by this time I was working in the Republic and had learned how to deal with some of their eccentricities—they were, shall we say, spirited ladies, with minds of their own that led to a lot of interesting problems for me and my brothers. For one thing, Georgia Sothern had a deep personal secret, which she didn't tell us for a year and which could have ruined us if it had come out at that time.

19

PHIL SILVERS: Did you throw that cigarette butt on the
  floor?
RAGS RAGLAND: What?
PHIL SILVERS: Did you throw that *butt* on the floor?
RAGS RAGLAND: What?
PHIL SILVERS: Is that your cigarette butt on the floor?
RAGS RAGLAND: No. Go ahead. You saw it first.

AS I SAID, we didn't know much about Georgia when she came to us from Philadelphia, and much of what I'm going to tell you I learned later on. She was born in Atlanta and her real name was Hazel Anderson. She worked for a few years with an uncle as a dancer in vaudeville, and when she was hired as a stripper by Izzy Hirst at the Bijou, she took the name "Georgia" for the state where she was born, and "Sothern," for the region. But when she signed the contract with Hirst, she misspelled the name "Sothern" and that's what it remained. She was a natural from the start and worked in a completely different manner from any of the other strippers. Here's the way she looked to an unbiased expert, Ann Corio, who was herself, one of the top strippers in burlesque history. Corio said in her book *This Was Burlesque,* "Georgia stripped and teased, but that was only a minor part of her act. Her music, "Hold That Tiger," was wild, the orchestra played at full blast and full tempo, and Georgia came on stage in full flight. And she'd work up momentum. Faster and faster the music would roar, and Georgia would be at the front of the stage, one hand cascading her long red hair over her face, the other outstretched to keep her balance as her hips blurred back and forth at a fantastic tempo. It was exhilarating, exciting—even forgetting the sex appeal involved. The mere sight of this red hot, red-headed temptress tossing her hips in fantastic abandon to the wild music of the band caught up everybody in its spell. You didn't shout from the audience to Georgia to take it off; there was no time, no pause and the music was too loud anyway. You just sat there and watched—and wondered how she could do it.

"By the time she was finished the whole theater seemed to explode in a sigh. The audience was almost as exhausted watching as Georgia was performing. She did an act that no one who ever saw would ever forget; she was a cyclone of sex and she literally blew the walls down."

She was only five feet in height but she looked taller in the high heels she wore in her act. She had a flat, taut belly and long legs. Her breasts were not too large, but makeup and her fantastic movement made them seem impressive. (After all, Gypsy Rose Lee also became a star with breasts that were more like molehills than mountains.) Georgia had been a big hit at the Bijou, and when her contract ran out, she was hired at a bigger salary by Harry Cohen of the Trocadero, the other burlesque theater in Philadelphia that was on the Mutual Circuit.

While she was still playing at the Bijou, she had a traumatic experience when she accidentally witnessed the machine-gun slaying of a gangland hood near the boardinghouse in which she was staying. Unfortunately, she knew the man who had done the killing. He was a boyfriend of her roommate's at Mother O'Brien's Theatrical Boarding House. The experience terrified her. But she was on a roll as far as her career was concerned and as soon as her twenty-eight-week contract with the Bijou ran out, she was signed up for a second contract as a star getting equal billing with Ann Corio and Carrie Finnell at the Trocadero. Everybody said that Georgia moved fast, but this was meteoric and her pay rise was equally impressive. By the time Billy got to offering her a contract, she was already sewed up by Cohen at the Troc. As we were adding theaters in Brooklyn and Newark, Billy's idea was to have a regular group of top stars that we would promote ourselves into celebrity status and that we could rotate from one theater to another.

I learned much of what I know of Georgia's early career in Philadelphia from Raymond Paine, who was working there as a straight man at the time but later became our principal straight man.

Georgia was an even bigger hit at the Troc than she'd been at the Bijou, especially since she was now in a star position on the program. Meanwhile, the gangster who she had seen murder another hood on the streets found out from her roommate that she (Georgia) had seen the crime and threatened her with death if she ever revealed what she knew. She was extremely worried but this seemed to have little effect on her act, which was as torrid as ever.

In Philadelphia, as in New York, there were various civic bluenose groups and police always watching the burlesque theaters to see if they could catch anything that violated somebody or other's moral code. Georgia was working in a pale pink chiffon gown with sequined rosebuds all over it. When she finished her strip, all she was wearing was the tiny G-string with three more sequin rosebuds sewn on its front. Somehow word got around about the hot, new stripper in town and just two weeks after Georgia started working at the Trocadero the theater was raided and unfortunately suffered a much worse fate than we had during our raids. It was padlocked and Cohen was out of business. The cops had managed to evade Cohen's warning-light system—we all had them—and it was Georgia that they caught. They got ahold of her after the raid and said to her, "Young lady, we're going to give you twenty-four hours to get out of town. If you're not gone by that time, you'll be put in jail."

I doubt that they could have made good on that threat, but it scared Georgia, who was still not very experienced. The night of the raid Cohen came to see her. He was heartbroken about the closing of his theater, but he did not blame Georgia. It was the fault of his "specials," who had not seen the police sneaking up the back fire escape.

What Cohen had done the minute he was convinced that his place was really going to be closed was to call Billy and offer to sell him Georgia's contract, and at a pretty stiff price at that. Billy told us about the deal, and though I was worried about the amount he was paying for the contract, he assured me that once I had seen her, I would be convinced she was worth it. And he was right.

So, Cohen telephoned us that Georgia would be on the next train, and we agreed that we would have the contract ready and waiting and a limousine to pick up our new stripper at the train.

Even then, Georgia was beginning to appreciate the value of publicity. The whole front page of the Philadelphia *Bulletin* was given over to her departure: GEORGIA SOTHERN GIVEN 24 HOURS TO LEAVE TOWN!

Another paper headlined: POLICE TO ESCORT MISS SOTHERN TO THE STATION.

Naturally, New York columnists got wind of this, and there was already a stirring of interest concerning her arrival in the city.

In New York Billy kept to his promise and gave her the full star treatment. He had his chauffeur pick her up in a big stretch limousine and drive her directly to the Republic. Just to give you an idea of how things looked from her point of view, this is the way she described her first encounter with Billy: "Billy Minsky was a flashy man, small but not too heavy, who always seemed to be wearing a cigarette as if it were a part of his face. He was a man sure of himself and satisfied with what he was. A man with brown hair and dark brown eyes. He always spoke with authority, yet never seemed less than warm and friendly.

"He was Mr. Minsky, the top man in his profession, and there was not a performer in burlesque who didn't want to work for him. He was Mr. Minsky, and he represented the big time. The pinnacle. The very top!

"He smiled, rose from behind his desk to greet me, and shook my hand. 'Welcome, Miss Sothern, welcome.' He let go of my hand and stood back to look me over. 'You look just as beautiful offstage as on.'"

Impressed she may have been, but she was a sharp little cookie. Billy had prepared a contract that provided for twenty-two weeks with a thirty-two-week option. But Cohen, who was fond of Georgia, had warned her. In the end, she argued down to a ten-week option and signed on the spot.

"Now, let me tell you what I'm going to do, Georgia," Billy said. "What I'm going to do first is advertise your name so big through the week that by the time you open, everybody in New York City will be fighting to buy tickets just to get a look at you. I'm gonna set this town on its ear." He pushed the intercom and asked for H.K.

and me to come into the office to meet our new star. Then he said, "You're a member of the family now, Georgia. You're one of Minsky's children. The first thing you're going to do for me is have your hair dyed. I want it bright red. A flaming red. Sure, it's red now, but I want it a flaming red so that you'll stand out in any crowd. And I want you to wear black mesh stockings and a garter belt. No matter what color your costume is, I insist on black mesh stockings and the garter belt every week. Understand?" And he offered to pay all the bills for hair dyeing and even for the new costumes, although usually the girls were required to pay for their own costumes. The hair color thing was important. There were certain general rules we Minskys had learned through the years that make for success with strip acts:

Hair: The stripper had to dye her hair a definite color. Red, yellow, or black. Theatrical lighting did strange things to the ordinary natural shades of hair, like honey and ash blond. Red hair in particular picked up wonderful highlights from our magenta spots.

Makeup: Minsky's supplied no makeup man to the strippers, nor did any of the other theaters. The girls had to learn how to apply their own makeup and get the best effect from experience and from the other girls.

Hands: Hands were important and had to be used gracefully, but not too much. That would distract. The less talented strippers simply didn't know what to do with their hands. Their idea was to stick out their little finger like a society lady drinking from a teacup. But Georgia, probably from her dance experience, had a natural grace in this respect.

The Walk: This was to fix the character—whether a demure stripper, a "hot" stripper, an ingenue type, or whatever. The idea was to know how to walk on a stage. Those who couldn't learn this stayed in the pony chorus or as show girls; they never made it as strippers.

Pace: A stripper has to maintain and sustain a definite pace, a tempo, from the time she appears until she exits. If she's a fast worker, she has to keep her foot on the pedal all the way—and Georgia certainly did that. If she parades as a tall and dignified show girl, like Gypsy Rose Lee, she can't throw in a little Suzy-Q or a trucking step at the end of her act.

Timing: A sense of timing is important. The stripper has to know when to take off what, how much to take off and how much to leave on, and what to do for an encore.

After Georgia had left his office Billy assured us that somewhere she had learned all these lessons and got top marks in all categories. "You'll see, she'll be pulling them in out of the hills, and she's a good contrast to Gypsy, who works in a completely opposite way," he said.

When we Minskys built a star, we didn't cut corners. We put Georgia up in her own suite at the Somerset Hotel, near the theater. We gave her the full advance publicity treatment, which I described before—the stilt walkers and a new item that we had introduced, a human "automaton" act that was so realistic the crowds would gather to see if the performers were real people or machines. There were life-size blowups of Georgia in front of the theater the week before she opened and huge signs announcing, "The Human Bomb-Shell to Explode Sunday!" There were also blowups of the Philadelphia newspapers about Georgia being such hot stuff that she had to be escorted out of town by the police. That didn't hurt any either.

The act with which Georgia had broken in down in Philadelphia was based on a chorus: "Clap your hands if you wanna see more of me!" It was a good act, but Billy and H.K. got together and decided that she would open with a popular standard called "I'm in Love With You, Honey!" To further coddle our new star I had two girls move out of one of the dressing rooms they shared and had it repainted and redecorated.

To get ready for her act Georgia, as most strippers did, coated herself from head to toe with a cosmetic called Stage White. It was applied with a sponge, and when a coating of this stuff was laid on, the girl was obliged to stand for a long time with her arms and legs spread apart until it dried. This made the girl's skin look like satin under the spotlight.

Georgia was standing that way, legs apart, spread-eagled, when Billy knocked on her door. He had a surprise for her, which he had only been able to arrange that afternoon. Perfectionist that he was, Billy worried that his new star still might not get as much attention as he wanted. That afternoon he got out and hustled up a gimmick that would even top the horse on stage.

"Wait'll you hear this!" He told the spread-eagled stripper. "I've just located an *elephant* for you to ride in the finale today!"

"An ... elephant?" The little girl from Georgia was dumbfounded.

"You know, where you were just gonna walk on and take your

bows? Well, it's all changed now. In the finale the girls are gonna do a jungle number and I've gone out and rented this elephant. You're gonna ride him out and he'll be backed up in the center of the stage and the whole cast will turn and hold their hands up to you and the curtain will close. We're gonna have the first elephant in burlesque! How about that?"

Georgia was speechless. And out in front of the house I was wondering what the comics would do for an ad lib if the elephant left a deposit on stage as the horse had. Oh, well, that's show biz!

CHAPTER
20

An Indian comes into court and says his wife has committed adultery.

JUDGE: Explain your problem.

INDIAN: When Indian plant corn, Indian *get* corn. When Indian plant wheat, Indian *get* wheat. But when Indian plant child, Indian get Chinaman???

GEORGIA WAS TEMPERAMENTAL and demanding, but she was good and we sold tickets. She had her own fan club. In 1932 she broke up with her boyfriend, a burlesque straight man, and got a little Pekingese dog named Okey to replace him. "So I won't be lonely."

But finally she got homesick and asked us if she could go home for a few months "to see her mother."

But in fact we knew that she had signed to do a road show for her old friend Hirst. After a certain amount of argument we let her go. She was a good attraction and there was no point in antagonizing her. She promised she would come back after her tour. In the end, the trip home turned out to be not so harmful, because she introduced her little sister, Jewel, into burlesque, and her sister wasn't a bad performer either.

By the time Georgia returned from her "trip back to Atlanta" and her southern tour, Gypsy was starring at the Republic, so we booked Georgia into our Brooklyn theater, the Werba. Georgia wasn't thrilled, although she was personally fond of Gypsy. She felt that she was no longer the queen bee. Even more galling to her was the fact that she had to compete at the Werba with a new star whose name was Margie Hart—a tall red-haired girl with a figure to make the customers' eyeballs pop. But despite her competitiveness, she became friendly with both Margie and Gypsy Rose Lee. (At the time, her sister, Jewel, was working at the Star in Brooklyn some distance from the Werba.)

During this period Georgia's boyfriend had gotten a job as a straight man at one of our theaters, although I was unaware of the relationship. But somehow the guy talked her into marrying him, and according to what Georgia later told me, "Less than eight hours later I hated my husband."

The day after her marriage, Georgia and Gypsy switched theaters, with Gypsy headlining at the Werba and Georgia again starring at the Republic. Her husband showed up for the opening night—Les Sponsler was his name. Georgia told him that she had not been happy with her honeymoon night. It turned out that she had been a virgin at the time and his lovemaking apparently had been just too violent and animal for her tastes. She told Sponsler that the love affair was over and so was the honeymoon and the marriage. The whole thing was a one-night stand.

It didn't surprise me she had been a virgin until that one-night marriage, since an astonishing number of our girls were virgins. Some of them were very young. And some of them were simply holding on to that good thing until the right man came along. After her scene rejecting Sponsler, Georgia went to Billy's office and told him everything that had happened.

"If you want, Georgia," Billy said, "I'll fire the guy right now. Pay him off and throw him out."

Billy did as he promised, and when Sponsler got the word, he went to Georgia's dressing room and beat her up badly. The next night, after she had gone out for dinner with a friend of hers from Philadelphia, Sponsler reappeared. He leaped from a doorway, wild-eyed, with a pistol in his hand. "I'm gonna teach you to make a fool of me in front of everybody!" He pulled the trigger and there was a blinding flash of light from the muzzle of the pistol and a sharp crack of the shot. Georgia felt the sting of a bullet against her chest and collapsed. Sponsler ran down the street. Her friend Angelina got her into a cab and unbuttoned her coat and suit jacket, looking for the place where the bullet had entered. But there was no blood, only a dull ache in Georgia's chest where the shot had hit her.

"Georgia," her girl friend said, "there are powder burns all in front of where your heart is, but there's no hole. Jesus Christ, it's a miracle but I think he missed you completely!"

Georgia sat up and examined her coat at the place where the material was charred by the pistol blast. As she examined her blouse, a small wad of paper fell from her coat into her lap. The two women stared at the paper that Georgia held in her hand and burst into laughter.

"A blank cartridge!" Angelina roared. "He shot you with a prop gun. Oh, Christ, what a goddamn phony!"

Sure enough, when they got to the theater they discovered that one of the prop guns was missing, but neither told the propman their suspicions.

Georgia managed to get through the show after all this excitement, but when she got back to Angelina's, where she was staying for the night, a policeman was waiting. At first, Georgia thought that he had heard about the shooting the night before. But that wasn't it.

"There's a man who says he's your husband standing on the ledge of the American Hotel. He told us he won't come in, and he's gonna jump if we come near him. He won't speak with anyone but you."

The officer seemed surprised that Georgia wasn't more upset, so she told him about the incident the night before. "Don't worry," she said to the cop, "I don't think he's got the nerve to jump."

But the cop was certain Sponsler meant business. Les had been on the ledge for several hours already. Wearily, Georgia agreed she would go back and try to talk him inside. When they got to the American Hotel, there was a huge crowd in the street staring up at Les, who was sitting on the ledge dangling his feet fourteen floors above 47th Street. There were news photographers packed around the entrance, grabbing shots of Georgia as she was hustled by the cops through the front door of the hotel. By now Georgia was certain that the whole stunt was an attempt to make her look bad. When she got to the floor where Les was, she smiled at him sweetly and said, "Okay, Les, I'm here. Now why don't you just jump?"

The cops were furious. "Look, lady, we didn't bring you here to make the damn fool jump! We thought you was going to talk him back to safety!"

But Georgia told them she knew her man and she was positive he would never jump. "If you leave me alone here for one minute, I'll have him back inside," she told the cops.

By this time the firemen had spread nets below and Les had made no move to prevent that. This made some of the cops think that perhaps Georgia was right and the whole thing was a stunt to attract attention. Reluctantly, the lieutenant in charge gave her permission. They left her alone, and Georgia walked to the window and put her head outside. Les glared at her, but she grinned back at him. "You phony! I'm not fooled by what you're trying to pull here. You might have fooled the other ones, but I know you too well. Any guy who'd shoot me with a prop gun wouldn't have the guts to jump."

Les was furious. "I'll jump all right and you're gonna look pretty bad when the papers come out in the morning. They'll fix your ass but good!"

"Too bad you won't get a chance to read all about it," Georgia said, mocking him. "You wouldn't miss that for the world, I'll bet!"

Now Les was genuinely angry. He began shouting at her and at the crowd below. He screamed that she was his wife and he had found her with another man. Georgia told him he was a liar. That all he wanted her for was as a meal ticket. They squabbled back and forth as Les clung to his perch and the mob cheered below.

One person in the crowd yelled out, "You burlesque tramps are no damn good!" Another one yelled, "Let the bum jump!"

Georgia looked at her husband of one day with scorn. "Jump or don't jump," she told him. "I don't give a damn, I'm going home."

And she meant it. As she turned to go, her infuriated husband leaped into the room from the window ledge and grabbed her before anybody could do anything, spun her around, and bashed her right in the eye with his fist. The cops came through the open door, jumped on him immediately, and dragged him off to jail, still cursing and swearing at Georgia. Downstairs, news photographers were waiting and Georgia didn't try to hide her damaged eye, which was already turning black. One reporter asked her with a grin, "You gonna work tomorrow night with that eye, Georgia?"

"Whatever Mr. Minsky says," she told him.

Another reporter asked, "Wasn't this all really a publicity stunt?"

But his photographer laughed. "If this is a stunt, buddy, she sure went about it the hard way. Look at that shiner!"

Billy was on the phone first thing in the morning. "Are you okay, Georgia?" he asked her.

"Well, my eye is closed shut. It's all purple."

"Well, you'll feel better when you see the papers. You're all over them."

Georgia apologized. "I'm sorry, Mr. Minsky."

"You're sorry? Georgia, this is quality publicity! How bad did you say your eye was?"

Georgia told him it wasn't really that bad. But it looked horrible, all purple, yellow, and black bruises.

"You can still do the show?" Billy asked her.

"What, with my eye like this?"

"Sure. If it doesn't bother you, it'll be great for business. We'll have to probably put on two extra shows to handle the crowds. We'll get you a rhinestone eye patch from wardrobe. It'll be sensational!" Billy told her to get to the theater early so she could talk to the reporters. And hung up.

When she had finished talking to him, Georgia sent down for the papers and it was as Billy had said—a sensation: MATE MAKES FAKE SUICIDE ATTEMPT FOR LOVE OF STRIPPER. There was a full story with a lot of pictures, including one of Les sitting on the ledge and a full-page shot of Georgia, shiner and all. The newspapers all seemed to take her side, and her husband looked like the idiot that he apparently was.

At the theater Georgia took off her dark glasses and let the photographers get a few more shots of the eye. Inside, Georgia took the rhinestone eye patch the wardrobe woman had made for her, slipped behind a screen, and got into costume, complete with the eye patch, and then came out and posed again for the photographers.

The matinee was a riot! People were yelling and cheering to the point where the strip act became superfluous. A radio news announcement had said that Georgia would remove her eye patch at the end of the number, and they were all there to see that, or most of them anyway. At the end of the act, where she usually gave them a little extra shimmy and ran off stage, Georgia held up her hand to stop the band.

"Okay, ladies and gentlemen. I know what you've come to see."

She paused dramatically and stripped the rhinestone patch, standing there in nothing but a G-string. The audience gasped and broke into wild applause. And that's the way it went throughout the day. As Billy predicted, they did four extra shows that day, and the actors were happy because they got an additional half day's pay for every extra show. The way they fit them all in was to cut several acts from each show.

After the afternoon show Georgia went in for a chat with Billy. She told him she wanted two weeks off to go home and get a divorce from Les.

Billy was furious. "How can you ask for time off without giving me notice so that I can reschedule the show? It's impossible!" He told her to read her contract. "You won't find anything in there that says that you should have time off for a divorce!"

Georgia slumped into one of the leather office chairs and began to whimper. But Billy was not easily swayed. He'd had the old waterworks routine from too many performers in the past.

"Cut it out, Georgia," he said. "You're gonna get your eyes all red and there's still one more matinee to do. It'll look terrible if you come out there with one eye all black and the other one all red."

Georgia ran from his office, still crying.

She was still crying when her cue came up and the comic stretched the scene and stretched it again in order to give her time to get ready. Billy, now furious, yelled over the intercom for her to stop the foolishness and get out and perform. Reluctantly and with difficulty she did so. Personally, I thought that Billy was being a bit rough on the kid. But he was running things backstage.

Later, Billy relented somewhat. He came backstage to see her and said, "Georgia, that was a good show, but you made us run late and that's not very professional. It's not as though you had an accident or something. I could have understood that. But you just threw a tantrum because you couldn't have your own way. I won't accept that and I never will! That's not the kind of action I expect from a professional in this business. It's unforgivable. Never do it again. Understand?"

Billy turned and started to leave, but Georgia reached over and caught him by the sleeve. She was on the verge of tears again. "Please, Mr. Minsky, it wasn't that I was just throwing a tantrum. I'm really tired and homesick. I want to see my mother."

Billy softened a bit, his face still stern. "Georgia, you're acting like a kid. You're a grown woman now. You got responsibilities, and this job is important."

Now Georgia followed him into his office and began to blubber in earnest. "I'm *not* a grown woman! I'm only fourteen years old!"

Billy practically fainted on the spot. He stared at her in astonishment. Then he softly repeated what she had said. "Fourteen?" He said it again aloud. "Fourteen? FOURTEEN! But you've been working for me for over a year. Do you mean to tell me . . . Oh, no! You can't mean it!"

Georgia heaved a sigh and then said quietly, "Yes, I was only thirteen when I signed that contract with you."

Billy slapped his head in astonishment. "Oh, my God!" This was worse than censorship. They could close the theater. Maybe send him to jail. "How could you do this to me?" he asked.

"I didn't think I was doing anything wrong. I had already been working in Philadelphia for a year. After all, you couldn't have known that I was underage."

Billy sank into his office chair with his head in his hands, muttering over and over in different intonations, "*Four*teen? FOURTEEN! Four-TEEN! This kid is only fourteen years old!"

While he was sitting there moaning to himself, Georgia ran upstairs to her dressing room and got something from her trunk. It was a piece of paper, which she brought back and handed to Billy. He looked it over curiously. "Where did this come from?"

"I got a whole trunkful of them," Georgia said. "When I was in vaudeville, my uncle Virgil used to have them made up in case we needed them. When I was only seven or eight, he was telling people that I was a midget." She showed him a whole handful of them. Billy examined them closely.

"You see. They got all the legal stamps and everything."

Billy examined them even more closely. "Nobody questioned these? They sure *look* legit."

"My uncle had them done by some guy he knew. He said the guy was a master."

Billy examined the documents even more closely. "Boy, he sure was. He sure *was*!"

Georgia wiped some of the tears from her stained face. "Is everything okay, then?"

Billy put his face up close to hers and looked into her good eye. "Yeah, it's okay, if you can keep your mouth shut. But how do I know that you can?"

Georgia started to cry again. "Because I'd lose everything if I told anybody!"

"You told me, didn't you?" Billy asked her.

"But that's different. You're my boss, right?"

Billy stared at her reddened eye a minute longer, thinking. Then he folded the phony birth certificate and slipped it into his pocket.

"I'll put this in the file with your contract. If anybody ever asks me questions, I'll tell them I didn't know your age when I hired you and that you gave me this as proof that you were old enough. I'll swear I never heard what you just told me today. Right?"

Georgia swallowed happily and nodded in agreement.

"How in Christ did you learn to strip like that at your age?" Billy asked. But before Georgia could answer, he held up his hand. "On second thought, don't tell me. I don't want to know. You win!" He sighed deeply and looked at her speculatively. "Okay, take the two weeks to go home to your mom. But remember, you owe me one!"

So that was the big secret that Georgia had kept from us for a year. Plus the fact that until that week she'd been a virgin. Now there was only one more thing that we didn't know about her.

CHAPTER

21

COMIC (*holding a hand mirror and crying*): Oh, no! It can't
be! No, no, this is terrible! This is terrible, this is
awful! I can't stand it!
STRAIGHT MAN: What's the matter?
COMIC: What's the matter? Look in this mirror. (*He
holds the mirror up for the straight man.*) What do you
see?
STRAIGHT MAN: I see me.
COMIC: Oh, thank God, I thought it was *me*!

THAT TWO WEEKS testifying before Geraghty's committee didn't do
anybody any good. My brother Billy was wearing under the strain.
For a while we thought that our whole enterprise—and we had
quite a few theaters by that time—was going to be wiped out. Furthermore, our admirer in City Hall, Jimmy Walker, was in plenty of
trouble. The newly formed Seabury Committee accused Jimmy
Walker of everything from accepting bribes to cheating on his in-
come tax. It was clear that the fabulous Jimmy was going to have to
retire under pressure, and that didn't spell good news for the
Minskys. At the time, Jimmy Walker was publicly squiring around a
fabulous show girl named Betty Compton. He was still married. In
actual practice people's attitudes could be quite liberal. But as for
burlesque, there was always somebody crabbing our act one way or
another.

As for the shows, we were doing good business, but it was true that they were sexier than they had ever been. Still, I think they cheered people up. After all, it was the Depression.

At night we were still attracting a mixed crowd. Maybe more mixed than before. There were plenty of women, usually accompanied by their husbands. They seemed to enjoy the strips just as much as the men.

We had a good lineup of stars alternating in our different houses then. Georgia seemed extremely distracted and hung around with some very unsavory men. But that was her business. If it didn't interrupt the show, we didn't meddle. But later I learned that the reason she was so nervous at this time was that the man she had seen gun down a gangland hood in Philadelphia had turned up in New York.

One thing about the Depression that operated to our advantage was that some very talented comedians who could no longer find work in the Catskill's Borscht Belt were turning to burlesque. One of the comedians who auditioned for us that spring was Phil Silvers, who was doing a double with another guy, Jack Albertson. I knew that Silvers had been making $200 a week in the Borscht Belt. But there was simply no work there. In his autobiography, *This Laugh Is on Me,* Phil remembers that day even more vividly than I.

"We had only two good scenes to present to H.K. and Harold at their Republic Theater on 42nd Street. (Silvers is confused here. It was H. K. and me or Billy. None of us ever worked with Harold, who was Abe's adopted son.) They were exuberant, honest men, and refreshingly theater-wise. Billy . . . practically invented modern burlesque. H. K. had a class complex: He dreamed of producing a clean Broadway show. But in laying out a burlesque show, the sequence of chorus, strip, body scene and so on to finale, he had no equal.

"The Minskys hired us for a road show. We did our two scenes, and developed a sequence that became part of the finale. I was just learning to noodle around on the clarinet; Jack performed a beautiful soft-shoe dance to my improvisations.

"We played six weeks in the Minsky eastern houses: Boston, Philadelphia, Albany, Baltimore and Pittsburgh. The comedians were good friends; it was cozy and fun—one big family. After we came back to New York, H. K. asked us to stay on, to play at the Gaiety, at 46th and Broadway. Jack didn't see any future in it; he thought he'd try to break into serious acting."

Well, maybe Albertson was right. In 1968 he got the Oscar as the best supporting actor for *The Subject Was Roses*.

In those days we would sometimes book into the Gaiety or other theaters on our circuit legit dance acts, which we called walking towels. This is because we used them to cool off the overheated audience between the strip acts. One of these was a tall engaging loose-limbed tap and soft-shoe man. His father ran the Biltmore Hotel chain, but the kid had run away from all that for a show business career. We liked Dan Dailey's act so much that we kept him on for an extra week. But somehow he never worked out in burlesque. I wonder whatever happened to him?

Phil stayed with us. One of his comments about burlesque was interesting. According to him there were two great myths that rose out of burlesque: (1) *It was a great training ground for comedians* (true) and (2) *most burlesque comedians were, therefore, great* (don't forget, this is Silvers's opinion, not mine).

"Most of them were hokey, rigid and vulgar. That's why they stayed in burlesque. The ones who rose out of it were able to build creatively on the basics they learned. Witness Abbott and Costello, Rags Ragland, Herbie Faye, Ted Healy, Bert Lahr, Red Buttons, Jackie Gleason, Danny Thomas, Bobby Clark, Ed Wynn, Red Skelton, Joe E. Brown, Eddie Cantor. And, Fanny Brice."

Not all of those guys worked for us, but quite a few of them did. In fact, Rags Ragland was with us right at that particular time.

We paid Silvers $62.50 a week in those days, and he was glad to get it. Three years later he was the top banana. (Actually, the term "top banana" was made up for the show that used all of our old burlesque bits, *Top Banana*. What we called them was first banana.) As our top comic he was making $250 a week, which was not bad for Depression years. Of course, our strip stars, like Margie Hart, Ann Corio, Georgia Sothern, Gypsy Rose Lee, were making between $700 and $2,000 a week. We had to pay them that to keep the big Broadway producers from hiring them away. Silvers worked with Rags Ragland at the Gaiety and established a friendship that was to last for thirty years. He'd met Rags in Chicago in 1930 working at the Star and Garter.

"I idolized Rags," Silvers writes in his autobiography. "What an exhilarating comedian. And what a man. Six feet five, lantern jaw, a loose-boned brawler and lover. He'd been a boxer of no renown in Louisville, but left town to escape a woman demanding a marriage contract.

"He used to hang around the burlesque house in Louisville. Encouraged by one of the comics, Rags joined a touring company on the assumption that the stage was easier than boxing. Or marrying. For him it was, because it gave him steadier opportunities to drink, in higher-tone places. To this day I cannot go into a bar and be at ease because whenever I was in a bar with Rags he was always in a fight. None of which he sought.

"I never drank. I'd just stand there while he drank away, and we'd talk. There was always some little man, fired up with booze, who wanted to hit the big guy. Rags tried to shrug him off, or walk away. If cornered, he'd break up the little guy and all his friends—and the bar. Rags was remarkably relaxed, almost languid. Burlesque was just a way to pay for his drinks. And he never hit a saturation point."

In his autobiography Silvers makes a point that I've stressed so many times, but it's nice to hear it reiterated by an old pro like him so you know I'm telling the truth. Here's what he writes: "Burlesque was a lot less nude and raw than Broadway or Off-Broadway today. It used the *promise* of nudity, suggestion, double meanings. Hypocritical by today's standards, but in the 1930s the audience—and the police who enforced the standards of taste—really believed in surface propriety. We worked within their frame of conventional morality."

Phil even cites an example of a skit he did to show what he meant by "double meanings":

> A comic walks out in an ill-fitting toreador suit. The straight man has convinced him he must fight the bull. He is terrified . . . a lot of comedy is built on fright.
>
> "It's nothing," the straight man says. "You just go out there and take out your machete [knife]."
>
> "In front of all those people?"
>
> "And you wave it at the queen's box."
>
> "What'll the king say?"

According to Silvers, one of our great burlesque fans was the British actor Robert Morley, who always caught our show at the Republic or the one at the Gaiety whenever he was in town. It was a new art form for him, and he was fascinated.

"Oh, jolly good!" he'd exclaim over any bit that intrigued him. And he had a big crush on Margie Hart. He even sent her mock mash notes like, "Petroushka, my sleigh is waiting. Let us fly into the night."

I'm not sure what Morley would have done if Margie had accepted his invitation. But you must remember that Margie, although talented and brilliant in her own way, was not a book reader in the sense that Gypsy Rose Lee, for instance, was.

Incidentally, since Silvers made such a big hit in the burlesque musical *Top Banana,* you might be curious about the skit that originated it.

Now, you have to picture these guys doing this with a stage Dutch or Jewish accent. And, oh yes, wearing funny costumes, baggy pants, and big shoes. So, there are three comics standing center stage. One of them holds up two bananas:

> FIRST MAN: I have three bananas here, and I will give you one.
>
> SECOND MAN: You only have two bananas.
>
> FIRST MAN: I have three bananas. Look, I'll show you. (*Holds up one banana in his right hand.*) One banana have I. (*Holds up one in his left hand.*) Two bananas have I now. One banana and two bananas makes three bananas.
>
> SECOND MAN: I only see two bananas. In your own words, I will show you you are wrong. (*He takes the bananas.*) One banana have I. Two bananas have I. One banana and two bananas . . . by golly! He's right! (*Aside to the third man.*) Would you like a banana?
>
> THIRD MAN (*nodding*): Okay. One banana for you. A banana for me . . .
>
> FIRST MAN: How about me?
>
> SECOND MAN: You eat the *third* banana!
>
> BLACK OUT

So, now you know how the banana bit started.

Phil left burlesque in 1938 for the theater and then Hollywood. Years later, when he became the star of the burlesque-inspired musical *Top Banana,* he was playing in a road company of the show in Salt Lake City, Utah. In the show he was called on to deliver this

line, which you must have heard by now: "Dis mus' be da blace!"
All of a sudden he was in deep trouble for that innocent line. How
could Phil have known that when Brigham Young first set eyes on
the site of Salt Lake City he had said, "This is the place!"

The line was even integrated into a song in the show. When Phil
heard what the problem was from a savvy theater manager, he ran
all over the theater from one dressing room to another telling anyone who had lines in the song "If You Want to Be a Top Banana,"
"Do not say 'this must be the place.' Substitute anything that
rhymes, whether it makes sense or not. 'You've got a funny face,'
'Set the pace,' 'Let's have a big race'—but do not say *this must be the
place!*"

At the time Phil came to us in 1932 we were not laughing. We had
beaten one rap, but now Mayor Jimmy Walker had been forced to
resign and had been replaced by an interim mayor, Joseph V.
McKee. God knows what sort of treatment we would get from him!
Meanwhile, despite police threats, and the Legion of Decency, we
were still expanding wildly in a time when everybody else was pulling in their horns. Billy had a million schemes, ideas, plans, and
flights of fancy so fantastic that he felt that they might ultimately
get him out of his partnership with Joseph Weinstock into the legitimate theater, where he, and above all his wife, Mary, hoped he
would some day be. He planned for us to set up a new wheel—the
Minsky American Wheel—from coast to coast. He had an idea to
take a burlesque company on a round-the-world tour. He even
planned to take over the Metropolitan Opera House for a season of
superburlesque. I am not kidding you. We already had an attorney
in touch with the opera company's people. In the spring of 1932 this
item ran among the personal notices in the *Times*: "To Whom It
May Concern: It is not true that Billy Minsky has acquired the lease
to the New York Public Library, corner of 5th Avenue and 42nd
Street. Signed: A Friend of the People."

So, all right, maybe Billy put the ad in himself. But it gives you an
idea.

Even though H. K. and I were on hand to supervise every possible
detail, Billy stayed through every minute of rehearsals. Meanwhile,
Mary, who had been coming to the theater in earlier years up at the
Apollo, stayed home in Seagate in Brooklyn, depressed and lonely.
She felt that Billy didn't need her. She was a stage widow and that

was true on the weekends too, when we held rehearsals that went through sometimes from Friday to Sunday night.

It was one of those Friday nights, I remember. The crew was clearing the stage after the final show. They were going to set up a lighting-effect number that Billy had seen in a Ziegfeld show and felt would be just right for the Republic. He was standing near the apron when the rig of a traveler curtain broke loose out of the flies and crashed onto the stage. Alarmed, Billy jumped backward into the orchestra pit and landed with his left leg doubled under him and badly wrenched. He was in horrible agony, but it seemed to be his shoulder that hurt worse than his leg. His main concern was whether he would be able to run the rehearsals the following day.

"Do you think anything's broken?" he asked. But how could we answer? Finally, we took him home to Seagate, where Mary was surprised to see him back so early, but deeply concerned about his injury. The doctor finally came. He found no broken bones, so he gave Billy a sedative and told him to lie flat until the "pulled muscle," which he diagnosed the injury to be, straightened itself out. The shoulder? Probably a bruise.

When Mary got up the next morning, she found that Billy was gone. Somehow he'd limped to his car and gone back to the theater to oversee rehearsals for the new show. Despite what the doctor told him, he would not lie flat. He found a cane in the prop room and managed to hobble around on that. Then finally he got impatient with this and threw the cane back into the prop room, determined that somehow he was going to make it on his gimpy leg. But the shoulder became increasingly painful.

A week later he was in agony. His shoulder hurt so badly he couldn't even get out of bed, let alone limp to the theater.

One month later we found out the cause of the pain in his shoulder. It was not a "bruise." It was Paget's disease, a bone malignancy for which no cure was known. He apparently had had it for months, maybe years. But it had been activated by the fall. The doctors were not hopeful. Billy knew he was dying. Mary and his son, Bobby, were there. So was my father, Louis, who was still mourning the death of his beloved Esther. We tried to be there as much as possible, but Billy would always get angry and chase us back to the theater.

"Who's minding the store, brothers?"

My father, who was a knowledgeable man, was not fooled by Billy's jokes. He knew that he was at the bedside of a dying son.

"Never work north of Fourteenth Street, right, Papa?" Billy kidded. My father tried to smile. Billy looked around the room. You would have thought he was counting the house. He looked at each person there—his wife, Mary; his son, Bobby; my father, Louis. There was an empty chair in the room, and he stared at it almost angrily. Billy hated empty seats. He frowned, angrily or possibly from pain, and started to shout something. "Why? Why . . ." and his voice faded away.

Billy was dead. The family, the burlesque business, the theater, all the wise guys up and down Broadway, the strippers, the comics, the straight men, the stagehands, all knew something had gone out of their lives. And above all, the family. In the whole time I knew and worked with Billy, we had hardly ever exchanged harsh words. I always tended to think he coddled me as the baby brother. But he gave me my chance from the start. There was no question that he had been the biggest influence in my life. I was heartbroken. As for my brother H. K., he could hardly speak. Naturally, we didn't go into the theater the next day. We turned the rehearsals over to a stage manager. But it was useless. Sunday morning he called us at Seagate, where we were sitting *shiva*.

"I don't know how to tell you this Mr. Morton, but I don't think we can work this deal without a Minsky. Things just ain't going right."

I sighed, looked at Herbert, and shrugged. "Okay," I said. "Call a full-cast rehearsal after the show on Monday night. We'll work until we get it right. I'll pay time and a half if I have to."

I don't know who said, "The show must go on." I never did. It wasn't because of that line, but I knew that Billy would have wanted it. It was the last show he produced, and I knew it had to be right.

CHAPTER
22

SCRATCH WALLACE: How's tricks?
RAYMOND PAINE: How's Trix? She's fine. She just had puppies.
SCRATCH WALLACE: Police dogs?
RAYMOND PAINE: No, they're too small to be police dogs. They're in the Secret Service.

IT WAS THE lowest point in my life to date. My daily life was so intertwined with Billy's life that it left me with a raw, open wound that forced me to think of his loss every day. But the show *did* have to go on. After all, it was bread and butter for the whole family. Now we had to find a way to apply the tricks, the gimmicks, the showmanship, the craft, and the talent that our brother had tried to impart to us. Perhaps there was no way that we could fill his shoes, but we had to try. We hardly had time to recuperate from our loss when we were hit with another giant blow. The new mayor, McKee, had us hailed into court again and was questioning the renewal of our license. This was in July, only two months after we had seemingly passed inspection.

The pressure on us was more economic than moral. It was the big-time producers who stirred up all those rabbis and reverends to come around. Sure, there was sex on 42nd Street and everywhere else throughout New York. People wanted it, they were willing to pay for it, and it was really simply a question of how *much* they wanted to pay. Ironically, our show was so tame compared with today's standards that it would seem like a Girl Scout picnic.

Certainly the area that *The New Yorker* had dubbed Minskyville had a carnival flavor. But that existed long before we arrived. There was a medical horror show on the block, with fetuses and two-headed animals preserved in alcohol. Hubert's Flea Circus down the street used two suckling pigs as sidewalk exhibits to call attention to their bounding performers. There were Indian herb doctors, gypsy seeresses, lecturers on golden medical secrets, strongmen, living statuary, and similar attractions along the Great White Way. Some were cover-ups for a certain amount of sexual display, such as the living statuary, which was always nude. Of course, there were penny arcades then, much resembling the video-game arcades that exist on that street today.

(Apropos of the Flea Circus, Professor William Hecker, who ran the one down the street, was feeling economic pressure during the Depression too. He said it cost him $3 to get a really good flea. His fleas were all from Europe, and he bought them from ship's cabin stewards. But because of the Depression not as many people were coming over, and it was difficult to find a good flea student. According to Hecker, the smartest fleas were Belgian, although French and Italian ones were quite bright. He felt that English fleas were basically stupid. Because of his patriotism, he said, he would not discuss American fleas at all.)

In addition to this, of course, there were phrenologists who could read the bumps on your head for personality traits, such as acquisitiveness, combativeness, and amativeness, which was their word for sex.

A few blocks north but still in the area defined as Minskyville there was an exhibit called the Salon des Arts. Somehow all the paintings in this salon were nudes. The masterpiece was a prewar (World War I, that is) Cleopatra that used to adorn Churchill's Restaurant at 49th Street and Broadway. There was also a pretty hot nude that once decorated the lobby of the Hotel Marguerey until customers asked that it be removed as being salacious. Originally the Salon des Arts had six artistic nudes, bought from various bars, restaurants, and hotels. By 1932 it had thirty, because they had discovered by this time that it was cheaper to paint their own masterpieces than to buy them. They even had an artist with a smock, beret, and a nude model working on the premises. He turned out four or five masterpieces a night, many of them bought for a good price on the scene by eager patrons of the arts.

There were peep shows then consisting of stereoscopic postcards in sequence of generously endowed beauties predating Sliding Billy Watson's time. If you turned a crank, the cards would flip rapidly and the odalisque would seem to be moving. But if you were really anxious to examine her at leisure, of course, you could stop turning the crank, which was controlled by the number of turns rather than the time spent peeping into the eyepiece.

Anyway, by September, Jimmy Walker couldn't take the heat and decided that it was a good time to resign and take a good long-awaited cruise to Europe. Mayor McKee, almost as soon as he got into office, and we had had some warning that he'd been waiting for this, declared war on burlesque houses. He said we would all have to clean up our performances—or else.

Within days of McKee's move into Gracie Mansion, the home of New York City's mayor, the *Times* published a four-column inter-view with Sumner in which he explained his mission in life. The way Sumner saw it, the breakdown in morality that followed Prohibition was only an omen.

"We are living in a strange age," he told the *Times*. "There has been a let-down in morals. This is not anything new in the world; it has happened before and will happen again. The pendulum swings from one side to the other and it seems to me that there is some kind of a stabilizer needed to prevent the swing from becoming too great in either direction. (Sumner, no doubt!) That is the part that this Society is trying to play. We feel that something must counter-act this let-down. After all, morals have played an important part in the development of any nation. Following the decline in morals there usually comes a decline in government. This played its part in an-cient Rome and also in the French Revolution."

I'm not sure what he meant about the French Revolution. But if he's right about the "let-down" in morals leading to the decline of Rome, this country better watch itself!

And, just to set an example, McKee now pulled the licenses of the Republic and the Eltinge. Lawyers got us out of that one and we opened after a brief closing but with much tamed-down advertising outside the theater. Now we were told we had to call out shows revues rather than classical burlesque, which we had been calling it up until then.

Meanwhile, the strain of running the theaters without Billy was telling on us all. All of a sudden Abe didn't like the way we were doing things, although they were just the way Billy had planned them all along. Of course, Abe had always had his own ideas, so now, in the midst of all this trouble, he decided to split completely and open his own theater, the Gaiety on 45th Street. He leaked the story to the newspapers that his show in the Gaiety, within a stone's throw of the Republic, was going to be classier than the one at the Republic. "I go my way and Morton and Herb can do as they please."

Things had been going sour between Abe and Weinstock for a long time. To tell you the truth Weinstock was not an easy partner. He was hard to get along with and fraternized more than we thought proper with the women in the cast. In addition, he had a couple of sons that he wanted to bring into the business as assistant managers. Abe also had an adopted son through Molly that *he* wanted to bring into the business. It just contributed to bad feelings. Furthermore, Abe was not too happy with H. K. either because of his marriage to Juanita. Despite his own checkered past, he had never forgiven H. K. for this. Partly that was because he had much respect for H. K. and felt that he was lowering himself to marry somebody from burlesque.

When Abe split from us in 1931, just before the Republic opened, he told all the papers that he was going to operate a strictly high-brow type of theater. But after the Gaiety was on its feet he decided to open a theater uptown, and he called it the New Gotham to compete with Billy and Weinstock's Apollo Theatre a few doors away. Despite his elevating announcement, Abe operated the New Gotham on a very low budget with minimum-wage strippers and $20-a-week chorus girls. One reason that he could get talent for those low prices is that he was still playing two-a-day instead of the grind policy that was beginning to take over all of burlesque. Oddly enough, earlier, the New Gotham had been the only grind house. But the two-a-day shows were easier on the cast, and some preferred to work less for less money rather than put up with the strain of four shows a day. So Abe got along without star names or elaborate scenery and kept his overhead down. He also ran a much rawer show

with shorter comic bits and very brief ensemble numbers. The inspectors for the License Bureau called it "a parade of anatomy." *The
Billboard,* the trade magazine, said, "Abe Minsky knows what they
want after twenty years in the business."

There were six or seven featured women, including a chorus girl
who did a strip specialty. Basically they simply removed their clothing without necessarily dancing and walked off the stage. It could
hardly even be dignified by calling her a stripteaser, but they got
down to bare skin covered only by a G-string in short order and
walked off jiggling as much as possible but without necessarily
dancing. Abe spent no money on advertising and didn't draw much
of a crowd, but his costs were so low that he managed to make a
profit of some sort for most of those years in the early thirties.

His wife, Molly, and her son, Harold, were also deeply involved in
the New Gotham. Molly was secretary and treasurer of the Burley
Amusement Corporation, which was the lessee of the theater. She
often conducted benefits there for the women's auxiliary of her local
synagogue. But Abe was drawing even more unfavorable attention
than we were downtown, and it became evident that he would not
get away with his low-down high jinks forever.

I remember telling Norman Klein, the newspaperman who interviewed us, about the split: "He thinks he can fill a burlesque house
with smart-aleck stuff like George S. Kaufman; he wants to give
them modernistic stuff.

"My friend," I continued, "you've gotta keep the laughs and routines down to a level. It doesn't pay to shoot above their heads. Abe
will find that out. You can't make a Broadway audience think. You
have to play down to them. We're the originals, and in two weeks
we'll have five burlesque houses running full blast.

"Listen," I went on. "Don't think Abe's going to make us look like
bladder slappers. We're specializing in good, clean fun. Why, the
jokes they tell at Park Avenue penthouse parties nowadays are too
crude for our shows. We don't let our girls wear as little as I saw on
bathers at Jones Beach."

Abe, playing the wise guy, would not say why he broke with H. K.
and myself. He told the reporter that he just *hates* publicity. "My
heart jumped," he said, "just hearing that a reporter wanted to see
me."

But he sicced the reporter onto Russell Carew, his house manager,
and Carew explained something of what Abe had in mind: "He

wants something sophisticated. He's tired of beefy or pony choruses too—our girls will make Ziegfeld look sick. The public wants to forget its troubles. Blondes? Sure, we'll have blondes in the posing numbers. You can't control blond chorus girls these days. They are blond today and red-haired tomorrow. It ought to keep the steady customers on the *qui vive*. You know?"

Carew told the paper that he was looking for new laughs "keyed to the modern spirit."

So let him give it a try, I figured. We had already found out that you can't tamper that much with burlesque humor. There were an estimated 400 to 600 bits that the comics and most of the audiences knew. They did not like too much in the way of revision. It made them uncomfortable.

Abe, who did not have much money himself after the 1929 Crash, had finally gotten financing from Harold Raymond of the Star Theatre in Brooklyn. Needless to say they had little success in competing with the Republic, which was established, traditional, and popular without being highbrow. Other burlesque houses were bitter about their inability to compete with us. One time Weinstock made a wisecrack about Raymond, who came from the garment business, being a "cloak and suiter," and Raymond punched Weinstock in the nose.

With all the harassment, business held up well. Some people said that the Depression was the savior of burlesque. Certainly, there was no time in American history when people needed a lift more than then, and we were giving it to them at a decent price. As if we didn't have enough trouble with His Honor Joseph McKee, who was followed by John P. O'Brien, another bluenose as far as we were concerned.

As I said, we managed to squeak through McKee, but our troubles never ceased. At the end of the summer months in 1933, Geraghty, who had supported the unsuccessful McKee against the new mayor, John P. O'Brien, was superseded as license commissioner by Sydney Levine, who at once proceeded to belittle his predecessor. The easiest way was through burlesque shows, which he termed morally destructive. "Geraghty," the new commissioner charged, "permitted obscene shows to go on running solely to embarrass Mayor O'Brien."

Levine served summonses to the burlesque houses that he considered indecent, which was practically all of them. He said that "hereafter there will never be tolerated the removal of clothes on any stage in New York City in an indecent manner." He conceded, however, that "immobile *tableaux* and statuesque presentations with distinctly artistic appeal provided the vital parts are clad in opaque raiments" would be okay. The way we read that, it was the first official sanction to bare the breasts on stage.

We were really dealt another body blow when the reformer and Fusion candidate Fiorello "Little Flower" La Guardia was elected mayor in 1933. He appointed a new license commissioner Paul Moss, a former Broadway producer, just one of the people who had always had it in for us as competition to their own high-priced shows. In October 1934, as soon as Moss came in, the Department of Licenses issued a list of restrictions, specifying what we could and could not do, and announced a set of rules. Among the items were:

1. No female shall be permitted on the stage in any scene, sketch, or act with breasts or the lower part of the torso uncovered, or thinly covered or draped as to appear uncovered.
2. Scenes, sketches, or acts in which a female appears originally fully or partly clothed and gradually disrobes shall conform to the above rules.
3. No vulgar or obscene or indecent language offensive to decency or propriety shall be indulged in by performers in any scene, sketch, or act or play.
4. The licensees of theaters will be held accountable by the Commissioner of Licenses for a strict observance of the aforegoing regulations in their respective theaters, and any willful persistent or habitual disregard of them may result in a suspension or revocation of the licenses.
5. Licensees of theaters shall cause to be displayed in the backstage portion of their theaters, in a conspicuous place where it can readily be seen by artists, actors, and other employees, a legible copy of this regulation, so that artists, actors, and other employees who have any grievance or complaint as to breach of contract or non-payment of salary might file complaint with the Commissioner of Licenses.

   Signed: Paul Moss, Commissioner of Licenses

Nevertheless, in those years we still didn't have too much to complain about. We had a good bunch of first-line strippers, some of whom we had developed or discovered ourselves and others that we had lured away from our competitors. Among the headliners were Georgia Sothern, Gypsy Rose Lee, Margie Hart, and Ann Corio, whom we had hired from the Eltinge across the street. For a minute we thought we might split our talents like amoebas. Georgia Sothern had already given us a clone or at least a talented stripper in her younger sister, Jewel. So when it turned out that Gypsy also had a sister, whose stage name had been Dainty June but who was now considerably beyond that, H. K. and I decided we might as well give her a shot. Show business was lousy then for chorus girls as well as for comedians. So H. K. and I told Gypsy that she could have her sister, June Havoc, come in for a tryout.

One thing about Gypsy you should know. Despite her reputation as an elegant lady and a member of the intelligentsia, her background was not refined. Her mother, depicted in Gypsy's own book and by Ethel Merman in the show *Gypsy*, was an ambitious, brassy, and pushy lady. But this was not the half of it. The old girl could kindly be described as an eccentric. And Gypsy, although extremely bright, had her idiosyncrasies too. I remember when she first appeared at the theater she had a monkey trained to do things that would have driven any of our license commissioners up the wall. However, she decided not to use that material in her act. As for her mother, by the time Gypsy had been working for us for a year, we had to bar her from the theater. Her river did not run to the sea.

Anyway, Herbert and I decided that we would give Gypsy's sister a try. She had been working the marathon dances that were so popular during the Depression. You probably saw what this was like in the film with Jane Fonda called *They Shoot Horses Don't They*. It was terrible work. And the pay was little. Frankly, when June showed up in the theater, she had bags under her eyes and looked a little skinny for the job. She also seemed taken aback by the kind of show we had.

I was in the box office talking to Rose, the cashier, when she arrived. The spieler outside was yelling, "Watch her! Like a banana, watch her peel! Watch Gypsy Rose Lee take it off, right down to the fruit."

June seemed not too sure about all this, but it had been her mother who had talked her into coming over to Minsky's for the tryout. Her mother had told her—and as far as I'm concerned it was true—that Billy Minsky's 42nd Street burlesque was equal to the best of Broadway.

"Why, burlesque is the womb that has borne great stars," her mother told her. "I can name you eight or nine easily, and the *Ziegfeld Follies* at the Winter Garden is no different in any way from 'Ada Onion from Bermuda' at Minsky's."

So, Dainty June listened to her wacky mother, as she always had. (Excuse me if I seem to keep harping on that, but I'll give you some examples that June described herself about her mother a little further on.) From what Gypsy had told her sister about the vicissitudes of stripping, it's no wonder she was nervous about her tryout.

Now, I haven't admitted this so far, but of course, among that audience of high hats, intellectuals, and jolly tradesmen there was an occasional creep or degenerate.

"Have you ever heard of any other public who sit with a newspaper covering their lap?" Gypsy asked her sister. June was a perfect foil.

"No," she answered.

"Oh, yes indeed." Gypsy was getting a big kick out of watching her baby sister's face. "You see, the reason for that paper is simple—it's because they're masturbating. That's right, and I guess they'd rather not be seen by the other Johns. God! All the stuff they bring in with them—it's an education! Milk bottles and raw liver and—you don't believe me? Check the alley. See what they sweep out of here at night." June wasn't amused.

"That's not an audience!" June told her sister angrily.

But maybe Gypsy was being kind. Maybe she wanted to dispel any illusions June may have had about burlesque. I'm inclined to think there was some sibling rivalry at work.

Gypsy pursued her educational discourse. "How would you know, June? Where have you been? What does your marathon audience bring in with *them*? Picnic baskets—so they can munch and crunch while getting their jollies watching a bunch of rejects degrading the human race in public?

"Well, let me tell you, June, my audience is no scabbier, no sicker, than yours, but my audience is more useful. Oh, yes—while they sit out there jerking off, I'm the one using *them*. Because there's another audience coming to watch my audience watch me!"

Now, this is a view of burlesque I've never had, but I felt I had to give it to you the way Gypsy gave it to her sister. As the fellow said, there's always a bit of dirt sticking to the spade.

June was intelligent and showed herself to be a good observer in her book *Cry Havoc.* When she showed up at the theater, she was told to wait in the dressing room, as Gypsy was performing. "I sat heavily on a backless kitchen chair drinking in the beloved clutter. Rhinestones and feathers, spirit gum and Sterno, perfume mixed in equal parts with death sweat. The never-stop cooking of coffee. This combination of intimate odors flowed in the atmosphere warmed toastily by circles of mismatched light bulbs framing the cracked mirrors. An array of brandy bottles littered the shelf, with lipstick smudged coffee mugs. Various plates piled high with cigarette butts completed the picture."

A good description of the chorus girls' dressing room. Gypsy had her own dressing room, freshly painted and shared with no one except her monkey. But the way June described the smells—that was accurate. And the brandy, that was accurate too. Gypsy could really put it away, and she often did, even between her acts.

Anyway, June didn't even try out as planned. H. K. and I, at Gypsy's urging, gave her a six- to eight-week contract sight unseen. Gypsy assured us she'd show her sister the ropes. Maybe she did and maybe she didn't. Maybe she didn't want her sister competing with her, although I really think the fact was that as far as stripping was concerned, Gypsy had a certain instinct for it and June didn't. We had to close her out in the middle of the first week, but we paid her full contract. Fortunately, she had plenty of other talents and succeeded splendidly on Broadway on her own, as she is still doing.

Gypsy, herself, was an original. In the beginning she had some very rough friends. First, a crooked Broadway cop. And then, the infamous gangster Waxy Gordon, otherwise known as Irving Wexler. This is where all that earlier gangster stuff ties in. Because Waxy got his start as a bootlegging partner of the famous Arnold Rothstein. By now, Arnold was dead and Waxy was considered one of the most important gangsters in town. He was famous for taking his unwanted friends for a nice ride in the fresh air to the Borscht Belt and leaving them in some of the colorful mountain lakes tied to a couple hundred pounds of cement blocks. Waxy himself was in a lot of trouble with the Feds. As in the case of Al Capone, the alcohol Feds were not able to pin anything on the elusive Waxy, so the tax men were called in to try and nail him one way or another. Besides, he was wanted on all sorts of charges, so he just sent his henchmen ahead of him to sit around and chat with Gypsy and presumably see

to it that she didn't get in any trouble. But that was a tough assignment. To keep them amused Gypsy brought in a little 8-mm projector and a trunkful of those movies where men are wearing black
socks, masks, and nothing else. I found out later that she got both
the projector and the films from her mother, who used to spend her
afternoons watching them in lieu of daytime television, which was
not yet available.

At this time Gypsy was living with her mother in a ten-room
apartment on Riverside Drive. She had a great sense of publicity
and had really developed an idea of the character that she was going
to be playing on Broadway—and it wasn't Mrs. Hovick's little girl.
She quickly got the idea from the ritzier people that attended the
show that if a stripper could speak even two lines of French, it would
be considered a miracle, and if she read even one book and quoted it
copiously, she would be considered an intellectual genius, so she
went about cultivating these talents. It was during this time, when
June was temporarily staying with her sister, that boyfriend Waxy
decided to present her with a complete houseful of furniture that
probably had to be handled with asbestos gloves. However, she gives
a good description of the notorious gentleman, whom she saw very
seldom: "He wasn't very tall, and he wasn't hefty, but the empty
room filled with his presence. He was well-groomed and nicely
dressed and the memorable thing about him, I suppose, was the
mustache. It was pointy. It was waxed." (This must have been a
temporary aberration. I never saw Waxy with a mustache.)

The dining-room set alone that Waxy presented her with consisted of at least thirty chairs and a table long enough to accommo-
date them. According to June, her mother seemed very taken with
Waxy. "Class. Class," her mother said firmly. "No pretense, just
honesty himself. In this world of stinkers, just give me a straightfor-
ward, true-blue gangster every time." And she left the room to
watch her blue movies. Shortly after that, apparently at the suggestion of Waxy, Gypsy's mother left the Riverside Drive apartment
and moved into one on West End Avenue. Gypsy moved into a penthouse apartment on Gramercy Square.

But though she was barred from the theater, it was hard to keep
Gypsy's old *yenta* of a mother out of the picture. She was there
whenever reporters turned up. But much of what she said made the
press, so I suppose we couldn't complain too much. "My baby is in-

nocent and pure," she told the reporters after a particularly galling raid on the Republic. That was the one where Gypsy told the press, "I wasn't naked. I was completely covered by a blue spotlight." She always had the gift of the gab. It was about this time that our star developed an ulcer. No wonder. Her boyfriend, Waxy, who was paying for her apartment on Gramercy Square, was not quite the sweet little musical-comedy-type hood that her sister June envisioned when she met him. Gordon was a genuinely vicious gangland killer, very high up in the mob world of the time—probably one of the two or three top bootleggers on the East Coast, if not in the whole country. After the death of Rothstein, he'd gotten into a squabble with Dutch Schultz, and several gangsters on both sides had been killed. Gordon never traveled without a heavily armed bodyguard, and sharing the same room with him could be something of a strain. Oddly enough he was a great fan of opera and classical music. But very few people would want to attend a concert with him. He also indulged in the importation of narcotics and other chemicals now called mood enhancers. Remember that even in the 1920s drugs were very popular, and the breakdown of law brought about by Prohibition encouraged the development of the drug trade. Drugs were popular backstage with the girls, at least some of them, but I just didn't want to know about it.

As for girls, these gangster types didn't want to know from the pony chorus. They wanted stars. Famous stars. Being seen with a woman known all over town for her sexuality gave them a big lift I suppose. Many of them got access to the girls by backing such shows as *Earl Carroll's Vanities* and the *Ziegfeld Follies*. But somehow they never came to us with their money. Meanwhile, Gypsy was cutting a wide swath through the city on every social level from top to bottom—and I do mean bottom.

CHAPTER
23

JOEY FAYE: My, oh my! Here comes a pretty girl now. Oh, boy! Hey! Honey, would you like to go to the park with me and watch the squirrels bury their nuts?

GIRL: Oh, I think I'm in love with you. Yes, I am—take my eyes. Take my arms. Take my lips.

JOEY FAYE: Sure, the best part you keep for yourself!

IN 1931, JUST before we opened the Republic, a small Italian congressman from New York named Fiorello La Guardia was pressuring Governor Franklin D. Roosevelt to clean up the city. It was Governor Roosevelt who in 1930 launched the Seabury probe of Walker. Sumner had been after the mayor almost as much as us and once tried to get a "Clean Books" bill passed. Sumner felt that the general public could not be trusted with the sort of material openly available in the bookstores. Walker said, "I never heard of a man or a woman who was ruined by a book."

When the censors and the reformers got after him about burlesque, Walker cracked, "A reformer is a guy who rides through a sewer in a glass-bottomed boat."

Maybe he shouldn't have been so sassy about the reformers. They were closing in on him fast. But we were still doing our best to give our audiences a good show. We hired a terrific, handsome singer as what some of the people called a "tit serenader," the tenor who sang the straight numbers between or sometimes behind the strip act. He was Robert Alda, who later starred in the title role of the film *The George Gershwin Story*. He was also the father of Alan Alda, who has become one of our greatest film stars following his success in *M*A*S*H* on television.

Bob Alda had a very sweet voice and was an excellent straight man in the skits. He really worked at his craft. Sometimes he did eight or nine parts in one show. He would sing fifteen songs a day, sometimes more. After he had left the burlesque circuit, Alda once said to me, "Don't worry, the more ex-burlesque people come to Hollywood the better."

Who was worried? What I was worried about was that Hollywood and Broadway were taking away our best talents. After all, we were only paying Alda $40 a week at the time. It didn't take much to tempt him. But for the girls it was a different matter. In the first place, they simply didn't get offers from Hollywood. Whether it was because their talents were of a different nature or what, I don't know. What they did get offers for, however, were the big girl shows, the *Follies* and so forth. But we weren't as threatened as one might think. The girl-show offers, although very pleasing to the ego of the performers, didn't pay their stars or even their secondary players as much as we did, and often they demanded a lot more from them. One of our girls explained her views in an interview by *Collier's* magazine in 1932. "I'd much sooner be in burlesque," she said, "than in the so-called girl-and-music shows. In burlesque your audience looks at you, yells at you"—she was rehearsing before a mirror at the time and the yells were understandable—"but they don't wait at stage doors or try to use influence to meet you.

"It's harder work. See, me, with one show over and another two hours away, and I'm rehearsing here and the girls are on stage learning new dance routines."

While she was telling the *Collier's* reporter this, thirty of the girls were rehearsing, led by our dance director, Rose Gordon, who was drilling the girls like a slave driver. I have to admit that many of them had less than ballet-level talents in the dance. The girl, whom the reporter did not identify, went on: "Those girls all talk nice and act nice. In the Follies and the Scandals and the Vanities it was different. Here it's business—both ways. When you're through with your stint, you go home—and you get your $150 a week if you're a principal and your $50 if you're a show girl, regularly without fail. And you don't have to stand for no bullying.

"When I was in a big Broadway show it was terrible the way we were driven. I've known fifty girls that start rehearsing at ten in the morning and not get through until five the next morning. And the language some of those dance routine bosses used to hand us on the big-time!

"That's one reason I prefer burlesque to the big-time shows. You've got to work harder here. You should see the way Minsky tosses out comics when they don't click! And then they're just as tough on the road. But when you make good it's a steady job. Hard work, but a steady job. And most girls like it. They're not bothered with stage door Johns or the manager's pals. Burlesque is rated a cut below girl-and-music shows for playboys, and that gives us a break. We don't have to buy our own costumes, and when there's a good week's run the management blows us to a beauty parlor service. I'm gonna have a free henna tomorrow.

"Why, this one girl got married last week to this big furniture man's son. He's giving us a party on his houseboat this week-end.

"Keep your high-hat shows," she concluded. "Give me burlesque."

That's the kind of girls we had working for us. They were, most of them, very young, often no more than eighteen. I would say the average chorus girl was in her early twenties. A lot of them came from the same Pennsylvania mining areas. They tended to be tall, with good skin and nice, fair complexions. And they appreciated a steady job, especially in those days.

Thus, despite all the annoyances, we were doing all right. At the Republic, for instance, which had 1,100 seats, we played six days a week at first because until 1933 they didn't allow us to do burlesque on Sundays. With two shows a day, that's a couple of thousand a day at the Republic alone. Multiply that by six, it would be about 12,000. Actually, we probably played to 11,000 a week, and the expenses weren't too high. Second and third bananas often were paid as little as $25 a week. And don't forget, we had a growing number of theaters all over the country.

I had to keep myself busy at the Republic. I'd get in about ten-thirty or eleven o'clock and the first thing I'd do would be to go up to the office, review the mail, and talk to the PR man and decide what we were going to run in the ads. Then I'd go over the bills and meet anybody who had to see us on business. After that I'd go down and check the theater. I wanted to make sure that everything was clean. We were very careful about sanitary conditions. This took in the men's room and the ladies' room. We were almost fanatics about that. The carpets had to be spotless, so I'd check that they were properly vacuumed or shampooed. Then I'd go down to see what action was taking place in the box office. After that it was time to see if the cast was coming in on time and if there were any absentees, and if so, what to do about replacements. While I was doing all this there'd be a million phone calls about structural changes, legal problems, bills to be paid, and so forth. I'd leave about five o'clock and drive home to 72nd Street for dinner and return by seven-thirty. Then I'd recheck the box office and see how the action was going. At curtain time I would stay to make sure that nothing was wrong. During the intermissions, if there were any celebrities, such as Fyodor Chaliapin, the famous Russian basso, or Brooks Atkinson, or Jimmy Cannon, the newspaper columnist who was then working for the *Graphic,* I might have them up to my office for a few drinks with H. K. Don't forget, it was Prohibition then so people appreciated getting the good whiskey that we offered.

Three or four times a week Milton Berle would show up with a pencil and pad and steal our jokes. But I didn't mind. He played to a different audience, and besides, we'd stolen them all ourselves in the first place. Milton never played in burlesque himself.

After the show was over we would audition new talent brought around by the agents. We would have advertised in *Variety* or *Zits Weekly,* which was a big show business publication at the time. We'd see not only strippers but dancers, singers, and comics. Sometimes we'd get a laugh even at that late hour. They'd be auditioning just under the work light with only a piano player, and I'd be tired; but still there was a lot of satisfaction in it. And you never knew when you would discover a new star. However, once you had found one, there could be problems.

Gypsy, for instance, was becoming not just a person but a *personage.* She hired her own press agent and pretty soon there wasn't a day that went by when you didn't read some new item about Gypsy. Of course, the striptease was still a new thing and any discussion of strippers was good copy for the newspapers. Remember, there were about twelve or fourteen newspapers competing for the readers' attention in New York at that time, including the new *Graphic,* which would run anything as long as it had sex. Gypsy attracted attention wherever she went. If she went to the opening night of the Met, and she did, she would wear a floor-length cape of real orchids. Don't think that wouldn't get plenty of attention. It was all over the papers that she lived in her penthouse and was absolutely dripping with diamonds and furs (paid for, of course, by Waxy). She told her sister, June, that she was so afraid of having her jewels stolen that she wore them all the time, in the bath and even to bed. Her parties attracted a lot of the most glamorous people, but also a lot of the sleaziest. According to June, opium and marijuana were smoked openly. Gypsy told her sister, however, that she was giving it up. "Makes me too agreeable," she told her sister. "I'm not giving anything away, I'm selling it. Sweet? Submissive? May as well be a housewife. Nope, it dims my luster, makes me resemble the others—that's the worst thing that could happen. Now, brandy makes me shine. I don't want my mind souped up or down. I just want my elastic tightened inside and out."

She had a way with words in both private life and public. She told one reporter that her favorite fan sat in the first row at every performance with a lunch box on his lap and his room number printed on his forehead.

June told her that she was becoming a fad. "Do you want to be a fad?"

"Of course not," she told her sister. "I want to be a legend. A fad is just one step along the way."

Publicity, of course, is a two-edged sword. All the items about her great supply of jewelry finally attracted some robbers. They took everything, even the pear-shaped diamond ring on her finger, which Gypsy tried to swallow. But one of the thugs hit her so hard on the back that she spit out the diamond and a few teeth as well—teeth that Waxy had paid for.

The rotten thing about it was that Gypsy recognized the crooks. That's what she got from hanging around with gangsters. But she could hardly tell the police who they were. Besides, if she admitted that she knew who they were, she might not be able to collect her insurance. Well, at least the thieves didn't take her mink-covered toilet seats. Who would have bought them? On second thought . . .

Robbery or not, it seems that Gypsy couldn't do a thing wrong.

The public was crazy about her, as indeed it was about all of the new star-style strippers. Shoes, brassieres, and chocolate sundaes were named after them. A department store in Kansas City featured the Gypsy Lee Strip Dress. This item fastened from the neckline to the hem with a zipper and it was for *junior misses!* The fact was that Gypsy thought zippers were vulgar and fastened everything with little snaps, buttons, or pins.

Nobody was ever able to analyze what special quality Gypsy brought to her stripping, but she had an undeniable *something*.

"I don't know myself what it is," she told me once. "I don't feel any spark of genius *here*." She splayed her hands over her undersized bosom.

"Most of the girls have better figures than mine. I can't sing, I don't dance." All true. But she had a way of talking a song that seemed to turn her audiences on.

I know that she had no real education other than a semester or two at a finishing school in Connecticut, but she could sure talk a good game. I think she went home and dug material out of books and then went out and quoted it to newspapermen. Whatever it was, they adored it. Once, after a public lover's quarrel, she was asked whether she didn't hate men.

"Why, the little rascals," she said. "I adore them—some of them. Let me freshen up a little on my philosophy. Wasn't it St. Augustine who said, 'Man is born in filth and predisposed to evil?'

"Well, I don't subscribe to that. I incline more to Clement of Alexandria, who wrote that 'man should not be ashamed to love that which God was not ashamed to create.' Meaning, of course women.

"Once in a while I hear that old chestnut popping out that us strippers—ugh—loathe the loathesome creatures. Males—ugh—the beasts! Say, am I loathing eighty percent of my audience? I'd make like a bigger fool than my mama taught me to be if I am. Why men are even kind of sweet."

With all this—the experimentation with drugs, the drinking, the cynicism, which I often thought was put on—Gypsy was a generous soul and well liked not only by her male fans but by the people she worked with. Georgia Sothern was one of her greatest fans, and despite their different tastes in social sets, Gypsy often invited Georgia to attend her parties.

"Gypsy's party," Georgia said after attending one, "was something else! It was a blast. There were all the people she said I would meet there and more. Mr. John, the hat designer. Some Broadway stars. A lot of names."

Of course, a lot of the names, which came from the literary and social worlds, Georgia would not even have recognized, such as Carl Van Doren, dean of the critics; William Saroyan, the author; and Peggy Guggenheim, the wealthy art collector.

But perhaps Georgia wouldn't have noticed anyway. She was teetering on the edge of a nervous breakdown. The gangster that her friend Angelina had been playing around with all these years had finally been reached by one of his rivals. According to Georgia, this man was a rival in love as well as in crime. On the night of Gypsy's party Georgia read in the paper that the man she'd seen kill another gangster in Philadelphia had been rubbed out in Central Park after both his legs and arms were broken. That was enough to make anyone nervous. This time when she insisted on being allowed to go home to visit her mother I thought it might be a good idea if I gave in. Besides, we finally found a new talent that we thought could replace her, or at least was worth giving a try. She called herself Maxine De Shon. A tall, beautiful blonde, she had a fashion-model look, as if she'd just stepped out of the pages of *Vogue* magazine, and unlike Gypsy, she had a terrific singing voice.

Things were going well enough that I thought it wouldn't hurt to give Georgia the time off she asked for, and H. K. agreed. Besides, we could both see that if we didn't, we'd have an extremely overwrought stripper on our hands.

Meanwhile, a young girl who had worked up at the Apollo for us in the box office and also here at the Republic spent all of her time hanging around backstage studying the moves of every stripper, particularly Margie Hart. She was a pretty girl, with long black hair, and ambitious as hell. She took on the name of Rose la Rose and soon was bumping and grinding her way to the top. But along the way she made an enemy that was to give her plenty of trouble—the fiery Margie Hart.

CHAPTER 24

MIKE SACHS: (*Staggers into the room looking like a corpse.
Lurches toward the straight man.*) Did you see a funeral
go by?
STRAIGHT MAN: No. Why?
MIKE SACHS: I just fell out of the hearse!

———————————————————•———————————————————

AS I HAVE already mentioned, in burlesque each stripper developed
her own technique, and most strippers were quite protective of their
own style. When Georgia was appearing in the Werba, she was
warned that Margie Hart, who was then still an up-and-coming kid,
was watching her act very carefully.

"Pretty soon she'll be copying your routines, honey," one of Georgia's friends warned her.

Georgia, a girl of great generosity, ignored the warning, and apparently it didn't harm her any. But now it was Margie's turn to be
emulated. Rose la Rose hung around backstage and watched Margie's every move. By this time, the tall, red-haired stripper was a
very big star. Part of the technique she had developed included a
certain persona that went with her act. She carried a Bible under
her arm at all times when she was not on stage and explained her
own personal success by saying, "Maybe it's because I'm just a
wholesome, clean American girl trying to get along." She also refused Hollywood movie offers because, "I don't like to be kissed
publicly."

But despite these demure protestations, Margie quickly gained a reputation for working "hotter" and showing more than any other stripper. She always had us worried. She popularized the type of trick dress that eventually became standard with all the advanced practitioners of her art. As it was finally developed, this consisted of narrow strips of silk that hung from the waist down the front and back with the sides bare. It was like a dress tied around the hips with the sides cut out. In this way she could expose her legs by intimately flicking the protective slips of silk back and forth with a casual twist of her fingers. This had certain advantages, as it did not call for the actual removal of the dress until some point near the end of the act. For the audience it meant that they didn't have to wait for that final split-second flash at the end of the act to get at least a glimpse of whatever it was they were looking for. It kept their interest riveted throughout the entire act as she ran her fingers along the edges along the narrow strips of dress and gave a special meaning to every second of the routine. Meanwhile, it was something that the censors had trouble dealing with since she was not taking the dress off.

However, the thing that brought mobs to see Margie was the rumor that she often worked without a G-string. God knows, I hope this was not true. I could never catch her actually coming on without one, but there was a rumor that she wore something called a Chicago G-string, which in some fashion could be stripped off during the act, and yet if somebody came to inspect her at the end, there it was. Anyway, the rumor was enough to keep her fans, who were mostly veteran burlesque buffs, avidly concentrating on every slight movement of her fingers as she played with her trick gown. They felt that they never knew when she might slip. A newcomer watching Margie's act would at first not understand the hush of expectancy that accompanied her routine. It looked like an ordinary one, with Margie parading around with a bare bosom. Generally, she didn't cooch or sing dirty songs or act arty the way Gypsy Rose Lee did or kiss the bald heads. All she did was to slink from one side of the stage to the other. But a keen-eyed observer might notice that the audience's eyes were fixed not above the waistline on Margie's rather impressive bosoms but a few degrees south of the border, where Margie, with a sly, saucy movement, was brushing away the slips of silk that remained between the audience and her innermost self.

Through clever manipulation of the complicated costume she always seemed about to give a glimpse of that promised land the audience was yearning to see—or possibly a reasonable facsimile thereof.

Margie didn't have Gypsy's press agent or Ann Corio's public image, but she was very proficient in her own simple, direct way and managed to get her name and her picture in the newspapers almost as much as the others. When she finally was busted in one of the raids that were now becoming habitual, she went to the courthouse and, in the anteroom adjoining the court in which she and the others were arraigned, stripped to the waist for the benefit of the photographers. When she went before the bar of justice, she was triumphant and self-satisfied as she calmly readjusted her shoulder straps. She knew now her picture would be in the papers regardless of the court's decision. She had already won the day.

And she was right. The press, although they didn't publish the actual shots of the strip, gave her all the space she needed. She was soon known as one of the leading strippers in the East.

But Margie, casual as she seemed, was a perfectionist. When she started to gain attention as a star, she had her slightly hooked nose straightened. She felt that in her business any imperfection would be noticed. As she continued to get newspaper publicity, she lost the air of the small-town, half-bright burlesque girl and even began to pal around with some of the literati with whom Gypsy was identified. She acquired a personality of her own, began to talk to the boys in the front row, cooched a little, and even talk-sang a few numbers à la Gypsy.

It was the nose job that led to one of the greatest feuds in burlesque between Margie and Rose la Rose. By this time, la Rose was doing pretty well herself, although she never achieved the popularity of Margie Hart.

Rose la Rose, who worked "hot" like Margie Hart, from whom she presumably had pinched much of her act, became a well-known stripper in her own right. She was called "a new and different exotic find" when she first appeared. Even Damon Runyon talked about her in his column: "Dreamed we nominated Miss La Rose for President."

Collier's later said this of her: "Known as the bad girl of burlesque because of her gay abandon on the stage, Rose more than any other dancer in the moulting business has city censors everywhere wailing—'is this strip necessary.' "

When I said Rose worked "hot" or "strong" it didn't mean that she actually stripped completely nude on stage. Rather, she developed the art of "flashing," and the guessing game between Rose and her eagle-eyed fans sold a lot of tickets for us and the others for whom she worked.

She would come out in a long, flowery dress that covered her body completely except for three strategic openings in front, two above and one below. The back of her dress had no midsection. Since many of her vital parts were exposed from the start, she could devote a lot of time to such tidbits as her favorite theme song, "Who Will Kiss My Oo-la-la."

Unfortunately, when she was planning her own routine she probably derived a few of her ideas from other strippers. They all did. But Margie Hart was particularly indignant because she felt that Rose had copied her style, gestures, and mannerisms. Apparently Margie made no secret of her feelings. When the two strippers spoke at all, the conversation was loud and angry. The argument finally reached the violent stage. Margie had had such success with her nose bob that Rose decided to emulate even this. She visited a surgeon, who rearranged her nose to more pleasing patterns. This was unforgivable to Margie. It broke the strippers' one unwritten law: copying a costume.

Shortly after this happened both girls were playing on the same bill at the Werba when the bag hit the fan. After a preliminary exchange of a few chosen insults, which hardly suited the Bible-carrying image Margie had affected, the infuriated redhead hauled off and hooked a right to Rosie's new nose, and blackened both eyes.

When the smoke had cleared, Rose la Rose had to lay off work for a month for repairs. She sued, but I never did learn what the outcome of the case was. I imagine it was settled out of court. Meanwhile, we were out a stripper for a month. (Rose, incidentally, went on to open her own theater in Toledo, Ohio, and made herself a small fortune teaching amateurs how to strip. I wonder whether she taught them any of Margie Hart's routines.)

Anyway, I had no time for these feuds. My mind was on one of the most exciting projects that H. K. and I had ever come up with. We decided in 1937 to open a theater-restaurant with burlesque on a pier in Miami Beach, and we wanted Georgia Sothern to open there. Unfortunately, we discovered that when she returned from her visit

to Atlanta, she had signed up with the Wilners, who were opening
the Apollo Theatre on 42nd Street, just down the street from
Minsky's Republic. (This was Stella and Max Wilner who had
achieved considerable success with the Irving Place Theatre on 15th
Street and had always given us a lot of competition for our strippers.) It didn't make us feel good. But at least we could remember
when the Apollo had been remodeled for George White and was the
location of his last *Scandals*. So, in any event, we had outlasted White
on 42nd Street.

CHAPTER
25

JOE WELCH (Jewish comic): (*Runs on stage shooting cap pistols and shouting.*) Vere's dot goil? Vere's dot goil? I vas to meet her here at halluf past six. It is now five o'clock. Vile I'm vaiting for her, I'll go home! How do you like my suit? A fine piece of merchandise. I got it in a restaurant. The fellow vas still eating.

THE EARLY 1930s were terrible for the country. Until 1932 the people were not really aware how much trouble the country was in. But by the mid-thirties we were surrounded by the Depression wherever we went. And it was happening all over the country, not just on Second Avenue. I was shocked when I went on the road to see conditions in different parts of the United States. And there seemed to be apple peddlers on every corner in every city. (The Apple Growers Association had made apples available as a subsidy to the poor, thereby decreasing their oversupply and helping somewhat in the tragic situation. Don't forget, this was before the Roosevelt administration had got its New Deal really under way, and there were very few support systems for the poor.) There were few jobs. There were breadlines wherever you went and men hanging around street-corners because they had no work and no place to go. But it was the best time for burlesque. Nobody could afford the legitimate theater, but burlesque was packing them in, not only at the Republic but in our theaters all around the country as well.

This is not to say that burlesque was equally popular all over the country. The deep South never really seemed enthusiastic over burlesque, with the exception of New Orleans, where it always thrived. An ambitious superburlesque show with sixty girls in the chorus, went down South in the 1930s. Called *Crazy Quilt,* it toured through Tennessee, Kentucky, Alabama, and Georgia, performing one-night stands. But there were repercussions in all the cities it played, and it was closed frequently. It was just too rough to cover all those distances at great cost and then risk having the show cancelled on the whim of a redneck sheriff or an irate minister's wife.

We had the money in those days and were using not only the top strippers but also the top comics of the era, some of whom we had developed ourselves, such as Phil Silvers, Abbott and Costello, and Rags Ragland. Rags and Phil were great buddies in those days, as I said earlier, and both were very decent men offstage. By that, of course, I don't just mean that they didn't crack dirty jokes but rather that they had excellent characters and were very conscientious at their work, although Rags always was partial to booze and the ladies and Phil enjoyed gambling.

I think one of their funniest bits was one that never actually appeared on stage, but which I heard about more or less on the burlesque grapevine.

As I have said, Rags was one of those lanky raw-boned people, and according to a legend about men who are built like that—men with large hands and feet—they are supposedly endowed with proportionately large sexual equipment. Anyway that was the rumor going around about Rags.

One afternoon, in a bar on 43rd Street, Rags and Phil were having a few libations between matinees. One of the musicians, who took considerable pride in his own sexual endowment, approached the two comedians. He used to boast that his personal equipment was as long as his clarinet. Anyway, the clarinet player challenged Rags to a showdown.

Rags, who was actually rather modest about his special gift, just laughed and declined. The man, who had had a few drinks, raged angrily and offered to bet Rags, first $50, then $100, that "his" was longer than anything Rags had in his baggy pants. Rags still declined, and the man really got angry.

Finally, Phil broke into the dispute. "Screw him Rags," he said, "just show him enough to win the bet!"

Of course, I wouldn't swear that it happened just that way, but that's the way I heard it, and I don't like to let go of a good story. Later Milton Berle, as was his habit, appropriated the joke for himself.

Anyway, it was not for that special talent that I hired the immensely comic and personable Mr. Ragland to go down and help me open the newest Minsky theater in Miami Beach, the Garden Pier. It was to be something totally different in burlesque and rather a novelty even in the theater business. With difficulty we persuaded Georgia Sothern to leave the Wilners to go down and open there.

My brother Herbert, who always had a yen to be more in the show biz end of things than in the business end, was so excited he even wrote a song for the new show called (okay, don't forget this was burlesque not Broadway) "I'm Umpa-Bumping All the Way From Gumpa." Georgia was to sing it during her strip act.

The new place had a large bar completely across the front of it, and instead of theater seats we had tables and chairs around the room all the way up to the stage. The stage itself was huge, with fantastic lighting equipment straight out of Hollywood and elaborate scenery to match. And practically in the laps of those sitting at the front tables was a small round stage that came up out of the floor. The girls would stand on the little round stage down front and do a sort of introduction, and then it would go down into the floor so they could go onto the big stage to do their strips. This rising platform was possibly even better than a runway.

But we had quite a bit of trouble at that theater right from the start. For one thing, several of the agents had signed girls on for the show without telling them it was to be burlesque. When they arrived in Florida and saw the huge Minsky sign on top of the restaurant, a lot of them rebelled. Finally, Herbert and I got them into our office and pointed out that this was a very elegant show and a fantastic showcase. However, in the end we were forced to up their salaries anyway, which were already higher than what any of them had been earning on Broadway. (Some of the girls were even from the *Follies*, but they still didn't earn the kind of money that the Minskys paid.)

Meanwhile, Rags, who had pursued the fiery Miss Sothern up and down the New York vaudeville circuit and into the hinterlands, had finally given up. Apparently there was to be no romance there. Besides, Georgia was carrying on with the owner of a Miami restaurant and had very little time for Rags. But Maxine De Shon was in the show, and once Rags set eyes on her, it was good-bye to Georgia Sothern anyway. So we were treated to the spectacle of a couple of love-besotted principals under the palms. It was, despite our difficulties in the theater, a delightful junket, what with the sun, the palms, the ocean, and the climate.

Rags told me that he desperately wanted to marry Maxine but that he'd been married before, when he was seventeen, and he was a Catholic. He was certain there was not the slightest chance to get a divorce. His wife was extremely religious, had not spoken to him since he had left her, and had not been willing to give him a divorce.

Naturally, this didn't sit too well with Maxine, and their arguments would often degenerate into brawls. By that I mean serious fights, with swinging fists. And let me tell you, Maxine held her own. But I was always worried that she, like Georgia or Rose, would wind up with some kind of a shiner that would create difficulties for the show. However, the brawls seemed to exorcise their passions, and at the end of each of these brannigans they would make up again and be gloriously happy.

At any rate, with a lot of money invested in the Miami operation, we had to go through with a full-scale publicity and promotion campaign such as was inspired by my brother Billy in the early Republic days. Low-flying planes with long streamers proclaimed, "Minsky's Garden Pier. Opening January 2nd. Starring Georgia Sothern!" We had the stilt walkers and the men passing out twofers on the corners and the rest of it.

The publicity worked like a charm and opening night we were standing room only. As far as I'm concerned, the show was perfect too. But Georgia Sothern later complained it was one of the worst nights in her life.

She made her introduction on the little round stage, and the microphone, which dropped down from the flies so she could sing her song ("Umpa-Bumping"), dropped a couple of feet too low and hit her right on top of the head with a crack that could be heard all over the theater. Georgia nearly went down for the count but managed to hang on long enough to recover her senses. She went to the edge of the little round stage and began to sing her song. Now, it must be admitted that the show had not been completely shaken down, particularly as far as the local techincal help went, and the little round stage with its dropping mike had given us headaches during rehearsal. But it really created a problem with a vengeance when during Georgia's second chorus the microphone rose right up into the middle of her long gown, which consisted of layers and layers of chiffon. As the mike rose, so did her skirts.

I'm not sure if the audience thought this was part of the act or not, but it certainly had them in stitches, and the boys in the band too were falling off their chairs. Meanwhile, the sound technician was still struggling with the microphone mechanism when finally he gave it one last violent tug and away it went up in the air and Georgia's skirts with it. She had had them all snapped together on a band around her waist for the succeeding strip act, but now she was standing there dressed only in the G-string and bra. Her lipstick was smeared; one of her false eyelashes was missing, and the other was hanging half off. Uncertain what to do, somebody started lowering the little stage back into the ground as Georgia scrambled off and onto the big stage, where she signaled the band, which went into another chorus of "Umpa." Georgia's problem was that she was already stripped down to her G-string and bodice and there wasn't much more she could do, so she gave them a long, hot chorus of "Umpa" and then went into the wild shaking and quaking dance with which she had first won her reputation. Nothing she could do helped. The audience was laughing and hooting crazily, and she could not seem to get them into a sexy mood. It wasn't until she went backstage that she discovered the source of the laughter. When the sound technician had pulled up the microphone, along with her skirts, he had inadvertently smeared her lipstick all over her nose, so that she resembled Bozo the Clown more than she did a strip queen.

These kinds of mishaps were not uncommon in burlesque, and the audience had come to expect them. The same kind of faux pas in a Broadway show would have left people shocked, but the burlesque audience always came ready for irregularities.

Georgia, however, was so upset by her reception that she went right out, looked up her boyfriend, and married him in a matter of hours. That was her third wedding. But it didn't last much longer than the others. Within a week she was on her way to the divorce court. I hoped the clumsiness of the Minsky sound technician had nothing to do with this.

Anyway, after the opening of the Miami theater we had several contractual run-ins with Georgia, and she left us for quite a few years to work for Earl Carroll briefly at a show he produced in Miami and for the Wilners again at the Irving Place and the Apollo theaters. Of course, this was part of the ongoing war we had with the Wilners for the top strippers, and they were giving us a hard time by at times offering double the price that we were paying for stars that we had actually developed. But there was no way that we could hold any of them to a long-term contract. That included not only Georgia, but Gypsy Rose Lee, Ann Corio, and Margie Hart as well.

We were having trouble from other quarters too. Gypsy's boyfriend, Waxy Gordon, had offered Florenz Ziegfeld $50,000 to star Gypsy in one of his shows. Fortunately for us, Waxy was nabbed by the Feds on a tax charge before this could take place.

Georgia seemed to be drifting out of burlesque. After her stint with Earl Carroll in Florida and another tour with the Wilners, she went to work in one of the NTG (Nils T. Granlund, a prominent girl-show producer at the time) *Revues* and from there into Billy Rose's nightclub Casino de Paris. But fortunately for us, these Broadway big shots were still not offering the kind of money we could pay. Even then Georgia pulled one of the stunts for which she was famous in the business. She doubled up, continuing to work for the Wilners without informing Billy and billed simply as "The Dynamic Redhead" rather than under her own name. She certainly was dynamic, because she worked for months like that, running back and forth from Billy's Casino show to the Irving Place. But finally we felt we needed her more than Billy Rose did and made her, as they say, an offer she couldn't refuse.

H. K. took her to dinner, which was unusual for either of us since we generally didn't get personally involved with the performers, and told her how much we would like to have her back in the Minsky family. Georgia knew in her heart that she was guilty in our contract disputes with the Wilners, and we knew that her contracts with both the Wilners and Billy Rose were running out. So she finally gave in and decided to play the Minsky circuit again. To us her appearance with the Billy Rose show had probably been a plus, since Billy had given her wide publicity as a star. Just the same, she enjoyed the sensation that so many other performers have of returning to what was essentially a family. There were the same stagehands, chorus girls, and comedians, including Rags Ragland, who by now had finally made a deal with his wife and gotten married to Maxine De

Shon. After her opening we had dozens of baskets of flowers sent to her over the footlights after each performance. There was a lot of stuff in the press about the feud between Georgia Sothern and the Minskys being over.

"My performances were me at my best," she later said, "and my audiences loved me and I loved them."

But another problem developed to interfere with a smooth and profitable routine. None other than Errol Flynn!

26

A burlesque bit player is waiting in the wings watching the first show and he sees a fellow "artist" made up with a red nose, blue wig, green makeup with teeth blacked out, baggy pants, funny hat, loud vest, slap shoes, large checkered coat, and a big, heavy watch chain. He turns to the stage manager and says, "By the looks of that guy he must be a very funny comedian."

The stage manager gives him a skull and whispers, "That's the straight man."

As I GET the picture, Errol Flynn picked up Georgia when she was having a late supper at Sardi's. He introduced himself, sat down at her table, and asked her companions to take a walk. Flynn was direct when he was after something. He took her home that night, but according to Georgia he never made a pass at her. The next day he sent her flowers, and what's more, he called for her backstage at the Republic. That made for some excitement among the cast! He was tall and deeply tanned from the California sun, every inch the matinee idol. Furthermore, he had been in the audience, watching every shake and quiver, and in Georgia Sothern's act that was plenty. Georgia made a date to go to dinner with him after the show and even broke a date she had with Phil Plant, a millionaire who had been courting her for several months.

Rags Ragland had seen the whole thing and was not too happy about it. "Do you know he's married?" he asked her. Georgia said she'd never thought about it.

"Well, think about it now," Ragland said. He was really obsessed with doing things right when it came to marriage. But perhaps Georgia, with three instant marriages behind her, was less conscientious. Georgia told him that she'd already been out with Flynn once and he hadn't even made a pass at her.

Rags only laughed. "That's the oldest gag in the world. Now you think he's a knight in armor, a gent true and blue, and next minute he'll be in like Flynn, and they didn't get that expression out of thin air."

Georgia protested that she was only seeing him for the excitement of dating a movie star and didn't intend to get into any trouble. But that seemed hardly likely to Rags, who, after all, knew something about seduction.

Flynn was backstage again after Georgia's last number the following day. When the finale was finished, she had Rags come into her dressing room for a drink with the movie star.

Although Ragland was very sour about the occasion, it turned out that he and Flynn got along very well. Flynn had already seen the show twice and again complimented Rags on his clever routines. Afterward, Georgia, anxious to retain Ragland as a buffer, asked him to join them at Sardi's after the show. When she was there, however, there was no need for a buffer because the little table gathering grew into a party of at least twelve of Flynn's friends and people he didn't know. Before anybody knew what was happening, there were twenty people around Flynn's table, including twelve women who obviously had eyes only for him.

After Sardi's, the three of them club-hopped around town until dawn. At daybreak, as the sun was rising over the skyscrapers, they left Reuben's, the famous late-night sandwich joint. Now Rags had his chance to play the buffer as had been scheduled. As they got into the taxi he gave the cabby the address of Flynn's hotel first.

"Hey, wait a minute," the film star protested, "I'm the guy that's supposed to take Georgia home."

"I figured you planned that," Rags said. "But Georgetown here has got a twelve o'clock matinee today. No way she's gonna do anything except go home and go to sleep. How about taking her home tomorrow night?" Flynn looked disgusted and just mumbled, "Yeah, maybe tomorrow night," and fell back in the cab's seat, drunk as a hoot owl.

By now, people were getting used to seeing Flynn backstage. He showed up for the second matinee that day behind a pair of sunglasses, which hid his bloodshot eyes. But he still looked plenty glamorous. He escorted Georgia from the theater that night, and I heard from people backstage that they'd gone to a little restaurant nearby. According to the way Georgia later told it to me, this is when he made his big pitch. He asked her not only to be his girl friend but to go back to Hollywood with him when he left town two days later. He even went so far as to promise her that he might make her his leading lady. It was an offer that would be hard for anyone to resist.

But Georgia was not at all sure it would be a good idea. In the first place, she had no experience as an actress, and in the second place, everything was so sudden. She'd only known the man three days. She decided to have a talk with Ragland that night between shows, in the Dixie Bar on 43rd Street. Over drinks, she told him the whole story, including Errol's last offer. When she finished, he asked her bluntly, "Have you been to bed with this guy, kid? Are you in love with him?"

Georgia said (1) she hadn't, and (2) she really didn't know. It was all so sudden.

"Do you think he's on the level?"

"I don't know. It's a heck of an offer. I would really like to be in the movies, and besides, I do like him."

Ragland sighed with exasperation. "If you want to know what I think, Georgetown," he said, not waiting for her answer, "I think you're either very naïve or very stupid. Can't you tell that this guy is a phony? He's a make-out artist. That's his whole career. I don't blame him for that too much, but if you believe those promises, you'd believe that a herring on the wall whistles."

Rags used every argument to try and talk Georgia out of her crazy obsession. During the conversation he found out to his surprise that she actually had had very few men in her life. According to her, three up to this point. I believe it. A lot of the girls that worked for me, including the strippers, were not necessarily loose or promiscuous. Then again, some were.

Rags kept trying to dissuade Georgia from this new romance. He finally advised her, "I'll tell you what you do. First, you give him a quick boff tonight, and then you wait and see if he's still serious about hauling you out to Hollywood with him when he leaves. When a guy gets the hots for a dame, he'll promise her anything just to roll her in the hay. But once he's got it, he cools off a lot. Get me?"

Georgia was not crazy about what she was hearing. Ragland was exasperated. "For Crissake? How can you believe that he'd really make you his leading lady? I never heard such crap!"

Of course, he was only telling Georgia what she knew deep down in her heart, but she was still tempted. When it comes to love, I guess logic is not always the strongest force.

Flynn was in the theater again the following night, and this time he watched Georgia from the wings. She was certain that this was the time when he was going to pounce for the kill. She hadn't really decided whether to take Ragland's advice and give him "a quick boff" in order to test his loyalty. She told him that she had to see me in my office, and Ragland showed up just as she left the dressing room.

Flynn, thinking that she was going to speak with me about leaving the show, offered to go in and talk with me himself, but Georgia told him that wasn't necessary.

Ragland, in the meantime, had found the bottle Georgia kept in her dressing room and poured himself and Flynn a couple of shots. It was obvious that Errol had already had quite a few, and as far as I could tell, he was usually drunk from morning until night. Finally, he was persuaded to leave the dressing room and go with Rags to the Stork Club, where Georgia would join them later. By now it was evident that he was so plastered that he could hardly walk without help.

Of course, Georgia didn't come in to see me at all. I doubt that she would have told me in advance if she was planning to quit burlesque and go to Hollywood. It wasn't her style, as she had shown on previous occasions. But in any event, she decided, reluctantly in view of Flynn's obviously drunken condition, to meet him and Ragland at the Stork. By this time the actor was so sozzled that it was necessary for Rags to half carry him downstairs so that he and Georgia could take to his hotel. There, while the comedian was busily pulling off the actor's shoes and covering him with a sheet, Flynn kept repeating to Georgia, "You are staying with me, aren't you, love?"

"Of course, love," Georgia answered. But before anybody could take advantage of anybody else, Errol went out like a light. Ragland grinned. "Well, Georgetown, time to go home with all your virtue intact." Together they left the hotel room.

But Flynn had not yet buckled his last swash.

Burlesque publicity shots promised much more than the show delivered. Dolores Le-
land as she supposedly appeared in the world premiere of Minsky's Every Inch a
Lulu.

Early burlesque soubrettes *generally displayed the same amounts of flesh and talent, as this 1921 picture reveals.*

Feathers were an important accessory to burlesque costumes (or lack of them). Rosita Royce and her educated doves were especially appealing to nature lovers; Lucille Ray's Jungle Fantasy was a cultural examination of the Dark Continent.

The big production number staged at the National Winter Garden in 1917.

The Minskys freely adapted the elaborate headdresses introduced by Florenz Ziegfeld. The young lady on the left represented Germany in a Minsky League of Nations revue; the photo on the right depicts the month of June in A Year of Beauty.

Rose La Rose, one of the statuesque beauties, gave Gypsy Rose Lee some real competition on the burlesque circuit of the 1930s.

Swan Lake or Leda, you had to have a gimmick!

THE FARMER'S DAUGHTER

(New Version)

Price 25c

"Send us textiles. My wives say they haven't got a thing to wear."

One of the naughty "French" booklets available to Minsky connoisseurs during the intermission. The accompanying spiel described the art as so racy, all future shipments were impounded by U.S. Customs. In fact, the cartoons were tame even then.

"Tell the draft board it's not that I'm unpatriotic, but I just don't want to go in the army right now!"

"Hello, room clerk? There are two strange men in my room – I want you to throw one out!"

BILLY MINSKY'S PLAYBILL PROGRAM

Devoted to Beauty and Slapstick in the New York Manner

FORTY-SECOND STREET & B'WAY · · · WIsconsin 7-1800

→ PROGRAM →

WEEK BEGINNING, MONDAY, JANUARY 30th, 1933

"WHEN THE MOON COMES OVER THE RUNWAY"

A typical Minsky burlesque in two acts and 28 scenes
Dance episodes conceived and staged by Palmiere Brandeau
Shoes by Selva
Scenery by Beaumont & Eclipse Studios
Dialogue staged by Al Golden and John Kane
Wardrobe by Mahieu, Tams and Morgan

Orchestra under the direction of Harry Rothfarb

Scene 1. OPENING "CIRCUS DAYS"—John Head, Isabelle Brown,
Sylvia and Our Clownettes
Scene 2. A DANCE SPECIALTY by Miss Hertel Collins
Scene 3. "MANHATTAN KISSES" with Joe De Rita, Jules Howard,
James Francis and Misses Wilson, Huff and Howard
Scene 4. "STEPS INTRICATE" by Minsky's Dancing Dolls
Scene 5. "WHERE IS OMAHA" with Lew Costello, Jules Howard
and Ray Parsons
Scene 6. "AVIATION" by Lester La Mont, Sylvia & Minsky's Models
Scene 7. "RED HOT TERPSICORE"—Ryan & Huff
Scene 8. "JUSTICE ALA THE BRONX"—Lou Devine, Al Golden & Co.
Scene 9. "MINNIE the MOOCHER"—Ray Parsons, John Kane & Sylvia
Scene 10. "THE CONTEST" with Al Golden and Joe De Rita
Scene 11. "AN ARTISTIC EPISODE" with John Head, Veto & Piri
and Our Prize Beauties
Scene 12. "A LESSON IN MAGIC"—"Al" and His Pupils
Scene 13. "REVERIES" by Miss Margy Hart
Scene 14. "THE HERO" by Ray Parsons, Lew Costello and Company
Scene 15. "NOW WATCH" Our Steppers
Scene 16. "IF YOU HAD A MILLION"—Lew DeVine and Company

Scene 17. Presenting Your Own Favorite—MISS DOROTHY M[...]
Scene 18. FINALE "A Gypsy Trial" with the Entire Compan[...]

— INTERMISSION —
10 MINUTES

ACT TWO

Scene 1. OPENING "LIFE"—John Head, Ray Parsons
Scene 2. "A STUDY OF ART" by Miss Tiny Huff
Veto & Piri a[...]
Scene 3. "THE NEW CHIEF"—James X. Francis, Lew C[...]
Helen Howard
Scene 4. "DANCEOMANIA" by Our High Steppers
Scene 5. "MR. BELL TELEPHONES" with Al Golden, L[...]
Scene 6. "CELLOPHANE" with Lester Lamont and Isa[...]
Scene 7. PAGE KING BEN" with Al Golden, Joe De Rita
and Misses Huff, Phelps, Howard, Wil[...]
Scene 8. "NOW GAZE AGAIN"—Miss Dorothy May
Scene 9. "TWO TIME MANIES"—Sylvia & Hertel
Scene 10. GRAND FINALE—The Entire Company

2 BIG SHOWS DAILY—2:30 and 8:30 P. M.
All Seats Reserved—Phone Special Box-Office Wisconsin 7-1800

AL GOLDEN AND HIS "GANG"

Jules Howard	Ray Parsons
Lew De Vine	Dorothy Maye
James Francis	John Head
Jackie Wilson	John Kane
Louise Phelps	Lew Costello
Joe De Rita	Hertel Collins
Helen Howard	Lestra La Mont
Elizabeth Brown	Sylvia La Vour

HERE'S OUR CHO[...]
DANCERS AND [...]

Valerie Vogelie
Ann Schaefer
Doris Mardell
Bee Warren
Gladys Lotz
Elsie Mardell
Sonny Delmar
D. A. Marvel
Violet Vogelie
Rae Cullis
Margie Lora[...]

"Beauty and slapstick in the New York manner" was Billy Minsky's boast in this 1933 program. "Lew" Costello was one of the featured comics, as was Jackie Wilson.

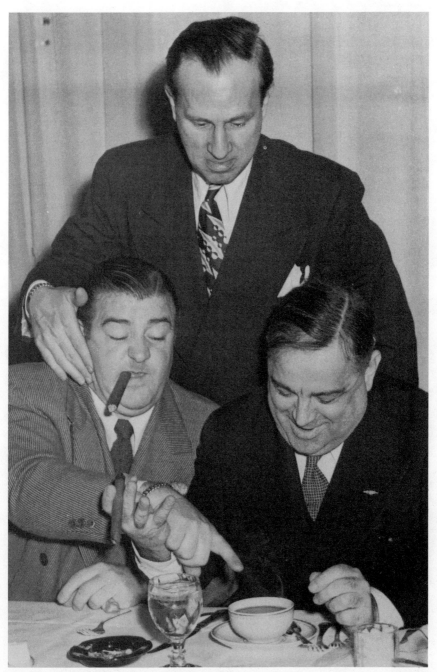

Bud Abbott stands behind Lou Costello and Mayor Fiorello La Guardia at a lunch honoring the two comedians. Ironically, it would be La Guardia who would crusade most vigorously against burlesque, where both Abbott and Costello got their show biz starts.

Pinky Lee, whose television successes were rooted in his years as a rough-and-tumble burlesque comic

Phil Silvers and Jackie Gleason were just two of the many comics who honed their talents in burlesque.

The USO wasn't the only show in town for the men who fought in World War II. Here Norfolk sailors with a weekend pass check out the new girls at Minsky's.

Ann Corio, right, parlayed a successful burlesque career into her own show, This Was Burlesque! *Here she checks the twirling quotient of a show girl's tassels.*

Ann Corio as she appeared with the Minsky troupe.

Gypsy Rose Lee, a burlesque original, in a publicity still from her short-lived stab at fame in Hollywood.

Nudity, in burlesque or in one of the uptown revues, was accepted if presented as a tableau or Living Statue. Any little movement had a meaning all its own.

The courts had ambivalent attitudes toward the "evils" of burlesque, but ultimately the reformers won.

Strippers and comics became suddenly shy when arrested in one of the reformers' many raids.

Fiorello La Guardia, "the Little Flower," was New York's reformer mayor. Under his administration, burlesque was to breathe its last.

CHAPTER
27

COMIC: What a hotel! The house detective wears a cow bell! He knocks on the door and says, "You got a woman in there." I say, "No." He throws one in.

FLYNN WAS TO be in town only two more days. The day before he was to leave, a gentleman called on us at our office. It was Johnny Meyer, who later performed similar functions for Howard Hughes. Meyer gave us his card with a Hollywood Boulevard address and told us he was Flynn's business representative. We knew that Flynn didn't want to appear as a tit serenader in burlesque, so it had to be about something else, and I had a feeling that I knew what it was.

"I won't beat about the bush, Mr. Minsky. Flynn wants to buy Georgia Sothern's contract. What will you take for it?"

"It's not for sale," I said, and to my surprise Herbert said exactly the same thing at the same time, as though we were one of those twin acts.

Now, it's always funny that when people from other entertainment media came to us, they always underestimated the kind of money our stars were making. Billy Rose had made that mistake in offering Georgia one tenth of what she was earning with us. And Georgia had retaliated by doubling up in burlesque while she was ostensibly Rose's principal. As for us, we weren't dazzled by the Hollywood aura. In the first place, most strippers simply did not have the talent or the acting experience for Hollywood. As far as I know, no star stripper ever did become a movie star, although some of the chorus girls did make it. Ethel Keeler started in burlesque as a chorus girl. She later became a star and married Al Jolson under the name of Ruby Keeler. But she was never a stripper. Lucille LeSueur danced for a while in burlesque, then on Broadway, before she became a movie star under the name of Joan Crawford. But strippers didn't seem to fit. Gypsy took a crack at it and failed miserably, and she was probably the most versatile of them all.

Meyer stared at us in astonishment. "You're turning down a chance to make a star out of Georgia Sothern? He wants to star her as his leading lady."

"So, since when is Errol Flynn a producer?" Herbert asked. "I really don't believe Mr. Warner would take his orders regarding a leading lady. It's going to cost him millions of dollars with an unknown star. Besides that, people might stay away in droves. A reputation in burlesque is not necessarily an asset in the films." When it came to show business, Herbert was by no means a dummy, and I agreed with what he was saying. It seemed obvious to me that Flynn, who was trying to get into Georgia's pants, was using the ploy of offering to buy her contract knowing that it would never happen or that he would accomplish his goals and then after a few weeks, the deal would "fall through." Jack Warner was not going to give a drunk like Flynn the decision in casting. No way.

"Look, Flynn swears that the girl has talent. We are prepared to offer twenty-five thousand dollars." H. K. and I both laughed.

"We're grossing more than twenty thousand a week with her act. She has a following, and we can move her from one theater to another when things are slow. There aren't that many striptease stars out there. A handful at most. You just don't develop them out of nowhere. She's worth a lot more than that to us as a peeler."

"Would you consider thirty-five thousand dollars?" I was tempted to ask him when the payment would be and in what form. I was sure that even if we agreed to $50,000, there would be some sort of letter of intent, with either a small down payment or none at all. Then, when Flynn had done his thing, the contract would simply not happen. This was typical Hollywood pie-in-the-sky talk. My thinking and Herbert's were always very much in line. We were friends and we understood each other, so Herbert did not even have to turn around to get my nod of assent before saying, "Mr. Meyer, I don't think we have anything to talk about. We have Georgia's contract. We fought for it, and we're keeping it."

Meyer didn't seem all that put out by our refusal, and I knew why. He just wanted word to get to Georgia that he had been in our office discussing buying her contract to show how sincere Flynn was in his respect for her. That would probably do as well as an actual contract. I didn't trust Flynn as far as I could throw him, and I'm no athlete. History has proved that I am right in regard to the mustachioed Lothario whose name became a byword for seduction, as much in his private life as in his film career. I will say that during the time that Flynn was hanging around the theater, I never saw him draw a sober breath.

When Georgia got to the theater for the evening show, H.K. sent a message that he wanted to see her instantly. He was angry not only at the offer but also at the cavalier way in which Flynn and Meyer had gone about it.

"Did you tell some clown named Meyer to come in here and offer to buy your contract, Georgia?" he asked her.

Georgia looked astonished and guilty at the same time. But she denied that she had done any such thing.

H.K. told her what had happened, without mentioning the amount. No sense giving her a swelled head. It could cost us money. Now Georgia seemed to understand a bit.

"I think I can explain," she said. "You see, I've been dating Errol Flynn, and he sort of mentioned that he might do something like this, but I never thought he'd actually try it."

H.K. was still not happy. "Of course, I knew about the two of you going together. It was all over town. But did you really think he'd buy your contract from me?"

Now Georgia told him the whole pitch that Flynn had laid on her. All the nonsense about how he was going to make her a big Hollywood star. The usual oleomargarine meant to lubricate the star's way into Georgia's arms, or more accurately, her bed.

H.K. reacted the same way that Rags had. "Georgia, I know you're younger than people think, but you can't be that naïve or that dumb. Do you really believe that line of malarkey? Can't you see that this is all a stunt? This guy collects women like those African hunters collect heads. Get the idea out of your head that Flynn is planning to go through with his word and make you a movie star. His plans are something else, and you know what they are."

Georgia started to cry. It seemed like half the time she was in our office she was in tears, usually because she was trying to change some aspects of her contract.

"I'm not really leaving, Mr. Minsky. It's all Errol's idea."

"Okay," my brother said, "just remember that. And if he tries any more stunts, you come and see me first."

Georgia seemed contrite. "Yes, Mr. Minsky. I might as well tell you that Errol said he'd be talking to you himself about my contract tonight."

H.K. sighed. "Let him talk. I'll handle him. Don't worry." But he could see that Georgia still had stardust laced with lust in her eyes. Women all over the country were being laid by Flynn either in their fantasies or in real life. Why should she be an exception? Women can be very dumb about love; becoming a star stripper doesn't make them any smarter, especially as far as men are concerned.

Sure enough, that night Flynn showed up again at least three sheets to the wind as usual. According to Georgia, she tried to stall him, but he insisted on going to see me and H.K. He wanted to take her with him to the West Coast the next night, he told her. Georgia protested, "But Errol, I can't go tomorrow."

According to Georgia, Flynn's face went tight. "Shut up!" he snapped. "You're leaving and that's that! I had my business agent drop in to see Minsky. By now he knows how much money he wants, so it's that simple."

I was in the front of the house, so it was again H.K. that Flynn confronted. While he was seeking H.K. out, Georgia was rehashing the whole matter with Ragland, who was truly concerned. She found him across the street in the Terminal Bar, his usual hangout. What she was doing was looking desperately for somebody to support her idiotic gullibility.

"Oh, Ragged," she begged him (I got all this later from Ragland himself), "help me!"

"Georgetown," he said, taking her hand, "you don't need my help. All you need is the balls and the brains to say no."

"But I'm so wound up now I don't know what to do. Errol is trying to buy my contract from Mr. Minsky right now."

"So, do you want Flynn to own you or not? It's your decision."

Georgia buried her pretty face in her hands. "God! I really don't know. Maybe for once Errol is telling the truth?"

Ragland looked at her with disgust. How naïve could a person be? "Don't be a jerk! You're just trying to talk yourself into this because you want to lay the guy. I give up on you! Do what you want to do, okay? As far as I'm concerned, you should stop all this bullshit and come back to earth. He's just setting you up as a pushover." Ragland started to leave, but Georgia begged him to stay. Finally, with resignation, he sat down again.

"Okay, Georgetown, you poor pigeon," he said. "Here's what you do. Tell Flynn that your mother is coming in tomorrow. Tell him you'll join him out in Hollywood after she leaves. At least that will give you a little delay and a chance to get over this crazy itch you've got. After that, you play it by ear. Is that okay for a start?"

Georgia nodded thoughtfully, neither acknowledging his suggestion nor rejecting it, and left to go back to the theater.

In the meantime, Flynn had been to see H.K. He burst in the door and stood there, slightly unsteady. "I'm gonna give your redheaded star the biggest break she's ever had in her life. It'll make Minsky's famous, and Georgia too. We're gonna buy her contract."

H.K. sat back in his swivel chair and smiled. He answered the star very gently. "In the first place, Georgia already is a star and has a big following and is making good money. In the second place, the name 'Minsky' is already famous. Having one of our stars appear in Hollywood wouldn't do anything for us at the box office. We need her here, not in Hollywood. Furthermore, I'm sure that your Mr. Warner would agree. And besides all that, the amount of money your Mr. Meyer offered is ridiculous! If you're trying to screw Georgia Sothern, you'll have to do it without our help I'm afraid, Mr. Flynn. Meanwhile, go out and enjoy the show. It's on us, so it shouldn't be a total loss."

Flynn looked absolutely dumbfounded. He stood there wordlessly for a moment and then rushed out, slamming the door behind him. He had already visited Georgia's dressing room while she was down at the bar with Rags, and when she returned, he was waiting for her impatiently.

"Where in hell have you been?" he asked her angrily.

Georgia told him that she had to make a call to her mother, who was arriving in town the next day. "So, I'm afraid there'll be a slight delay, until I can join you out there," Georgia said as she stripped out of her street clothes and began to get into her costume.

"Jesus!" Flynn said. "That's really one for the books! First a cheap burlesque owner tells me where to go, and now you come up with a stupid excuse to keep from going with me. OK sweetheart. Let's just forget it; I have more dames around me right now than I can handle. I really don't need any more." He spun on his heels and ran out of the dressing room, slamming the door behind him for the second time in five minutes.

It was a good thing that Georgia wasn't yet in her stage makeup because she began to bawl like an infant, and I believe it was real tears this time.

I was delighted to be rid of Flynn. We got a little publicity out of it—there were some gossip items in the papers about him and Georgia. That didn't do any harm to our image. But he was a nuisance to have around, and I was glad to see him go. So was Rags.

But Georgia wasn't through with the film star yet. Just three days later he called her from California. That Flynn must have been some sweet talker. He told her that he really believed the story about her mother coming to visit, and since she was probably gone by then, he expected her to come to the West Coast when her contract with us had run out. There were in fact only a few weeks to run on Georgia's contract. Her mother and her sister, Jewel, who had also achieved some success as a stripper, actually lived in California. So when her contract with us ran out a few weeks later, she came to see me and H.K. and told us that she wanted some time to think, but that she would be back to renegotiate her contract with us in a few weeks.

"So you're really swallowing all that banana oil that Flynn has been handing you?" H.K. said.

Sothern flashed him an angry glare and then smiled guiltily. "Come on! Who could resist it? And who knows, maybe he's telling the truth this time?"

H.K. looked at her cynically. He wasn't worried about her trip to the Coast. She'd be back when Flynn was through with her.

"Go then, and God bless you. I'll leave you with a quote from the Talmud that my father often cited to me: 'What he *says*, he doesn't mean, and what he *means*, he doesn't say.' "

Sure enough, with or without our advice, Georgia flew to Los Angeles with stars in her eyes. Of course, she told everybody that she was just going to San Francisco to see her folks.

Flynn had not sent her the cost of the plane ticket, as he had promised he would. Furthermore, at the last minute he told her that he was very busy on a film he was shooting at the time, so that instead of meeting her himself, he'd send an envoy. Still our red-haired stripper didn't see the light.

CHAPTER
28

STEVE MILLS: Listen, cutie, would you like to make a bet? Bet a nickel I can kiss you without touching you!

CURLS MASON: OK, I'll take that bet.

STEVE MILLS: Get ready. This is going to be a cinch! (*He kisses her on the lips several times*).

CURLS MASON: You lose! You touched me when you kissed me!

STEVE MILLS (*shrugging*): Ok. Here's your nickel.

I SAID BEFORE, Minsky's was like a family, and in a sense the whole burlesque business was. Whatever happened eventually got back to me or Herbert. So I won't bore you with telling you how I found out what happened on Georgia's trip. Just think of it as a Hollywood fable.

In Hollywood Georgia was met, as promised, by a representative of Errol Flynn, a guy with a pompadour in the latest Hollywood style.

On his home ground Flynn had really laid it on. There was a beautiful hotel suite, the biggest one and the most luxurious at the Beverly Wilshire. Flynn's envoy was named Eddie. In the hotel he mixed her a drink and told her that he had been commissioned to take her to dinner. Georgia was shocked. She had been under the impression that Flynn was absolutely on tenterhooks to see her, and now he was not showing up until later in the evening.

Georgia, not particularly taken with Flynn's flunky, decided that she would have room service send her a meal. She told Eddie that he could take off and amuse himself elsewhere.

"I'm afraid I can't, Miss Sothern," Eddie said respectfully. "I was told by Errol not to leave you alone for a minute until he gets here." Georgia took in this information and felt just a twinge of that other side of her hot nature beginning to perk up—the side of the terrible redheaded temper.

"What does Flynn think I am anyway? His slave?"

Eddie looked miserable but stuck to his guns. "I got my orders," was all he said.

Georgia had a bite to eat with her unwanted guest and a couple of more drinks, gradually developing a slow burn over Flynn. He finally arrived at nine o'clock, "bounding into the room like he was jumping off castle walls," Georgia said.

He grabbed her, waltzed her around the room a couple of times, kissed her on the neck and the ears, and told her he was thrilled to see her. Eddie got his cue, mixed a drink, and drifted off into the Hollywood night.

Georgia was positive that Flynn was going to try to jump on her right at that minute, but he told her to get dressed for a night out on the town.

This was just the right coolant for Georgia's rising temper. It made her feel important and that Flynn was really serious about her.

He showed at least the intensity of his feelings when Georgia finished dressing carefully in an emerald green silk crepe dress, long beige gloves, and a mink stole, set off by a string of pearls, a diamond bracelet, and a dinner ring—all compliments of her millionaire lover in New York. It was when she started to pin the orchid her friend had sent her at the plane that Flynn reacted. He grabbed the flower from her hand, threw it across the floor, and then trampled on it savagely.

"When you're with *me*, you wear *my* flowers," he said. "Not some jerk's from New York!" Georgia said he was livid with anger. In fact, he was so mad that he slammed his glass against the table so that it shattered and fell to the floor, cutting his hand rather badly and causing it to bleed. Then, ignoring the blood, he strode to the door, opened it, and slammed it behind him. He was a master of explosive exits. Georgia decided she had had enough and would pack and go see her family in San Francisco on the nine o'clock plane the next morning. She had just started to undress when Errol returned, looking somewhat chastened. He threw a box on the bed. "Your orchids madam," he said. "Now get yourself back in gear. We're going out!"

But Georgia wasn't so easily mollified. She grabbed the box and threw it in his face. A corner of it caught him in the eye and drew blood for the second time that evening.

"Not the face, dummy, not the face!" Flynn said. "If I have to go to the studio with a black eye tomorrow, you're gonna be sorry!" But Georgia wasn't through with him yet. She reached for a jar of cleansing cream from the bureau and shied that at him too. "Here, have another black eye!" she screamed. Flynn ducked just in time. (Flynn must have been used to dodging flying missiles. Maybe he even enjoyed it, since his wife, Lili Damita, was notorious for tossing crockery and all other portable impedimenta at her playboy husband when she was in a pet.)

Then, for a while, they chased each other around the room until Georgia's foot caught on the carpet and she fell on the floor and Flynn stumbled after her, landing on top. Georgia said she was terrified. She was certain he was going to beat her. But somehow they made peace over a couple of drinks. By my count, according to what Georgia told me, that was at least the eighth for Georgia and God knows how many for Flynn. Finally they made a truce and Flynn picked her up, just like in the movies, carried her to the living room, and laid her on his lap on the couch, petting her until she finally stopped crying. Now they finally got around to their first really passionate kiss, and Georgia thought that the inevitable was going to happen right then. What with the drinks and one thing or another, she was about ready for it. But at the last minute she remembered that Flynn had promised to show her the town, and she'd never been in Hollywood before. She cleaned herself up, put ice on her eyelids to bring down the swelling from all the crying, and pinned on Flynn's orchid. They hit every place in Hollywood, having a few drinks in each, Chasen's, the Brown Derby, the whole works. Toward the early morning Flynn showed signs of wilting, although Georgia was just getting her second wind.

"I'm really loaded, honey," he told Georgia, "and I've got an early studio call tomorrow."

Georgia, who knew about show business, apologized for being so inconsiderate and had the doorman hail a cab. But even then, barely able to walk, Flynn insisted on hitting three more bars on the way back to the hotel.

"When we got back to the hotel," she told me, "I didn't know what to do with him. He was bombed out of his skull, falling asleep. I couldn't take him to his home because I had no idea where he lived; I wasn't sure but what his wife might be there."

So she took him to her room, and as soon as he saw the couch, he flopped onto it and passed out. In a way, Georgia was relieved. A couple of hours later, Eddie, Flynn's boy, came to help him pull himself together and leave for the studio at 6:00 A.M. So Georgia had spent her first night in Hollywood in a hotel room with Errol Flynn and not even gotten pinched.

The next day, Eddie showed up again on Flynn's orders to feed her breakfast and take her shopping. He flashed a wad of bills as thick as a can of Campbell's pea soup. But the gesture just made Georgia angry. Again he was treating her like a cheap bimbo that he could buy, and Georgia didn't like it. She pulled a roll of traveler's checks from her purse and waved them in Eddie's face. "Anything I want I can buy for myself. Flynn doesn't owe me a thing, so why do you think I'd let him buy me my clothes?"

Eddie got angry. "Listen, baby, don't get so goddamn high and mighty with me. I know all about you. You're nothing but a goddamn cheap stripper from New York!"

So, they argued back and forth, with Georgia trying to get away from him and go out on her own. In the meantime, he told her some home truths that gave her an idea of what she was involved with. It seems that the suite in which she was staying was not registered in her name but was a place that Flynn kept permanently for any dames that crossed his roving eye. Eddie hinted that it may in fact have been paid for by the studio. Georgia had had it. She made a reservation on the afternoon flight to San Francisco. She left Los Angeles without even having felt the tip of the hero's sword.

The hotel suite, in fact, was one that belonged to Warner's and that Flynn made occasional use of for his escapades. Even when engaged, as his fiancée Nora Eddington once wrote, he might be romancing three or four different women in such a fashion, using the same old technique of promising them parts in his films. Nora Eddington wrote of him: "He was changing women as fast as Alex, his valet, could change the sheets."

Errol said of himself: "The public has always expected me to be a playboy and a decent chap never lets his public down."

There's no use in telling you I told you so. As they say nowadays, nobody loves a smartass. But the combination of the problems we had with Georgia in Miami and this Errol Flynn escapade cooled things between the Minskys and the fiery redhead for some time.

For Georgia, there would be no Hollywood career. And it wouldn't be long before Georgia was back on stripper's row, where she belonged.

CHAPTER

29

JOEY FAYE: Listen, I'm gonna go out and get a drink. I'm thirsty.

STRAIGHT MAN: Drink? What are you going to drink?

JOEY FAYE: Whiskey.

STRAIGHT MAN: Why?

JOEY FAYE: I'm thirsty.

STRAIGHT MAN: You're thirsty? If you're thirsty, drink milk. Milk makes blood.

JOEY FAYE: I'm not bloodthirsty.

STRAIGHT MAN: Look at me—I'm in fine physical condition. Thirty-nine years old, never drank a drop of whiskey in my life. How do I look?

JOEY FAYE: Listen, I had an uncle Max who drank a quart of whiskey every day of his life. He lived to be eighty-three. Three days after he died, we dug him up and he still looked a whole lot better than you do right now!

THE DAY THAT Gentleman Jimmy Walker resigned was a black day for everybody in burlesque. Mayor McKee and his license commissioner, James Geraghty, got onto our backs immediately. Harassing burlesque was a sure vote getter. Who was going to come out for sin? And they certainly tried to make us look like veritable dens of iniquity. Despite the fact that they never quite succeeded, their constant vigilance about racy jokes and exposed flesh was like having a trolley car growing in your stomach. Geraghty got us to tone down our jokes and strip acts, and people stayed away in droves. The New York *Herald Tribune* did all but hang black crepe on us: "The year about to sign off [1932] will be remembered as the year when the burlesque shows were forever stopped; when owing to the resignation of Mr. Walker as Mayor graft and corruption came to an end; and when Prosperity, long dead of vertigo induced by corner turning, turned in its grave."

You've heard of the prophet Jeremiah?

A piece in the *World Telegram* by A. J. Liebling was headlined AU-DIENCES PLEAD BUT IN VAIN FOR STRIP ACT AS BURLESQUE DECIDES TO PULL DOWN THE SHADE.

"Sure it was a clean show," Liebling quoted a house manager. "It had to be."

Liebling continued, "After the show at the pretentious Republic on 42nd Street, operated by Les Frères Minsky, Le Père Weinstock and Le Fils Weinstock, there was speculation as to the future of burlesque strippers." Liebling, a longtime fan of burlesque, had spoken to Herbert the previous night: " 'Last night I refused to make a statement,' said Herbert Minsky, the producer. 'And a reporter quoted me. I would make a statement to you if I were not afraid that you wouldn't quote me. So I'll refuse to say this to you and then I know it will get in the paper.

" 'Burlesque will be improved. The strip was unimaginative. It was limited. We will replace it with a high form of folk art.' "

All right, so a little hype verbally never hurt business. Meanwhile, the paper itself estimated that 400 strippers were being put out of work in the middle of the Depression.

Here's how another paper reviewed Georgia's act at the time:

> Georgia Sothern, billed as the 'human dynamo,' appeared in a voluminous gown and furs and sang a song to the effect that if 'you want to see a little more of me then clap your hands like this.' The audience clapped its hands. She repeated the song. There was more hand clapping. The song was repeated again, but in the end the singer made her exit without a stitch less than she wore when she entered.
>
> Life in a burlesque theater appears to be filled with such disappointments.

Even the eminent theater critic Burns Mantle, writing in the *Daily News*, was concerned with the negative effect on theatrical employment of Geraghty and McKee's vendetta on burlesque:

> With less than thirty out of sixty Broadway theaters operating it is no small matter to tell the owners of one of the thirty that he cannot open his house to an entertainment the courts have, in effect, approved.
>
> What in general is to become of these vacant theater properties?
>
> They will, you answer, go to the banks that hold mortgages on them.

In September McKee's office won a court decision that closed us down and ordered us to clean up our act before we could reopen. In October we reopened with the results you heard about. There was a little humor or almost irony in the fact that in May 1933 Geraghty, still in office, closed down several more theaters, including the Irving Place Theater on 15th Street, which he discovered too late was owned by the then district attorney, Thomas C. T. Crain. In that case, the licenses were suddenly renewed again for a while.

Well, thank God McKee didn't last very long in office, but unfortunately he was succeeded by another short-term mayor, John P. O'Brien. Geraghty was replaced as license commissioner by Sydney Levine, who instantly tried to upstage his predecessor. He put out a big puff piece in which he described burlesque as morally destructive.

"Geraghty," the new commissioner charged, "permitted obscene shows to go running solely to embarrass Mayor O'Brien." So the new license commissioner started serving summonses to all the burlesque houses that he considered indecent, which was practically all of them.

It was finally 1933, and we had Sally Rand prancing around with her fans in New York. This seemed to get the wind up with License Commissioner Levine, and he ordered Sally to get bigger fans. He also told the Republic and the Irving Place to eliminate "indecent and immoral features."

The Republic Minskys weren't the only Minskys with troubles. In November Levine launched a probe against Abe's New Gotham

Theatre. The hearings were, as usual, comic fodder for the press, pointing up how stupid the censorship was.

Joe Rose, who doubled as first comic and manager at the New Gotham up in Harlem, where they really did work quite "hot," appeared for Abe at the hearing. He told the commissioner that although the people out front thought they were seeing nudity, in fact they were not, and he set out to prove it. Rose pulled out four pieces of wardrobe while being questioned on the stand—two sets of brassieres and trunks. One of them was made of rubber and the other of net. The rubber ones, Rose explained, went on first, and the net ones followed. Then there was a coat of powder, and the stripper was all set to strip.

"That's how they do it at the [New] Gotham," Rose said with a straight face. But Levine was no dummy.

"Isn't that powdering meant to give an effect of nudity?" he asked.

"No, sir," Rose answered, "that's to keep them from *shining.*"

Rose then proceeded to struggle into the strip garment over his suit to show the commissioner that it wouldn't fool anybody. Levine noticed that there were certain trimmings on the brassieres and asked what their purpose was.

"Those," Rose answered, "are rosebuds. My girls are never without these rubber undies if I have anything to say about it. However, they may not be so careful when they are a little drunk."

The commissioner was aghast. "You mean your actresses sometimes get drunk?"

"Hell, yes!" Rose replied. "And when they're liquored up, they don't know *what* they got on! That's why I watch them."

Now I know Joe and I know what the Gotham was offering up there on 125th Street. If those girls were wearing rubber undies and fishnet leotards, I'm the herring on the wall that whistles for sure. Despite Abe's claims of being interested in highbrow burlesque, the New Gotham was notorious for running the rawest shows in town. Of course, we're dealing in a world of illusion, and if the customers at the New Gotham *thought* they were seeing actual nude flesh, then what's the difference, right? It was said by some people in the business that the reason Margie Hart had such a big crowd was that people were always sure that she would flash some pubic hair at the end of her act. But it was also said that she had ordered a special

G-string that was tufted with *artificial* pubic hair, so that if the authorities actually nailed her, she could prove that she had not shown anything forbidden. It gets complicated, doesn't it? Others who had seen Margie completely nude backstage assured me that she was a natural redhead from what they could see of her nether regions. But here again, illusion can reign. Who says that a girl can't dye *all* of her hair? Illusion, illusion, that was my business; but even I didn't sometimes know how the illusions were produced. I know that Margie Hart's hair, or the display of some of her hair, made *my* hair turn gray at times. (But it isn't *all* gray even yet, so how much of a headache could it have been?)

As it turned out, no matter what Joe said, and it was a pretty good act, Abe's place was locked for a short period.

But Levine's reign was a blessing compared to what was to come. In 1933 La Guardia was elected on a Fusion ticket, and he appointed a former theatrical producer, Paul Moss, as his license commissioner. Now the artillery started to get heavy.

Moss started in with a vengeance. He even closed several Broadway shows because of "immorality," such as *Wine, Women and Song*, and he ordered the removal of lighted runways. Said they were fire hazards. What could we do? We tried to survive. We dimmed our lights, we cleaned up some of the sketches. Moss denied a license to the Irving Place again, but they managed to beat that rap in court.

Surprisingly, in response to the request of a religious organization that burlesque be banned altogether, Moss contended that burlesque had its place, if properly supervised. (By him?)

Commissioner Moss was spreading a wide net throughout the city. It wasn't just burlesque that was on his mind. He was also clamping down on vendors of "obscene magazines," racing tip sheets, pinball machines in Coney Island, junk shops that bought from children under sixteen, pinball-machine distributors, ice companies that gave short weight, sidewalk photographers, used-car dealers, and theater booking agents and employment agencies engaging in sharp practices.

He was obviously building quite a job for himself. As far as censorship was concerned, he insisted that he was not a censor but merely "planned to educate theater managers to the realization that if they wished to make money they must produce clean plays."

All these attacks made life complex. I often thought we should have put revolving doors on the box office. We were open and closed so many times. Here a technicality, there a technicality. Once, when the electricians and stagehands went on strike and were picketing the theater, Moss tried to close us up for obstructing the sidewalk! But through the harassment our loyal friends remained loyal, and many people who were not otherwise favorable toward burlesque were stirred to our defense by the obvious violation of our civil and business rights. Our old-time friends from Second Avenue shifted their loyalties to the Republic when we moved uptown, which for many of them was an easier trip. Most of the theater critics and writers were either fans of ours or at least defenders of our right to present the sort of theater we thought our public would want without continual harassment. Now, in addition to our old fans like Otto Kahn, Condé Nast, George Jean Nathan, and Henry Louis Mencken, we were attracting some of the newer crowd—Walter Winchell, Mark Hellinger, and Robert Benchley, people like that. I remember one of our fans in those days was the stage designer Norman Bel Geddes (the father of Barbara Bel Geddes, the actress who later won fame on the *Dallas* TV series). Bel Geddes was always accompanied by a small but beautiful girl friend, whom he called his little puddle jumper. I was never quite sure what he meant by that, but she was a darling little girl, and they would both come to our office as others did, including Jimmy Walker, even after he retired, and the new, bright young Broadway columnist Leonard Lyons, and of course, our old friend A. J. Liebling. The custom of having a drink in our office started during Prohibition, when it was pretty hard to get one, but with the election of Franklin D. Roosevelt, repeal came and with it the reopening of bars. Still, people liked the coziness of coming into the office for a quiet little drink and a talk.

One night Brooks Atkinson dropped in. "How are you getting along?" he asked H.K.

"Well," H.K. said, "I still have a very serious interest in the theater."

"So do I," Atkinson said quietly.

We had the Rosebuds, so we had to expect thorns in the form of a constant assault by the Church and authorities. Nevertheless, we were making a pretty good buck in those days. In 1933 they were holding a world's fair in Chicago billed as "The Century of Progress." Despite the Depression, people were flocking to it. Some

61 million people managed to visit the fair. A lot of them were attracted by an act there called "Sally Rand and Her Fan Dance." It occurred to H.K. and myself that we might send a unit out there to cash in on all the publicity Sally was attracting. It must be remembered that it was allegedly at the world's fair forty years earlier that the cooch dance was originated by a performer named Little Egypt. Even in Chicago Sally's dance attracted the usual shocked attention of various bluenose groups. A lady attorney named Mary Belle Spencer complained to a local judge that "lewd and lascivious dances and exhibitions" were being held at the Streets of Paris concession on the Fair's Mid-way. She was particularly shocked by Sally Rand's dance.

But the Chicago judge was less easily swayed than the New York judges. "If you ask me," said the bored Judge Joseph B. David, "they are just a lot of boobs to come to see a woman wiggle with a fan or without fig leaves. But we have the boobs and we have the right to cater to them. Case dismissed." Nobody seemed to notice the judge's inadvertent pun regarding the boobs displayed by Sally Rand.

After kicking the idea around the block a few times, we decided that the safest thing would be to have a tryout nearer to home. We decided to lease the Auditorium Theatre in Baltimore to put on the supershow that Billy had always dreamed of. And we would call it the *Billy Minsky Follies.*

George Alabama Florida, now the manager at the Republic, was certain that Baltimore should be the place for the tryout. "You can always pay the nut in Baltimore," George advised us. So we made him the manager of the show. We dug up a $40,000 budget, which was big for that sort of thing. For another $60,000 you could put on a musical in those days. We told George not to stint on the show. But maybe he took us too seriously. What he didn't stint on was straight bourbon whiskey. But we didn't know that at first.

We signed on an all-star cast, which included Gypsy Rose Lee, Margie Hart, Red Marshall, Murray Leonard, Joey Faye, Jack Diamond and his new bride—Ethel De Veaux—and Robert Alda. We also had as dance acts two fantastic black tap-dance teams, the Step Brothers and the Berry Brothers. For the girls we even got a ballet master from the Paramount Theatre. It was going to be fantastic. There were two pit orchestras, a special arranger, a set designer, a

costume designer, and a lighting specialist. We got Sammy Tim-
berg, a very hot composer in those days, to work up an original score
for the show. We would also have a chorus of thirty-six girls and a
crew of New York stagehands, who would need to handle six full sets
and thirty-two drops. Altogether, the troupe would have 300 costumes. This would be everything that Billy had ever dreamed of.
And more. We figured it would knock their socks off when it got to
Chicago.

We had discovered a new comedy team when we opened the Republic, and they were wowing the audiences there. Their names
were Abbott and Costello, and we decided to add them to the
troupe.

Lou Costello had been working around the burlesque and vaudeville circuits as a slapstick comedian. He'd already developed his tag
line "I'm a b-a-a-d boy!" He'd been featured on The Mutual Wheel
with their ace shimmy shaker Peaches Strange. Meanwhile, Bud
Abbott was working for us as a treasurer in the front of the house.
He was a fast talker and seemed as though he might have talents as a
straight man. Lou, who came from Paterson, New Jersey, had a
quick and provocative style that was already catching on.

When Costello was working at the Republic he got together with
Abbott mainly so that they could discuss horse racing, which fascinated both of them. All the money they earned they were constantly
putting into the hands of the bookies, and consistently losing. So
they would show up at the office practically every other day to get
advances on their salary. They were even willing to give us tips on
their horses. Such a favor! Pretty soon they were so far ahead in
drawing advances on their salary we didn't know how we would
ever collect. Anyway, they started working together and clicked as a
team right from the start. I must say they almost always used clean
material, which might account for their later success on radio. But
they were still using routines that had been batting around burlesque for generations. For instance, the "Who's on First?" routine,
for which they became famous, had in one incarnation or another—
including the baseball setting—been a favorite among burlesque comedians as long as I can remember. I remember seeing it as a skit
called "Who Is the Boss?" as far back as 1919. Steve Mills tells me
there was a sketch ten years earlier than that called "The Who and
Dye Cleansing Company." And Weber and Fields, way back around

the turn of the century, were doing a gag that started "He Works on Watt Street."

This is no knock on their talent. They were very, very funny men and deserved the success they got. It's simply that all burlesque comedy seems to derive from earlier material. The "Ghost Scene," which they popularized and also made into a movie, had been kicking around since the eighteenth century according to some students. "Handful of Nickels," which they performed on *The Kate Smith Show*, was also a standard. Anyway, they were included in this monster, hoped-to-be boffo Baltimore tryout troupe.

So after all this planning, we had George Alabama Florida down at the Auditorium Theatre. We had equipped him with all the necessary publicity posters, two sheets, three sheets, ten sheets, and George wired us from Baltimore, LET 'EM COME.

So we put this huge show on a B & O special train and settled down at the Republic Theatre to wait for further word from Baltimore as to how advance sales were piling up and, of course, how rehearsals were going.

George was very happy with the dress rehearsal, but his telegram made us nervous regarding sales: B.O. STARTING SLOW BUT BOUND TO SNOWBALL *STOP* This was not great news, but we were still not alarmed. But the next telegram made us somewhat uncomfortable: ADVANCE SALES STILL SLOW SEND DOWN MORE 3 SHEETS STOP

So I got together a batch of posters and sent them on the next train. Now we get a telegram: WAITING FOR IMPACT OF 3 SHEETS WILL SEE RESULTS ON ADVANCE IN MATTER OF HOURS STOP

Quite a few hours went by and we still had no good news. Finally, another telegram: EVERYTHING GOING GREAT EXCEPT LAG IN ADVANCE SALE STOP NOTHING TO WORRY STOP.

But I felt there *was* something to worry about, so I went down there to check on advance sales. To reach the lobby you had to climb fourteen steps in front of the theater. I remember chasing up the steps to inquire how many tickets had been sold for the opening night. The treasurer said, "Forty-three, but don't worry—Baltimore people buy tickets at the last minute."

The last minute? Opening night came and it turned out that people didn't buy tickets at all. It was 1933, the week the president closed the banks. Baltimore was a disaster area. We were playing to twenty customers a night. I called New York and asked them to have the man we called Oscar Skyhook, the tallest stilt walker in history, to come down and see if he couldn't attract a little attention. Perhaps he would liven things up.

We also had other problems. Our assistant manager, who was related to some of our backers, could never get over the excitement of working with all these beautiful girls. Somehow one of the snoopers that are always on our backs found out that he was spending the night in a hotel room with one of the *soubrettes,* and the next thing we know the house detectives raided the room and the kid was arrested for adultery. Did we need this on top of everything else? Finally, with a little payola to one of the cops that I had gotten to know when setting up the show, he was released. In those days adultery was a big thing and you could actually get arrested and prosecuted for it, especially if you were with a bunch of wise-guy New York burlesquers.

So Skyhook arrived the next day. I called George Alabama Florida at the theater but was unable to reach him. A strange voice told me that Mr. Alabama Florida had left word that he was busy giving press interviews. I tried to reach the assistant manager who had gotten in the jam at the hotel room, but he wasn't around either. I wondered if he was back in the sack with the *soubrette.* One guy got on the phone and told me that the only person backstage was the fire marshall. Now what? Had there been a fire? No, all he was doing was making a list of violations. Aha! Another payoff on the way. Finally I called the hotel. Was there anybody there from the Minsky Company? The clerk said he was sorry but since the arrest all service had been cut off from the troupe's rooms. What about Mr. Alabama Florida? He, the clerk said, could be reached at the Police Department drunk tank. Disturbed, I left my hotel and ran over to the theater to see what was happening. By now I was prepared for the worst, and it's a good thing I was. There lay our distinguished stilt walker plastered, out cold, stretched the length of the fourteen steps leading to the box office. His head was pillowed on his bashed-in opera hat, and he was positioned just above the empty box office. Eleven feet down the steps from the box office his huge prop shoes were leaning against each other like the feet of a drunken giant. Some kid scrawled something in chalk on the soles of the huge shoes. On one shoe was written "Hellp! Hellp!" and on the other shoe were the words "Too Late."

Was I too late! I made my decision then. I ran into the hotel immediately adjoining the theater and told the hotel not to advance any monies to the company. I called the railroad and made arrangements to bring back the company and scenery the cheapest way. That was a 1:00 A. M. excursion on the B & O. I paid the company out of what little cash I had brought from New York and gave them IOUs for the difference, which we would settle up when they got back to the city. I arranged for the scenery to come back on Davidson's Trucking. I'll never forget coming back to Jersey City at seven in the morning and having to take the ferry back to New York City, arriving practically at dawn at our apartment on 72nd Street.

We took a $40,000 bath on that one. A lot of money any time. After that disaster we thought we might be better off opening a branch theater in San Francisco or Chicago. We started making inquiries about a suitable location, and it turned out that the first available theater for our purposes was the Park Theatre in Boston. Boston had always been well inclined toward burlesque, and the Old Howard, which had been operating there successfully for years, was a standard extracurricular course for the Harvard students. Ann Corio was a particular favorite in that area, as well as Carrie Finnell of the rotating tassels.

We leased the Park, which had been a movie theater, and spent quite a bit of money altering it to Minsky standards. We had to put in a stage and a runway, as well as repaint and redecorate the whole place. The Park was on Washington Street, Boston's main drag for department stores, and there were also several legitimate theaters on the street. When we opened there as a Minsky showcase, we got a lot of publicity and we gave a party at the Statler for some of the local people. In turn, we were given a party by an elite social group in Brookline—I can't quite remember the name of it, but it was a black-tie affair. There were a good many guests there and it was very warm, so I thought I would go outside and get some fresh air. I had had a couple of champagnes—perhaps they had gone to my head also. Anyway, I sat down in the front seat of one of the chauffeur-driven cars belonging to one of the guests. I was sitting there by myself and suddenly one of the butlers from the party came out and asked me whether there was something I would like. I'm sure he thought I was drunk. Anyway, he invited me to go up to one of the bedrooms in the house to rest. Ruth had no idea where I was. She thought I might be involved in a publicity conference or something of the sort. When I got to the bedroom, I took off my shoes and my jacket and stretched out on the bed. I fell asleep right away. Finally, Ruth, not seeing me anywhere, began to worry about me and asked around until one of the servants told her I was up in a bedroom. When she got up there, she took a look at me and was furious. "Do you know," she said, "you're wearing brown socks with your black tuxedo?" Very embarrassing for a Minsky. I usually dress impeccably.

Anyway, we stayed in Boston for a few more days, and after that I would go there about every ten days, since it wasn't that far from New York. Even in those days it was only about a four-hour train ride. We had plenty of competition from the Old Howard and were considered interlopers by the traditional Bostonians. Somehow the grandeur and panache of our show, with Abbott and Costello and Gypsy Rose Lee, was untraditional and offensive for Boston burlesque. In any event, the Old Howard, which had plenty of political pull in town, started agitating to have us closed or censored. In the end they brought enough pressure through city authorities to make us stop operating. Around that time life was not exactly a bowl of rosebuds. However, we continued trying to expand and had some success when we leased the Shubert Theatre in Philadelphia. Then we went back to Baltimore, this time with a theater of our own, the Palace, formerly a legitimate playhouse. There was another burlesque theater in operation at the time, the Bijou, where Georgia Sothern got her start, but it didn't seem to be too much competition. After that we went up to Albany and took the lease on the Capitol Theatre; then we went to the Erie Theatre in Pittsburgh. By the time we were finished, we were operating shows in about thirteen theaters, including theaters in Brooklyn and the Bronx, as well as three theaters in Manhattan and the rest out of town. So now we were a wheel ourselves, which we called the Eastern Wheel, and we sent our shows around to all these theaters, which put us in a very good position in terms of booking top acts.

But the more complicated and extensive our operation became, the greater the friction between Weinstock and Herbert and myself. He simply wasn't our type. He smoked big smelly cigars, he flirted with the girls, and perhaps more. He disagreed with us on almost every point of artistic judgment. We had made our reputation on putting on the most lavish and spectacular burlesque shows in the country. Weinstock was always trying to cut corners and get things a little cheaper. That wasn't how you got where we were. Billy, the late, great impresario, had managed to keep the rift between the Weinstocks and us from widening. It didn't help any that Weinstock's wife and sons were also involved in the bickering. It soon became clear to H.K. and myself that we would have to sell out our share and go off on our own.

CHAPTER

30

ETHEL DE VEAUX: Hey fellow, do you know the difference between mashed potatoes and pea soup?
JACK DIAMOND: No.
ETHEL DE VEAUX: *Anyone* can mash potatoes!

THE PERIOD BEGINNING on Christmas Eve, 1931, when the Republic opened on Broadway, certainly ushered in the high point of the burlesque era. The Minsky's expansion into other theaters around town and out of town, the development of the Eastern Wheel, and the opening of a number of competing houses on Broadway and elsewhere, not to mention Abe running his own Minsky operation, made our name more of a byword in the field than it ever had been. Let me give you a view of what burlesque looked like from the inside in those days. Take the backstage scene, for instance, so endlessly and occasionally accurately depicted in various shows, which purported to give the lowdown on burlesque. (The earliest one I can remember was the 1927 show called *Burlesque,* which starred Barbara Stanwyck.)

Of course, I can only speak for our own theaters, and although I personally spent very little time backstage, over the years I got some idea of what was happening. In the first place, the famous scene in which a gentleman appears backstage with flowers or whatever and the girls start shrieking in alarm, "Eek! Eek! It's a man! Cover up girls!" Well, I can only say that it must be some Hollywood writer's idea of the backstage scene.

Our girls were by no means tramps, nor were they loose with their affections; but as far as modesty, that was hardly their business. They were used to walking around without their clothes on and it took a lot to alarm them.

Of course, the backstage area was out of bounds to anybody who was not legitimately in the company. But even when an occasional newspaper columnist or an inordinately wealthy stage-door Johnny managed to worm his way into the area, it was hardly grounds for a wholesale panic. Generally the girls went on inspecting their makeup, adjusting their minimal garments, reading, knitting, napping, or whatever else they were doing between shows. The only one that I can remember who wore a robe and seemed a bit modest backstage was the extremely attractive stripper Sherry Britton, who did not really get into burlesque until the mid-1930s, right out of high school.

The backstage area generally consisted of two large dressing rooms—one for the chorus and one for the men in the show—plus a number of more lavish dressing rooms for the stars, and a few that were shared by two or three people. As I said, nobody got too excited by the presence of men in the backstage area if they were authorized, and I even remember way back, when I was in college, I used to take one or two guys backstage with me. They would be thrilled at the sight of hundreds of square feet of rounded flesh in various stages of undress. But most of them never would dare to start a conversation with these glamorous ladies of the runway. As for the girls, far from being abashed, they would no doubt have been thrilled to make the acquaintance of a "college" boy. That was much more of a rarity in those days than it is now. If my friends had only known!

The girls were from various walks of life, although most of them were from the lower class and uneducated. Burlesque was a step upward for them, socially and financially.

A sociologist named David Dressler attended a thousand burlesque performances in the 1930s and wrote a hundred-thousand-word doctoral thesis on the subject, "Burlesque as a Social Phenomenon." As far as I am concerned, he didn't learn much from the thousand performances, but he did do some research that provided statistics that I certainly never gathered. Basically my concern was the box office. Dressler, a rather prissy character, was a moralist wearing an academic cloak, but even he had to see that there was nothing especially immoral going on backstage in burlesque. "Actually burlesquers have a life organization about as stable and free from abnormality as is the case in other branches of the theater," Dressler wrote in his thesis. "As individuals, burlesquers cannot be considered a 'menace' so far as their personal lives are likely to go. They are not vicious or vice-ridden, as individuals, even though as a group, based on what they perform, they can be classified as purveyors of vice." (By Dressler, purveyors of vice; by me, strictly working girls.)

I am quoting this academic fuddy-duddy only to show that my statements concerning the propriety of life backstage in general are not strictly to protect my family image.

"Where here or there one hears of what may be termed delinquency on the part of the performer, it is the exception rather than the rule and is likely to be associated with one of the less intelligent girls least able to organize her life habits," Dressler observed.

Here are a few more of his observations. "The burlesquer has achieved part of her life pattern from her experiences prior to coming to the stage. But the life of the theater has made significant changes in her.

"This is only natural since it is an adult group. The strippers and the men may be in their thirties or even older, but the chorines are in their teens practically without exception. This has been true since the early days of the Depression when unemployed girls flocked to the stage in lieu of anything else to do. They replaced the former type of burlesque chorine, who was older and less pulchritudinous.

"One should not assume that this burlesque girl is *ipso facto* a demoralized person. Such a generalization would be as misleading as most generalizations. The burlesque girl must be thought of as a member of a particular social group.

"She therefore acts largely in terms of what would meet approval of that group. Her morals are no better or worse than what is sanctioned by the *mores* of her group."

Dressler quotes Fanny Brice speaking of her days in burlesque: "Out of eighteen girls in the chorus, sixteen were virgins. They worked hard always taking care of families and saving their money. They didn't go to parties. . . . I never learned about life in burlesque." So if you can't believe Baby Snooks, who can you believe? Even *Fortune* magazine, which sent a reporter to cover burlesque, observed "some virgins, no professionals."

So now you have a serious scientist's confirmation of what I've always said. The Minsky girls, while a few of them might have had their wild moments, were essentially as moral as any other working girl, maybe a little better looking.

By the way, Dressler, though he spoke through pursed lips, was surprisingly generous to the Minskys and other burlesque operators: "The operators in metropolitan New York are, with few exceptions, men of good family backgrounds, in that they were raised in at least adequate, comfortable homes, with opportunity for education, emotional and economic satisfaction. Operators need to be fairly intelligent and good businessmen.

"Five operators, for instance, are college graduates, one being a Phi Beta Kappa. One, now deceased, was a Ph.D."

I don't know who that Ph.D. was, but two fifths of those five college graduates were myself and H.K.

When I say that the theater contained elements of bedlam, I am not exaggerating. You have to remember that the theater, especially during the grind era, was in use practically the whole day. Rehearsals were conducted between shows and after shows, and in many cases we had shows at 12, 2, 8, and 10, seven days a week, with a midnight show on Friday and a new show every week.

Fortunately, most of the girls clubbed together to live in hotels or rooming houses near work. There was hardly time for extensive travel to the job.

Although our girls were paid better on the average than most, I do not kid myself that they were becoming wealthy. But they got a lot of presents from admirers and spent most of their money on clothes, hair-dos, and cosmetics, letting such nonessentials as food and medical expenses take care of themselves.

Most of them who did not become stars only stayed in burlesque for ten or twelve years and then left to get married or take a job in some other field.

For the chorus cuties and the show girls it was possible to earn a little extra money by getting tips from the strippers as "catchers." They would stand in the wings and collect each item of clothing that the star peeled off during her act. In this way they would have a chance to watch how the stars worked and perhaps learn some of those tricks. Probably those that lasted longer, aside from the top strippers, many of whom had amazing durability (some were still able to perform an incredible strip in their sixties, notably, Ann Corio and Sherry Britton), were the talking women, who came close to being talented actresses or comediennes. Some of them would work their way into the sketches and often managed to tie into a particular comedian and become, in effect, straight women.

One comic named Mike Sachs, a jolly red-haired old-fashioned comic, who in private was a middle-class husband and a devoted father, derived most of his comedy by pointing with great exaggeration as he talked to the breasts and other anatomical parts of the women in bits with him. Finally, his wife, Alice, who had been in burlesque, got tired of this sort of carrying on and decided that if anybody was going to get poked in the bosom, it would be her. They became a team, and after that Mike left the other girls alone.

Part of Mike's woman-baiting act was a tongue-tied eye-blinking routine that was very funny the first few times it was seen and heard and helped to make him a headliner. What the audience didn't know was that the eye blinking had not been all comedy. Mike had a serious eye condition and was subsequently stricken blind. Even after that he still worked as a comedian. Alice knew the routines and helped him through, and the audience was none the wiser. When Mike quit the stage, Alice later appeared in bits with other comics. Occasionally they would poke her in the bosom or in the fanny or take liberties with her that were not in the script, as Mike had done. But Alice would have none of it. "Stop padding your part," she would tell them.

The girls in the chorus and the show girls very seldom, if ever, went out with any of the stage-door Johnnys. If anybody was sexually warped, it was probably these characters that hung around the theater, kept regular seats, and hoped in some way to connect with these fantasy creatures bathed in the magenta light.

Often the girls would get to know their special fans and would tease them and sometimes come down into the aisle and plant a kiss on their head or tickle their ears. But I don't think I know of any case of an actual romance resulting from this.

Occasionally they would become friendly with some of the tradesmen in the area. Back at the National Winter Garden there was a man who operated a cigar store down there. His name was Rudy Kahn. He, I believe, had a romance with a couple of the girls. Also, the guy who operated the livery service near the theater dated some of the girls. His name was Dave Goldberg. There weren't that many cars around in those days, so when people went out for a night on the town they would often hire a car with a chauffeur. Dave had a fleet of about three cars. Also Fred Spitz, who ran a flower shop, would usually have a romance going with one or another of the girls. Spitz was the score keeper of the girls' popularity because whenever any of the stage-door Johnnys wanted to send flowers, they would come to his shop two blocks away. The girls kept an informal tally, and whoever got the most flowers was considered the popularity queen of the week. Of course, if we were building up a girl, we'd often buy flowers and have them delivered on stage with great panache.

There was an easy friendship too between many of the straight men and the chorus girls. But many of the stars—the strip acts— considered the comics to be competition. And *vice versa*. Often when the comic was several lines into his act, the members of the audience, if the girl was popular, would continue clapping their hands until she came out for a bow or to remove one more garment. This was great for the stripper. It made her look as though she was stopping the show.

As a matter of fact, the star strippers were a whole different thing from the rest of the people, who might be called the enlisted men, whereas the strippers were more or less the officers. In the joint dressing room, which I would call the troupe's barracks, there was generally a friendly spirit and much less jealousy than there was between the principals. The girls would watch out for one another, lend one another money, and console one another in romantic problems. Cleanliness was important to them too. Conditions were crowded, and the sanitary facilities primitive, to put it mildly. If a girl was not fastidious in her personal habits, fellow performers quickly termed her a slob and would often see to it that she got fired.

Of course, because they spent so much time in the theater, strippers didn't have much time for shopping. For the most part they counted on various peddlers to come to them. There was one called Mother Haines, who sold net pants to all of them.

Sometimes when I was hanging around backstage I would hear

remarks that gave me an idea of the goings-on and the interchanges between the girls.

"They're fresh tonight," one of the strippers might complain as she came offstage with a bare breast and a jewel decoration across her hip. "Wise guys in the gallery."

Sometimes the girls would talk about guys they had spotted in the audience. "There's an old guy in the front row, a linotyper on some big paper," a girl might complain to me. "He's seen the show at least six times. Can you imagine that? Gray hair. Old guy. Sends me presents of fruit, and sometimes a dirty picture."

Once I heard one of the girls do a rundown of the sort of gentlemen friends that the chorus girls wound up with. "Bellhops, racketeers, small merchants, policemen, firemen, federal agents, men looking for adventure, taxi drivers, waiters, aspiring artists, and sailors when the fleet comes in. Also occasionally some old men who . . . Oh, never mind."

Occasionally the girls would get letters from their fans. A member of the audience would offer a girl $5 to roll her stockings below the knee or to throw a high kick in his direction.

I get asked a lot about what the girls were really like. What can I say? The stars were different, more intelligent, often a little bizarre in their behavior, but the run-of-the-mill burlesque performers were human beings who had the same desires as any other group. They wanted to succeed, they wanted to have fun out of life. The comics, in the main, were married. Their wives were either in show business or just homebodies. The comics who weren't married or weren't known to be married would carry on with the chorus girls and have their affairs like anybody else. It was as normal an existence as in any other field. But not *more* normal. I was aware, though I never saw it, that there were always a certain number of people backstage who favored smoking marijuana and sniffing cocaine even back then. After all, they didn't write that line in the thirties, "Some get a kick from cocaine," for nothing. Phil Silvers worked the Gaiety for two years and while there he learned about marijuana backstage. There was a comedian booked into the Gaiety named Tommy "Moe" Raft. He looked like George Raft and he called everybody Moe. In fact, he was Mexican. Silvers observed that he was high most of the time. "I am very innocent about that aroma," Silvers comments in his autobiography. "Whenever I come into his dressing room, I inspect his rack of clothes. I think they are burning."

So a Sunday matinee rolls around. It was tough because they had done six shows the previous day and Phil was hung over. He finished his first scene and went to his dressing room for coffee. The stripper came off and then the music cue began for the next comic scene. In the dressing room Silvers became aware that the cue music was repeating like a broken record. He sensed that something was wrong: "I run out to the stage. It's empty. I recognize the props for the 'Ice Cream' scene. In burlesque, you don't ask questions. I figure Tommy has missed his scene, so I do it.

"Every time I come to the blackout, someone else walks on. Tommy has done so many variations, nobody knows where he belongs. I'm going out of my mind—I can't end the scene."

Finally he came off the stage and growled to the assistant manager, "Where is that son of a bitch Tommy?" The manager called Raft's hotel. He wasn't there. He'd disappeared. Silvers gulped down some more coffee and went out for his second comedy scene, which made three in a row for him now. He was tired and he was furious.

An usher put his head in the door. "You looking for Tommy Raft? He's up in the mezzanine."

"The mezzanine? That's a weird place to be even for a guy like Tommy," Silvers said to himself. He slipped out front and climbed up to the mezzanine. There he found Tommy in the front row with his feet up on the railing. But he was on another planet. His eyes were glassy.

"I tapped his shoulder. It takes about thirty seconds for him to turn and put me into focus."

"What are you doing up here?" Silvers asked.

"Just wanted to see how I look from out front!"

Another time Phil was working with Rags Ragland, and Rags in turn was working with a Yiddish dialect comic named Bobby Morris.

"Bobby is the busiest comedian I've ever seen," Silvers recalls in his book. "His tie revolves, and his fake nose lights up. He has a shoe gimmick, too. The soles have a hook which locks into a special screw in the stage floor so he can sway dangerously over the footlights. The Leaning Tower of Pisa bit."

Rags came into Phil's dressing room afterward. "What do you think?" he asked Phil.

"He's very good," Silvers answered. "But when you have a joke—

he's catching flies all over the stage." This means that he was distracting Rags's punch lines by working his various gimmicks, rotating his tie or lighting up his nose or simply moving on Rags's lines. Rags was generally a good-natured person but very professional, and he hated to have his comedy scenes loused up, particularly by a third or fourth banana.

"Oh, he was doin' that?" he asked, boiling with anger underneath. As he waited for his second scene, Rags spoke quietly to the young comedian: "Don't move on my lines or I'll nail you to the stage."

The kid shrugged off this threat because Rags had a reputation of being a nice guy who didn't really care whether someone else got the laughs or not. When they went back on, Bobby went into his busy, busy routine. Rags held up his hand to stop the action. He called offstage for Carlo the carpenter. He'd planned this all in advance. "Give me the hammer and the spikes." Carlo handed out the necessary material. Rags kneeled down and nailed Bobby's shoes to the stage. The audience broke up, thinking it was part of the act. Rags finished his comedy scene and walked off. Silvers told his own straight man, "Just pretend the kid is not there," and went on with his scene.

"Bobby tried to take off his shoes. They're hightops, reaching up to his knees, in order to grip him as he sways, and the heavy laces are tangled. He claws away unsuccessfully at the laces.

A stripper is next. As she parades around, the spotlight picks up Bobby, sweating, squirming, pulling his heels to lift the spikes. But of course, the stage hooks still hold. He's trapped."

According to Silvers, the gag ran through the rest of the show, with the cast watching from the wings.

"We all [felt] a little sorry for the kid, but Rags is Rags, and you just don't interfere with his Thing," Phil writes in his book.

When the feature film came on to cover the hour-and-a-half break for dinner, the screen came down and missed Bobby by about an inch. He found himself in front of it blinking into the projector light when the manager finally took pity on him and came out with a crowbar to release him.

"Rags was a man of his word," Phil told me. "He didn't think his gag was funny or not funny. But he warned the kid."

Phil loved to tell stories about Rags, his best friend. He remem-

bered a night at our theater in Philadelphia, the Shubert. There
was a drunk and noisy heckler in the audience. Sometimes comics
were able to work with these guys and get laughs even better than
those written into their scenes. But sometimes the heckler could
ruin things too. This one would yell out every time the comic came
to a punch line: "Aw, bring out the girls!" Phil, who had been away
for a week with pneumonia, was watching the show from out front,
wondering why an usher or manager didn't shut the heckler
up. Rags came on with Russell Trent, his straight man, for one
of the few musical scenes he did in burlesque. In this scene, the
straight man scolds the comic, "You ought to be ashamed of yourself, the way you treat the girls!" This leads into a song that they
sing together:

> TRENT: . . . And who is to blame
> if the child has no name?
> It's a man every time,
> It's a man!
> RAGS: What did I do? (*This goes on another eight bars.*)
> TRENT: It's a man every time,
> It's a *man!* (*He slaps Rags.*)
> RAGS : Hey, I'm a citizen. I didn't—

In the second chorus they switch roles—the comedian sings the
lines and gets the part where he slaps the straight man, but he gets
slapped anyhow. This time, as Trent started his swing, Rags stopped
the action. He stepped down to the first row and slapped the heckler
instead. Hard. He climbed back onto the stage, sang another eight
bars, stopped Trent, came down again to the heckler, and whap!
whap! The first slap put the heckler, who is drunk, away. He lay
there with his mouth open, out cold. Rags packed quite a punch.

Silvers left the theater to go back to his hotel for a shower. On the
way, he stopped at the cigarette counter, where he overheard two
salesmen. The first salesman said, "Seen any good shows in town?"
The second salesman replied, "You'll get a kick out of the burlesque
show at the Shubert. Just don't sit in the front row. They got a big
comedian there that slaps the hell outta you!"

One of Phil's favorite stories when he reminisces about burlesque
was the time that Boob McManus, who was according to some people the lewdest comic in burlesque, nearly ruined us with just one

clean line. Boob was an Irish comic with a hoarse, loose whiskey voice, red fright wig and all. But he was funny. He was also a drunk. He was seldom on time for any curtain, even on payday, and he lived right next door to the Oxford Theatre in Brooklyn, where he was playing. Phil remembers it this way. "H.K., in his relentless clutching for class, refurbished a large plush theater in Baltimore. Baroque gold and red, only two shows a day and all seats reserved. It was to be the Palace of burlesque. And, incidentally, a gold mine because this was an old port town, and burlesque had built up a loyal clientele over many years.

"H.K. invited the leading Baltimore politicians and other aficionados of culture to the opening. Among them was a local movie censor, a high-busted, pince-nez kind of woman. She took the show as a personal insult and stormed out of the theater. Next day the police raided us. They surrounded the stage and called out the names of all the actors on the program. They were to appear in court. Except me. H.K. had hired me only the day before to 'boost some weak spots,' so my name was not in the cast list.

"Everybody walked to court, since it was near our hotel. I followed behind Boob to see the show. Boob veered off here and there, to reinforce himself for the ordeal. The manager had rehearsed everyone on court behavior and where the courthouse stood; but Boob's eyesight dimmed when his blood count reached 86 proof. He entered a large building with a facade of columns and statues, and called out 'I demand justice!' It was the public library. I pointed Boob in the correct direction, and then hurried on to catch the courtroom scene. Boob shambled in late, of course."

When Silvers got to the courthouse, our defense attorney was cross-examining the chief prosecution witness, a well-rehearsed police officer.

> DEFENSE: Your complaint specifies that you saw bare breasts on the show girls. In fact, your Honor, they were wearing thin mesh nets as brassieres.
>
> OFFICER: I didn't see any mesh nets. Just bare flesh.
>
> DEFENSE: Where were you sitting?
>
> OFFICER (*arrogantly*): Fifth row, right on the aisle.
>
> DEFENSE: Then we better test your eyesight. You also filed a complaint against the straight man, Russell Trent. Mr Trent is here in court. Would you please point him out?

So the officer looked around vaguely not certain of himself. Russell, like the good straight man he was, looked around the room also. The cop was baffled.

> DEFENSE(*triumphantly*): Your Honor, if he can't even recognize a six-foot straight man, how could he recognize a little bare breast?

The officer became angry and glared at Phil and then even at Boob, who was so fried he couldn't sit up in his seat. It looked to Phil like we were winning this race by half a furlong. But suddenly the red-haired boozer Boob came to life. He leaned forward and tapped Trent on the shoulder: 'Russell, he's looking for *you!*' " And the officer said, "That's him!"

So the case was closed and so was the theater, for a couple of days anyway. Phil says, "It was the only clean line I ever heard Boob utter."

Ah, those comics. They were a world unto themselves. A few of them were a little crazy. But what a world of talent, timing, skill, and history went into their work. Let me give you an idea.

CHAPTER
31

BOOB COMIC: Is this a first-class hotel?
STRAIGHT MAN: First *class*? Why, the Hit and Run
   Hotel is the only hotel in town with hot and cold
   running chambermaids. On a clear day you can see
   the bed. Our mattresses are the playground of
   America! (The phone rings.) You say there's a rat in
   your room? Don't call me! Call room service, and
   have a cat sent up.

PERSONALLY I HATE to talk about comic technique, because deep in
my heart I feel that all great comics are born not made. Still to get
ahead in burlesque comedy you had to know your ABC's. It is said
there are 200 basic burlesque bits. I don't know where that figure
came from, but it's somewhere in the ballpark. After a year or so on
the boards, every comic knows these bits and can ad-lib variations of
them. If he comes to a new theater, he just has to have a chat with
the resident comics and they will decide they will do the "Hold the
Car Bit," "How High Is Up," or "A Handful of Nickels."

Steve Mills, one of the great burlesque comics, who never made it
into the legit, described what happened to a new comic this way.

"On Monday we'd get to the theater around ten o'clock in the
morning and the first banana would say, 'Well, Steve, what are you
gonna do for scenes?' I say, 'Maybe we do the rose bit.'

"Maybe the first banana doesn't know this one, so he says 'How does it go?'

"Well, we blow on stage and we kibbitz around out there for a while and finally the girl comes on. You turn to the girl and you say, 'Hi ya, miss' . . . and so forth. I'd give him the skeleton, and he could fill it in himself from what he knew."

One standard was called "Crazy House," and it was a catchall into which any kind of business or stock joke could be included. Basically it was an extended sketch involving a man who applies for a job in a mental institution and is mistaken for a patient. As played by Steve, in an old-fashioned nightshirt and a derby hat, he's kept in a constant state of bewilderment by a ridiculous doctor, a sexy nurse, and a bunch of patients in weird clothes who run through his room uttering non sequiturs.

A woman in a very short skirt runs out, followed by a man running after her in a Grouchoesque crouch. His attention is briefly deflected by what we called in burlesque a nance character waving a scarf. The chase stops in midpursuit, and the comic takes off in the opposite direction after the fluttering scarf.

A peculiar-looking personage in a shaggy sleeveless fur jacket, sometimes played by Harry Conley, appears, greatly upset.

CONLEY: Oh, why did he die? Oh, why did he die? Oh, why did he die?

STEVE MILLS: Why did who die?

CONLEY: My wife's first husband. Why did he die? (He exits.)

ROBERT ALDA (Yelling from the wings): Hey, fella! Don't send any more letters to Washington!

STEVE MILLS: Why not?

ROBERT ALDA: He's dead you know!

Any variation could be run on these bits within the framework of the "Crazy House," or the "Dr. Kronkite" skit. So while the audience was often essentially getting the same gags over and over again, they would often be in different contexts.

Mills had played around, hopping back and forth from vaudeville to burlesque, as so many comics did in those days. When he came to us, he had been playing the Columbia Wheel, which was dying a slow death out in the boondocks.

For one thing, the style of comedy they featured was getting old-fashioned. It was a pun-laden old style consisting of minstrel and variety skits, ethnic characters, and slapstick comedy. It all began to seem, in the new age of radio and talking pictures, as dated as the horse and buggy. Mills had been featured in a revue called *Mr. Basko,* which although playing the regular Broadway circuit, was described enthusiastically by *Variety* as a genuine burlesque show, which ordinarily would be right on the money. Ordinarily is the key word here. *Mr. Basko* may have been funny, but what happened at the box office was not funny to the producers. It was suggested to Mills that he see my brother Billy. This was in 1931, when he was beginning to pull the Republic show into shape. Billy saw his talent immediately and signed him to a contract. Says Steve, "The Minskys believed in me. No matter how many of the old-timers they had in there, like Joe Rose and Walter Brown, who was a big favorite, they believed in me. I had quite a good routine of scenes from 'tab' (a shortened version of a Broadway musical) shows and the Columbia Wheel. . . . Now the other guys used a lot of pretty rough stuff . . . like Walter Brown always wore the big pants out to there, grabbing at the women, 'Arroowww, come on baby!' . . . You know what I mean? . . . And would see my scenes and say, 'You can't do a thing like this in burlesque, they'll razz you off the stage.' But Billy Minsky would say, 'Put it on, son; if the producer can fix it up for you, put it on.' And if a scene was going really good, he'd tell me, 'Open up, Steve. Put some more stuff in there.' That's the way it was."

Things were undergoing continual change in those days. First, there was the Americanization of the various ethnic groups. Whereas previously much of the comedy was based on Jewish comics, Dutch comics, Irish comics, and so forth, as each minority achieved increasing economic and social status its members began to perceive the dialect characters as insulting. Then, comics adopted the guise of an eccentric character, which meant anything. A guy with funny makeup, big shoes, anything to make sure the audience knew he was a comedian. Toward the last days of burlesque many comics would just use a funny hat to make them look different from the straight man, or nothing at all. You just had to tell by the fact that he was funny.

One of Mills's standard routines, which he honed and adapted through the years, was done with Ann Corio, who would include the routine in her *This Was Burlesque* show some years later. How could she not?

It went like this: There is the sound of a boat whistle in the distance. Raymond Paine, the straight man, is waving good-bye to someone leaving on the boat.

> PAINE: Bon voyage, Jackson! Give my regards to Leicester Square! Lucky dog. Jackson's going back to England, while I have to stay here for three years more. Seven years I've been on this island, seven years of hell. . . . This intolerable heat, the damned dry rot that gets into your bones, nothing but natives to talk to, and the lousy native liquor to drink. (*He sits on a box and pours himself a drink.*) Well, if I'm going to endure it, I might as well stay drunk.

You see how this is a takeoff on all of the tropical island dramas, including Somerset Maugham's *Rain,* which had been a recent Broadway hit.

Steve enters. He's wearing a pith helmet and a Hawaiian shirt, but no baggy pants. ("I don't play that type of broad humor," he explains, "because you're not going for belly laughs here, see? It's an acting scene. . . . Real burlesque. . . . That's why I like it.")

> STEVE: I'm the new overseer, sir, sent here by the company in England to take charge.
> PAINE (*laughing uproariously*): Ha, ha, ha! So you're the new man?
> STEVE: What are you laughing at? (*He does a dignified but outraged take.*) Did you ever get a look at your mug?
> PAINE: I just wanted to know why the company didn't send me a *man.*
> STEVE: Well, all the men . . . (*He catches himself.*) *I'm* a man, what do I look like?

He goes on to rhapsodize over the glorious tropics, which he sees as a veritable paradise, so different from the cold and fog of London. Paine just laughs. "Paradise? Well, I've got a bit of history . . . that's if you care to hear it." He starts a long speech about how much in love he was with the island when he first came and then his disenchantment: "The tropical heat, the damn dry rot that eats into your bones and seems to crush and smother the life out of you . . . and then," he goes on ominously, "there are *other* things." Steve asks, "What do you mean by other things?"

Paine tells him about the native girl Tondelayo—that's Corio.

"After you've spent many weary days here and countless sleepless nights, when the monotony of it all casts its spell over you, when the touch of a woman's hand, the sound of a woman's voice, means all eternity to you, when you would sell your chances of ever getting into heaven for a kiss from a woman's lips, it is then that *Tondelayo* will come into your life. . . . She'll kiss you, caress you, fondle you, and then comes the inevitable *mammypalava* . . . some call it love, some call it passion, some call it fascination, but no matter what they call it, my friend, it means one thing, my friend, it means you're going *native!*"

Steve swears he will be loyal to his sweetheart back home and Paine exits, raving out of his mind. Now *Tondelayo* appears. She is barefoot and semidressed in a sarong, which shows her legs up to the top of her hips and a good part of her upper portions also. Steve keeps a stiff British upper lip resisting her charms: "They told me everything about you, Tondelayo: They told me *everything.*"

Corio begins to swing and sway seductively, undulating her hips as Steve's eyes follow her every move. More undulation.

> STEVE: Everything except *that*!
> (*Tondelayo continues to rotate her hips, moves closer, and puts her arms around him.*) Go away, Tondelayo, go away! (*His voice is desperate, but his resistance falters. He throws his arms around her.*) Tondelayo, stay away from me as close as possible!" (*Laughter, usually. A lot of it.*)

Steve exits arm in arm with Tondelayo to her hut, and Paine reenters, sees where Steve has disappeared to, and laughs triumphantly. He summons another comic, Bob Nugent, who appears dressed as a native in a hotel bath towel, derby hat, modern shoes, and socks with garters, and carrying a spear. They talk in native gibberish and then it seems they are actually speaking in some Jewish dialect. This ends with Paine saying, "Englishman, Tondelayo, hut!"

Steve reenters and is introduced to the new arrival.

> PAINE: Tondelayo's jealous lover, Unga, from the neighboring tribe of Hunga. He wants to know, did you go into the hut with Tondelayo?
> STEVE: Yes. (*Paine turns to Unga and talks to him in gibberish. Unga goes*

bananas and tries to attack Steve in a jealous rage. Paine stops him.
There is more gibberish with much waving of arms.) What did he say?
PAINE: He wants to know, did you *kiss* Tondelayo?
STEVE: Yes.
PAINE: (*speaking to Unga*): Kissy, kissy. (*More gibberish and arm waving.*)
STEVE: (*worried*): What did he say now?
PAINE: He wants to know . . . did you and Tondelayo . . . *mammy-palava?"*
STEVE: Twelve times.
PAINE: (*with excitement*): Twelve times?!!! (*He turns to Unga and interprets all this in that weird lingo.*) Englishman, Tondelayo, in hut
. . . Inka, Chinka, Flinka!
UNGA (*with amazement*): Inka, Chinka, Flinka?!!! (*He runs to the side and gets a loving cup from the propman, hands it to Steve, and kneels at his feet drawing out the last word in worshipful tones.*) *Minkkka!!*

BLACKOUT

This routine, which changed a lot over the years in burlesque, originated in a Broadway show called *White Cargo,* which had the character Tondelayo in it, but the Unga sequence was probably taken from a previous comedy skit called "In Africa," which played the Eastern Burlesque Wheel way back in 1910.

So you can see that the skits, while they had a sexy undertone, certainly were pleasing visually with the presence of Ann Corio and were about as off-color as a Hope-Crosby road show.

Although the jokes were often old and frankly corny, the comedians never lost sight of the old concept of burlesque—to do a take-off or satire of an existing show. Aside from the competing Broadway shows and *Follies,* they would keep track of new developments, and as movies and radio became increasingly prevalent, they worked their routines around these mediums as well.

I remember a short sketch called "The Good-bye Scene," which Mills often performed, which revolved around a movie director and a comic who was to appear as a ridiculously unsuitable "new leading man." One short section, I remember, went like this:

MILLS: I was in another picture once too . . . a picture in which I starred.
STRAIGHT MAN (*playing the director*): You *starved.*

MILLS: No, *starred.*

STRAIGHT MAN: Oh, what was the name of that picture?

MILLS: The name of the picture was *The Millionaire's Daughter and the Butcherboy.*

STRAIGHT MAN: *The Millionaire's Daughter and the Butcherboy?* What part did you play in that?

MILLS: I delivered the meat!

STRAIGHT MAN: Oh, I get it. Another small part.

MILLS: Small part, hell, you should see me.

STRAIGHT MAN: Well, never mind that. . . . Now, this picture that we're going to do is a love picture, so when we get down to the love scene, I want you to give me all you've got.

MILLS: Don't worry, I'll stretch a couple of inches for you.

Okay, so, it's a little suggestive. After all, it *is* burlesque.

They had a big show on radio in those days called *Stop the Music.* We developed a funny skit revolving around that radio program, which I understand has been revived on television recently. Here's how that one went: The straight man enters and walks to the center of the stage with his microphone.

STRAIGHT MAN: Good evening ladies and gentlemen, this is your announcer Harry Vonzelly broadcasting for the *Adam Hat Quiz Program,* where each and every week we give away thousands and thousands of dollars. Will the contestants selected before the broadcast kindly step on the stage? (*The comic enters, very shy and bashful.*) Don't be bashful. Step right over to the microphone, please. My name is Harry Vonzelly, and yours?

COMIC: Burns. They call me Fat Burns.

STRAIGHT MAN: Fat Burns? Well, it *does,* doesn't it? Now. Have you ever appeared on a radio broadcast?

COMIC: Yes, I was on the *Take It or Shove It* program.

STRAIGHT MAN: You mean *Take It or Leave It.* Tell me, do you work?

COMIC: No, sir, I own two pinball machines. (*This was also partly a joke on the bluenose La Guardia, who in addition to attacking burlesque, was spending a lot of time breaking up pinball games, which he said were ruining our students.*)

STRAIGHT MAN: Are you single or married?

COMIC: I'm married.

STRAIGHT MAN: How long have you been married?

COMIC: Fifteen years.

STRAIGHT MAN: Any children?

COMIC: No, sir.

STRAIGHT MAN: Married fifteen years and no children? What's wrong?

COMIC: My mother-in-law's very strict.

STRAIGHT MAN: Well, let's get on with the contest. We are going to give away thousands of dollars and we hope that you take some of it home with you. Will you please send out the other contestants? (*A man and girl enter and walk toward the straight man.*) Now I would like to introduce you to the sweetheart of the *Adam Hat Quiz Program*　Miss Adam Hattie. (*A girl dressed as a page enters and stands alongside the straight man. She is holding a box with questions in it.*) We will start the contest with contestant number one and that is you, sir. (*The second male contestant walks to the microphone.*) Now, all of the questions are in this box and you may select your own. (*The man reaches into the box and gives a question to the straight man, which he reads.*) Now, your question pays five hundred dollars if you answer correctly. Here it is, so listen carefully. In what year was the war of 1812 fought?

MAN: 1812.

STRAIGHT MAN: Correct! You win five hundred dollars, and here it is! (*Gives the man the money and he exits. The straight man now addresses the girl who came in with the man.*) All right, miss, you're next and good luck to you also. Please select a question. (*She reaches into the box, picks a question, and gives it to the straight man.*) You have selected a very difficult question, and here it is. What famous general is buried in Grant's Tomb?

GIRL: Grant!

STRAIGHT MAN: Correct! Here is your five hundred dollars. (*She takes the money and exits stage right.*) Now, we're up to you, Mr. Burns.

COMIC: (*overjoyed*): Oh, boy! This is a breeze—War of 1812 ... Grant's Tomb.

STRAIGHT MAN: Select your question, sir. (*The comic takes a question out of the box and gives it to the straight man.*) You're very lucky, sir! Your question happens to pay five *thousand* dollars.

COMIC: Five thousand dollars!

STRAIGHT MAN: It's so easy that a child of three could answer it. Your question, Mr. Burns—listen carefully—is: What was the name of the foreman of the construction gang that built the Egyptian pyramids? (*The comic faints, and the straight man and page girl hold him up.*)

STRAIGHT MAN: How do you feel?

COMIC: What happened to 'What general was buried during the War of 1812?'

STRAIGHT MAN: Those questions are over with.

COMIC: Maybe I didn't hear you right. Would you mind repeating the question?

STRAIGHT MAN: Not at all. Here it is: What was the name of the foreman of the construction gang that built the Egyptian pyramids? (*Aside to the audience.*) No prompting, please.

COMIC: No prompting? Who in the hell would know? No, let's see—construction gang—foreman . . . Was it the day or night shift?

STRAIGHT MAN: Swing shift.

COMIC: Aw, nuts!

STRAIGHT MAN: No. But you were close to it. It was Ah Kublican Nuts! Too bad.

COMIC: Gimme another chance.

STRAIGHT MAN: No. I'm sorry. (*He takes pity on the comic though.*) You haven't won *any* money yet, have you?

COMIC: No, nothing, and I need it to make a six-horse-show parlay.

STRAIGHT MAN: Very well. I'm going to give you another chance to win some money, and here is your question. It's so easy that we can only afford to give you two thousand dollars.

COMIC: Only two thousand dollars? That's all right, I'll accept it.

STRAIGHT MAN: This is so easy that a child of three—

COMIC: Yeah, I know, a child of three could answer. Please make it easy. I'm a mental midget.

STRAIGHT MAN: Here it is. With which hand do you stir your coffee?

COMIC: (*relieved*): That's easy . . . my right hand.

STRAIGHT MAN: You lose—most people use a spoon.

COMIC: (*aside*): This guy was after me, that was a trick question.

STRAIGHT MAN: What do you mean a trick question?

COMIC: I'll show you. I'll ask you one. If you were a farmer, would you put fertilizer on strawberries?

STRAIGHT MAN: I certainly would.

COMIC: I'd rather put sugar and cream on mine.

STRAIGHT MAN: Now I see what you mean by a trick question, so I'm going to give you another chance. (*To page girl.*) Miss Hattie, would you please select the next question for him? (*She does and exits.*) My friend, you are fortunate, you have selected the Jackpot Question and it pays *ten thousand dollars*!

COMIC: Oh, boy! Ten thousand bucks!

STRAIGHT MAN: And you don't have to answer any question. All you have to do is repeat a simple little verse after me. Listen carefully, as I will only say it once. Here it is. "One smart fellow, he felt smart; two smart fellows, they felt smart; three smart fellows, they all felt smart."

COMIC: (*The audience here is in on the gag. It is almost impossible to say these words without saying "smelt fart," twisting the consonants around. But the comic goes on bravely.*) One smart fellow, he smelt fa . . . (*He stops himself in the nick of time.*) I bet you thought I was gonna say the wrong thing, didn't you? Okay. Here goes. (*He milks the gag all he can until he finally says it right.*)

STRAIGHT MAN: Correct! You win ten thousand dollars and here is your money. (*He gives him money.*) You can thank Adam Hat for that. Adam Hat, first in style, first in quality, first in everything.

COMIC: Adam was first in *everything*. In fact, Adam was the first man.

STRAIGHT MAN: You're absolutely right!

COMIC: Adam was the first man and we're all related to Adam.

STRAIGHT MAN: (*looking interested*): Are *you* related to Adam?

COMIC: Yes, of course!

STRAIGHT MAN: I'm sorry, but you lose the money. (*Takes the money from the comic's hand.*)

COMIC: Why? I lose? Why? Why?

STRAIGHT MAN: No employees or relatives of Adam are allowed to enter this contest. (*Exits.*)

COMIC: (*looking in stunned surprise after the departing straight man*): Me and my big mouth!

So, that was one in which they parodied radio. There was also a pretty good skit called "Cease the Melody."

So girls or not, there was still a certain amount of burlesque left in burlesque comedy. If burlesque were going today, they'd be doing takeoffs on *Dallas, Hill Street Blues,* or *M*A*S*H.* Everything was grist for the burlesque comic's mill.

In the 1930s and 1940s it was considered that in order to keep the box office going and compete with the strippers, every comic had to "shovel a little." But this wasn't true in the Minsky circuit. There was a lot of double entendre, and there were some that went in for pulling pants and hitting fannies and ogling bosoms; but dirty, filthy comics didn't last long. Most of the comics weren't all clean

. . . but they weren't downright dirty. They were earthy, and mainly they were very broad, with the baggy pants and the crazy shoes that they'd slap and pop onstage.

Some people accuse burlesque comedy of being sadistic. Sure! We laugh when a man slips on a banana peel although he might wind up with a sacroiliac condition.

Joe Weber of the famous comedy team of Weber and Fields, which started in burlesque, once said, "I never could understand it, but everyone always wanted to see Fields beat the hell out of me. Every time Fields would conk me with a stuffed club or bladder, the audience would howl."

It was true with the Greeks, it was true in Punch and Judy, and have you ever seen a Bugs Bunny or Road Runner cartoon? Sure, it was always good for a laugh. Perhaps when people are feeling low and suffering, they like to see someone *else* get the business for a change.

Harry Fields was known by the unlovely handle of Stinky; along with his partner, Shorty McAlister, he was a big hit at the Republic. I'm not saying that we told them what to say, but I'm quoting his view, as a comic star of the famous Stinky and Shorty team.

"What the Minskys wanted," he told a reporter, "was low slapstick. So Shorty, being a veteran of the Keystone Kop days who had thrown thousands of custard pies, cooked up an act with me.

"The very first night we wrecked the Republic stage. We threw pies, hit each other over the head, chased each other through the audience shooting guns, climbed up the scenery, and almost killed each other. And the audience loved it! From that night we played the Republic five solid years and then went over to the Apollo with the same act for two more."

To understand the universality of this humor, and the difficulty of putting it into print, try describing Chaplin's *Easy Street* or his hilarious *The Gold Rush* and see how many laughs you get.

The burlesque audiences were often rowdy, sometimes drunk and always uninhibited, perhaps more so than the performers. For extreme cases we always had the security guards, but sometimes the comics, with their endless inventiveness, could manipulate the rowdy drunk into being part of the comedy skit.

In the first place, the fact that there was practically no audience turnover in some of the grind houses—in the orchestra at any rate—

made it very tough for comedians. If they tried to speed up the performance by "scissoring" a bit, the regulars reminded them in loud voices that they'd left out a line or bit of business.

"You forgot the one about the bear and the traveling saleswoman!" a jerk would jeer from the second row. Or maybe somebody in the house would deliver the punch line before the comic got to it. The comic was left with lame retorts, such as, "You *ought* to know. You've been here since eleven this morning!" This was often answered by the rude witticism of a flatulent Bronx cheer. The audience, which was on the jerk's side, laughed like crazy.

A typical contretemps in which a member of the audience would throw the comic off might go like this: The straight man and the hobo comic are doing the bit where they meet a "fairy princess," who gives them the power to make four wishes. If they don't get all they wish for the first time, the second wish brings the rest.

> STRAIGHT MAN: Look! She's got a wishing wand.
> COMIC: That's nothing. *Lots* of people think they have wishing wands.
> STRAIGHT MAN: Hers has a star on the end!

So the skit is going along all right; but at this point a crowd of men who have reserved seats in the first row trail down the aisle after an usher. Unnoticed, a drunk staggers in their wake, his ticket in his hand. The six newcomers are seated and the usher goes back up the aisle. The drunk reels around looking first at his ticket and then at the occupied seats in the first row. He turns around and yells after the retreating usher, at the top of his lungs. This brings the comedians to a halt on stage. The usher turns around.

> DRUNK (*with a sweep of his arm*): C'mere!
> STRAIGHT MAN (*speaking to the usher*): A guy wants to talk with you.
> (*The usher runs back down the aisle.*)
> DRUNK: Where's m'seat? "S'm'b'dys innit." (*He looks at the faces of the seated customers belligerently.*)

Somebody in the balcony yells, "Siddown! Let the show go on." The usher checks all the tickets and chases out the man who is in the wrong seat. The drunk takes his place, but he's not finished yet. The skit continues.

STRAIGHT MAN: All right, make a wish. (*He's going on with the skit, see?*)

COMIC: I wish, I wish, I wish. (*A wallet comes flying through the air. The straight man picks it up. It's empty.*) Now, you *wish*. The fairy princess said if we didn't get it all the first time, we'd get the rest the second time.

DRUNK: (*getting into the act*): The second time? (*Now that he's got the stage in focus he wants to show that he understands what is going on.*)

STRAIGHT MAN: (*ignoring the drunk*): I wish, I wish, I wish. (*A roll of bills sails from the wings and lands at his feet.*) See? We got it this time.

COMIC: Bah! Stage money! (*But the drunk is interested.*)

DRUNK (*yelling*): Give it to me! (*Now the audience is with him. They're laughing. The comics try to go on with the skit.*)

COMIC: Make another wish.

STRAIGHT MAN: I wish, I wish, I wish. (*A bundle of something white is tossed from the wings. It looks like a towel. The straight man opens it. It's a huge pair of drawers. This should be a laugh line. But the drunk butts in again.*)

DRUNK: Oh, boy! (*He's really in the skit now.*) Wish again!

COMIC: (*going along with the new member of the team*): "I wish, I wish." (*One of the strippers walks onto the stage. The drunk starts to get up. Somebody pulls him down by his coattails. The comic looks the stripper over critically, thinking about what he'll get on his next wish.*)

COMIC: (*finally deciding*): I don't want it.

DRUNK: I'll take it!

And he means it. He struggles away from his neighbors, who are trying to hold him down, and staggers up the steps onto the stage. A propman, the stage manager, and a fireman appear as if by magic, grab the drunk by the arms and coat collar, and hustle him off into the wings. The drunk lurches back for an encore.)

"M'hat!" he shouts, struggling desperately. "I left m'hat on m'seat!" An usher retrieves the hat and the curtain comes down abruptly as the chorus trips out after a roaring round of applause for the drunk's return. The chorus and the band make a lot of noise but not enough to completely block out the sounds of an angry scuffle somewhere offstage punctuated by continued shouts diminuendo for 'M'hat!" Nobody knows if it is all part of the show or not. It isn't, but the skit gets as many laughs as it might have anyway.

Well, the burlesque comic's turns were certainly not engraved in granite, and they were not on tape either. If he made a mistake or was fouled up by a jerk in the audience, he always had the next show to recover in and the next and the next. A burlesque comic always had to be ready to cope with an emergency, and so did the straight man.

CHAPTER

32

STRAIGHT MAN: How'd *you* get in here?

COMIC: I got pull.

STRAIGHT MAN: What do you mean?

COMIC: The backdoor was unlocked, so I pulled it open.

STRAIGHT MAN: If you don't keep quiet, I'll have the ushers take you out!

COMIC: I don't go out with ushers.

STRAIGHT MAN: Wait a minute, why are you tipping your hat to that girl?

COMIC: My brother knows her.

STRAIGHT MAN: What's that got to do with you?

COMIC: This is my brother's hat.

STRAIGHT MAN: What did you come in here for anyway?

COMIC: I came here to sell you an old suit of clothes; but I see you got one.

●

YOU HEAR A lot of talk about the first banana, or the top banana, as he became called thanks to Phil Silvers's masterful recreation of burlesque in the musical *Top Banana*.

But you don't hear that much about the third banana. Generally, the third-banana spot was an unfortunate place to be and an uncomfortable position from which to come up in the trade. He was the catcher for all the rough stuff. He took the pie in the kisser, the seltzer in the pants, the hatchet in the leg. If he didn't react properly and get a few laughs when this happened, the first banana would often continue to knock him around—hit him on the head with a baseball bat or a bladder or a slapstick. Of course, for the rougher tricks the comic usually wore a steel protector under his wig, but it still jarred him when he got hit hard enough.

Part of his training, in addition to the obvious—learning to tell a gag—was learning how to point and how to skull it. A skull is a mug or a double take. The gag is told and the comic leers to the audience or registers pain or looks around him, pretending to be innocent. The joke must be emphasized so that the audience, which is not *entirely* made up of intellectuals, gets the point. "Pointing" a joke means emphasizing the right word by giving a certain inflection so that it becomes funny—much in the way that I sometimes will emphasize a word in the text here by italicizing it. You can point a line by shrugging your shoulders or by using your voice. You can also take the heat off the joke, for instance, one with a salacious intonation, by more or less "depointing" it.

Most of the humor in burlesque was not really gag humor. It was not the jokes but, rather, the situations that mattered. Getting back to the "Crazy House" scene, for example, the point of this was that anything can happen. One nut thinks he's a fireman and squirts water in your pants. The doctor thinks you're one of the nuts. The nurse tries to seduce you and you're unable to perform. These aren't jokes. The audience is laughing along because of the situation.

I remember once when Lou Costello and Rags Ragland were doing the "Crazy House" scene—this was before Lou teamed up with Bud Abbott—I was watching from the back and was surprised to see Ragland running in through the door, run past the bed where Costello was being visited with all the irregularities of the "Crazy House" personnel, and keep running off the other side of the stage.

Although I was used to anything happening in the "Crazy House" skit, this particular bit surprised me because Rags wasn't even supposed to be in the scene. Lou, still startled by this impromptu appearance, was even more surprised when a girl raced through the door behind Rags. She was waving what looked like a real pistol and shouting, "Stop, you son of a bitch or I'll shoot!" But Rags didn't stop, and the girl chased him right up the aisle. The audience thought it was hilarious. A great finish for this sketch. But I found out later that it was no gag. Rags was the most famous ladies' man in burlesque, and apparently he had broken someone's heart, and this lady was apparently not going to take it lying down.

Another important talent for any comic, and this is something that is hard to teach, is timing. Now, I'm talking not only about timing in delivering the punch line, but knowing how to wait for the laughs, how not to step on your own line just when the laugh is building. Also important is how to stretch the bit. That's one real test of a burlesque comedian.

Say the comic and the straight man are there, building their way to the boffo finish and blackout. Just when the straight man is about to hit the cue for the punch line, the stage manager waves frantically from the wings. The straight man looks at him, and the stage manager lays the palms of his hands together and separates them widely. S-T-R-E-T-C-H the bit, that's what the signal means. Something has gone wrong backstage—maybe the stripper has busted a zipper, or someone's taken sick or is drunk.

Now the comic and the straight man have to keep the scene going until whatever has gone wrong has been straightened out. Like Phil Silvers earlier, when Tommy Raft didn't show up for his scene. He may have to prolong the bit for ten minutes. If he can't be funny, he at least has to be believable enough that the audience doesn't begin to clap for the next act or boo.

One of the techniques is to lecture on the straight man's skull. Or, if the talking woman is still on the stage, he can bring her into it because even if she's dumb, she'll have enough sense to answer yes or no, which is all she's called on to do. It's the guy that's doing the lecturing that has the whole creative burden, and most of them have a bagful of these lectures in their repertoire. Sometimes the silent partner can make the joke even funnier simply by his reactions.

One of the oldest "skull" lectures was called a "Handful of Nickels" and was popularized by Abbott and Costello and later introduced into their routine on *The Kate Smith Show*. It went like this:

> **ABBOTT:** How can you possibly be so dumb? You must have had to go to high school a long time to learn to be so dumb! Suppose I put a handful of nickels in your hand. How much money have you got? You don't know? That proves how dumb you are. Suppose you go down to the station and buy a ticket and

you give the man your handful of nickels. Where are you going? Where's your ticket to? Are you taking a train or a bus? How much change did you get? Is that all you can say? "I don't know." Okay. Now suppose you go to the ball game. You buy a ticket. You go in, and you sit down. Who's playing? You don't even know that? Then why did you go to the game? Do you know why the Giants can't play pinochle anymore? No? Because the Cards are in St. Louis. Okay. Here's an easy one. If you can't get this, you've gotta be the dumbest fellow I've ever met. Now, there's a man who's in love with a girl. He wants to marry her but he can't, because he's too old. He's forty and she's only ten. He's four times as old as the girl, right? So he waits five years, until he's forty-five and she's fifteen. Now he's only *three* times as old as the girl. But he's still too much older to marry her. He waits fifteen more years. Now he's sixty and the girl is thirty. He's only *twice* as old as she is. So here's the question: How long will he have to wait until they become the same age? You don't know? It shows how dumb you are!

. . . and so on and on and on. A good burlesquer could keep this going until whatever the crisis was backstage was resolved.

If there were some props on stage, a talented comic and straight man could improvise indefinitely on them. If there was a bed, the problem was solved. There would be endless oiling of the springs with a locomotive engineer's squirter, examining the sheets, puffing up pillows and placing them in the center of the bed with shouted snatches of love phrases from popular songs.

If there's a bottle of prop whiskey around, for example, the comic could do ten minutes on that. First, in order to get up the nerve to kiss the talking woman, he's got to take a drink. The bottle may be on a table or the straight man offers it to him. He looks at it fearfully. He walks away. He comes back again. Finally, he thrusts out his chest in exaggerated bravado, strides up to the bottle, and tosses down a mouthful. It's too strong! A shower of spray covers the straight man. The comic doubles over, his hands at his throat. He's choking. He coughs. He's going to throw up. He shivers. After about three minutes of this he straightens up, takes a final gasp, and says, "Gee, that was good!"

So now he's got a new bit that he can milk for quite a while. He's drunk. He staggers around. Maybe he seems to wet his pants. He shakes his leg. The straight man gets a bottle of seltzer and squirts it down his leg to sober him up. It's all part of the game.

There's one other trick that a burlesque comic had to know—and that was how to cover up for unexpected accidents. Maybe the third banana had accidentally gotten knocked out by a fall or a crack on the head. I remember once when Scratch Wallace was doing a drunk act and he had a prop bottle of whiskey in his hip pocket. Steve Mills, playing a cop, smacked him on the head with a night-stick. Scratch went down, falling on the whiskey bottle, breaking it. Steve had to keep Wallace's backside, which was turning red as the blood oozed through his pants, away from the audience. He had to make up a bit while he dragged Scratch off and did a solo finale. And he had to time this so nothing seemed to have gone wrong. By the time he'd gotten Scratch off, the stage manager was already te-lephoning for the doctor to come and pick the glass out of Scratch's backside.

Every burlesque comic also had to cover for others by doing the scenes of some of the other comics if they didn't show up. This wasn't tough, since they all knew the various parts, but it required experience.

They had a lot of words that were strictly backstage slang. Some of them have become popular, so there's no longer a need to explain them. But some never got out of the backstage vocabulary. "The Boston version" meant "clean it up, the cops are coming or are out there." "Detracting" was when one comic stooged for another. If a comic said he was "painted on the drop," that meant he had no lines in the bit. A comic who couldn't learn anything was a "liver-head." If he mumbled or stammered his lines, he was a "flannel mouth." A new man in the house or just anybody whose name wasn't known was called "Jake the Plumber."

The one person who appreciates a good straight man, maybe more than his wife or his girl friend, is the comic. The audience never quite understands how important the straight man is. But as Joe Laurie, Jr., the famous show-business critic, once said, "A good straight man can make a fair comic look good and a great comic look better."

There are basically two types of straight men: one called the legit, who would have a background in or a manner suitable to the legiti-mate theater, like Raymond Paine, and the other, what I would call the character, who might be a little eccentric and even comic himself, such as Bud Abbott. Probably the two greatest straight men in the business were Minsky's Raymond Paine and Al Golden, Jr.

In the burlesque world the straight man was always the fast-talking sharpie, the swindler, the con man who in at least two bits out of three had to be outsharped, swindled, and conned by the comic. Raymond Paine was the legit type. In fact, he could do comedy as well as anybody, but he had always had an ambition to be a serious actor—even Shakespeare! The trouble is he was only about five feet two, and who would want to see a midget King Lear?

He was a serious actor, but no producer would take him seriously, despite the fact that he had a deep, resonant voice that would have been perfect for Othello. He was even too short for drawing-room comedy or melodrama. If he had come up through the movies, he could probably have stood on a box like Alan Ladd and played dramatic parts, but he came up in the legitimate theater, where stature could only be modified with high heels or stilts. One tactless manager once told Raymond, "If you hadn't grown that last foot, I might have used you in midget parts. But now you're too big." Raymond says it was this that drove him to drink. Well, *something* did! But drunk or sober, he had an elegant finger-snapping strut, an oily and rapid-fire con-man spiel, and he could roll out the five-dollar words like the Royal Mint.

But even the most masterful of straight men and comics can be broken up once in a while by an unexpected bit from the audience. I remember Raymond once introducing a beautiful new stripper whom we had hired straight out of the *Ziegfeld Follies*. She had adopted the name Sharmaine. Raymond said, "And now, the original Minsky Brothers proudly present the lovely charms of the inimitable, delicious, *Shar* . . . maine!"

As she paraded out slowly in an undulating fashion, as luminous as the morning star and as sexy as Eve, an entranced voice called from the audience, "If that's chow mein, I'll eat it!" Phil Silvers, standing in the wings, nearly dropped his spectacles over that one. But Phil Silvers himself was another number.

I remember when he first came out to us for a tryout, in 1932, just after we opened the Republic.

"Do something funny," Billy asked him.

Phil stumbled out on the stage, accidentally knocked his glasses off, got down on his hands and knees, and started patting the floor looking for them. "Where did everybody go?" he asked. It broke Billy up, and Silvers was hired.

Silvers, like Milton Berle, Mickey Rooney, Judy Garland, and many others, was a child star. He was discovered by Gus Edwards and was a working singer and comic by the time he was twelve and a has-been by the time he was twenty. For his second career, in vaudeville, he hooked up with Mildred Harris Chaplin, a beautiful woman who was billed as "Charlie Chaplin's First Wife." She'd been a bit player in the silent days, but her divorce from Chaplin got her more attention than she'd ever enjoyed in her film career.

In those days champion prizefighters, explorers, attractive lady murderers, mistresses of famous gangsters who had made the papers, anybody who had achieved a certain amount of fame and notoriety, might get a booking on the vaudeville circuit, and occasionally even in burlesque. I remember in the 1920s trying to book Peaches Browning, the teenage bride of the millionaire "Daddy" Browning. But Peaches wouldn't take the bait and went into vaudeville instead.

Anyway, while working with Mildred, Silvers found himself booked by his manager into the Star and Garter, then regarded as one of the raunchiest burlesque houses in Chicago. However, it gave him a taste of what was to come. Phil's act was a total flop at the Star and Garter. So the manager asked Mildred to strip. She did it willingly, if in a somewhat aimless way. *Variety*'s front page was appalled. Headline: MILDRED HARRIS PEELS! The Orpheum Circuit, which had booked Phil's act, cancelled the contract by invoking a morality clause. But the act introduced Phil to Herbie Faye (not to be confused with *Joey* Faye) and they became lifelong colleagues and friends. Twenty years later Herbie Faye worked with Phil and Joey Faye in *Top Banana*.

"To seize attention of the predominantly male audience, a comedian had to make his presence felt. And fast," Silvers recalls in his book. To buck the appeal of the increasingly nude strippers, the men had to go on with their only weapon, comedy.

"The management was not interested in how funny you were," Silvers once wrote, "Just how *often* you were funny."

In an era in which all the comedians, just as the strippers, had their own special bits, which were frequently included in their name—such as Harry (Hello, Jake) Fields, Peanuts (What the Hay) Bone—Phil Silvers just played himself, a funny-looking kid with a big nose and horn-rimmed glasses in a pin-striped suit.

"Paradoxically," Silvers writes in his autobiography, "burlesque gave me a lot of freedom. I could improvise anything I wished—a new bit here, a couple of lines there didn't matter to the others in the scene, as long as it got us all to the blackout. The only critic was the audience. If you failed, the show did not close. This was a big, wide-open world for a young comedian. I had a stage, costumes, lights, music, a friendly company and a captive audience. The management gave me all this to play with—and even paid me."

It was at the Gaiety that Silvers first worked with Rags Ragland and established a thirty year relationship. He'd met Rags during his disastrous run at the Star and Garter in Chicago and had instantly taken to him.

In his book Phil gives a rare insight into backstage life as he saw it: "The code of morality among the performers was strict and monogamous. Strippers usually married straight men. It made sense, it was frugal—they could always be booked together. Casual bedhopping was rare. When a man went with a girl they were considered a couple. Another man in the same show would never infringe. There were no class distinctions, based on salary or billing, in pairing off. The couple would break up only when one partner chose to do so. Pairing off was simple and direct. No games. The man would say to the girl, if she was not tied up, 'Would you like to go out for a drink?'

" 'Sure.'

"If she went that far, you were paired."

According to him he was, like many of our performers, a virgin until a year or so after he was in burlesque: "The refined ethics of the burlesque world freed me from much guilt and repression. I had been an emotional virgin till I was old enough to vote. Now I began to *enjoy* sex. On benches, dressing-room tables, a heap of drapes in the scenery dock. Even in a bed."

Phil was still working at the Gaiety on 46th Street when he was approached by his old friend, Lew Brown, one of the top song-writing team of DeSylva, Brown, and Henderson. Brown had become the writer, director, and producer of a new Broadway musical called *Yokel Boy*. He had cast Jack Pearl, then a top Dutch dialect comedian, originator of the line 'Vass you dere, Sharlie?" and the

comic character Baron Munchausen, as the star. Playing the juve-
nile part of a young dancer discovered in the mountains of Virginia
was Buddy Ebsen, who had just quit his contract to play the Tin
Man in MGM's *Wizard of Oz* because he suffered from a skin allergy,
which made the silver makeup painful. (Recently Ebsen said that he
believes that some of the early scenes in the original *Oz* were of him
before he quit.)

Anyway, there was a small role for a brash comic in the show, and
Lew, who was fond of Silvers and watched him at the Gaiety all the
time, asked him to read for the part. Silvers did so, got a laugh, and
was hired immediately at $150 a week, a $125 cut from what we
were paying him at the Gaiety. Still he was getting tired of burlesque and wanted to break into the big time, and this seemed to be
a good chance.

As it happened, Pearl couldn't seem to ignite the audience with
an old-time Dutch dialect comedy. Ultimately, the show was rewritten and the character turned into the sort of brash Broadway sharpie that Silvers always played. The name of the lead character was
changed to Punko Parks, and the whole show was rewritten around
Silvers. Silvers had bet on the right horse this time, and it really
turned out to be his big break. After that he came back to the Gaiety
only once—that was on the night of the opening of *Yokel Boy* at the
Majestic Theatre: "I walked over to the Gaiety to say hello to my
friends. Rags was there, and Hank Henry. I said, 'Rags, let me do
your scenes.' I did two of them, and the audience never knew I'd left
the Gaiety. They never ventured into Broadway shows. The laughter and warmth loosened me up. Relaxed and confident, I strolled
back to the Majestic Theater—I couldn't wait to go on."

Phil was cool as a cucumber in his performance, but the show was
panned by the critics. Nevertheless, Phil emerged unscathed. Herbert Drake of the *Herald Tribune* noted: "The hero of the evening is
Phil Silvers, a burlesque emeritus who carries just enough of the
gutter savoir faire of his favorite art to give *Yokel Boy* a little tang. He
is all the comedy there is." If you'd like a little clincher for the anec-
dote of Phil's breaking into the big time—guess who financed *Yokel
Boy* and Lew Brown's previous production, *Strike Me Pink*? None
other than the famous beer baron and mob battler, Waxy Gordon!

In 1946 Monte Proser was producing shows for the Copacabana
in New York. He had a wonderful idea. He wanted to reunite Phil

Silvers and Rags Ragland at the Copa in their old vaudeville act. Phil, a habitual gambler, was chronically out of money and it seemed a great idea to him; besides, he loved working with Ragland. Furthermore, they would practically not have to rehearse since the routines were all ingrained in the little grooves and crannies of their brains.

But before they could open, Rags collapsed in terrible pain. His years of hard drinking finally took their toll on his liver. Phil stayed by his bedside almost every moment. He died weeks later at the Cedars of Lebanon Hospital in Los Angeles, following a seven-day coma.

Dejected as he was, Silvers was a trouper and did not want to let Proser down. But he didn't know where to turn. He was sitting there dejected and heartbroken when the door opened and in walked Frank Sinatra. "Well, when do we go on?" he asked Silvers.

Sinatra had heard about the situation and left the set of the film he was shooting in Hollywood and flown to New York that day to help out. For years he and Silvers had played most of Rags's bits on tour and at parties. They quickly outlined a routine by two old early troupers, and Sinatra went on that night without advance announcement. He brought down the house. And that opening night it seemed that every comic in New York wanted to become a one-night-stand burlesque clown. Jackie Gleason came to heckle and stayed to play out the bits. Milton Berle came along to heckle Gleason. Joe E. Lewis joined in. Henny Youngman picked up a violin and went into his routine. Gleason turned a seltzer bottle on Berle, who slipped to the floor and they went into an improvised artificial resuscitation bit.

The audience howled with glee.

The show ended in a chorus of laughter and tears, and Gleason, who had learned his craft in burlesque, also finished out the run with Silvers just for the price of his drinks, which, come to think of it, was considerable. Like I said, burlesque was one big family. . . .

CHAPTER
33

STRAIGHT MAN: (*running his hand over the bald comic's head*): Ya know, Charlie, your head feels exactly like my wife's backside!
COMIC: (*running his hand over his own head*): Ya know? You're right!

ALL RIGHT, all right! I know you're getting impatient with all this talk of comedians and family affairs. You want me to tell you about the *girls*. Especially the *strippers*.

Okay. So for the moment leaving in abeyance the question of whether the strip was invented by Hinda Wassau or by some bare-topped waitress in Kansas or by Mae Brown at the National Winter Garden, there was no question that from the late 1920s on, strips began to dominate the business. Strippers became the highest paid people in the game, after the producers, naturally. It is interesting, when I think back, to realize that one of the reasons we were getting better- and better-looking girls from the 1930s on is because of the Depression. There were so few jobs that a lot of people who ordinarily would not have thought of working in burlesque came down from the hills and were delighted to work in our shows. And we were delighted to have them. In those days a lot of them were from Pennsylvania mining towns, quite a few of Polish extraction. They were magnificent to look at. They were all blond and had lovely features.

They'd wind up at our theater on their own or through an agent. In those days you would advertise in theatrical publications, such as *The Billboard, Variety,* or *Zits Weekly.* It was a matter of chance whether a girl wound up at Minsky's or in the *Ziegfeld Follies,* because we were all drawing the same girls from the same mining towns in Pennsylvania.

We'd hold auditions for these girls between shows, at five-thirty in the afternoon. The girls would come in and appear onstage and line up, and the dance director would do just what they do in all those musical movies, ask them to raise their skirts and show their legs. H.K. or I, or Abe or Billy in their time, would look them over and just say flatly, "You're acceptable," "You're not." That's the way it was. Pretty tough, not too much sympathy for the girls. But they never gave up hope; they just kept doing the rounds and answering the ads. Sometimes, if we were hiring for the chorus, we'd ask them if they could do a couple of simple dance steps. When the strippers became the big thing, there were agents all over the country scouting for talent in Chicago and the Midwest and sending their clients' pictures to Minsky's in New York. Sometimes, if we knew a girl's work or had read reviews of her act, we would hire her just from the pictures the agent sent, for a short contract anyway.

There will always be critics who will decry stripping as "indecent"; but I think it's all a matter of perspective and degree—and also timing. What one era considers filthy, the other considers barely suggestive. Psychology and Freud are soul mates of the stripper, whether the girls know it or not. It's that one percent physical and ninety-nine percent mental that works for the stripper. Margie Hart once said to me, "You undo the first bit of clothing and the audience does the rest."

Several popular songs come to mind in trying to explain what makes one stripper so much more appealing than another. I remember the song popular in the 1930s "It Ain't What You Do, It's the Way What You Do It!" The other song was almost part of Minsky legend, "You Gotta Have a Gimmick," from the show *Gypsy.* Our own Mae Brown, for instance, was known as the Dresden Doll. She would roll down her tights and have the orchestra leader poke his baton just where the back ended and the top inch of where the tights should have begun to descend into two plump areas of popular provocation. Sally Rand, of course, became famous for her fan gimmick, and Zorita, for the doves that flew in and out and revealed strategic parts of the anatomy on cue. Lois DeFee capitalized on her height—she was six feet four and weighed a couple of hundred pounds. Once, for a publicity gimmick, she actually married a midget. It immortalized her name in burlesque. The gag went around about how they consummated their marriage: "Somebody had to put him up to it." Of course, they used that joke about Billy Rose too. Later on there was Tirza and her wine bath, Dorothy Henry and her milk bath, Faith Arden's Leda and the Swan. (She used her right arm for the swan's head and her hand as the head. Then she would manipulate them in a reenactment of the original Greek story in which Zeus makes love to Leda in the guise of a swan. Very classical, right?)

In addition to the gimmick, there was also the personal style of the girl. Some had a special way of executing the basic movements of the strip. Some were slow workers, some were fast, some were sexy and promised more than they delivered, and some unfortunately delivered more than they should have from the point of view of the law. It often became a competitive thing. Each girl trying to outdo the one before her. We always had to watch out for that sort of thing.

There's a basic dance step in the strip, but each girl does it according to her own personality. It's whatever she feels. There's the walk or strut, and then the dip, and then the grind, and then the bump! But each stripper would elaborate on this. Some people used furs, some used animals, some had a chair. The thing is the tease. It's not so much taking it off, it's teasing, which is really the most important thing. So they would take a lot of time, because once they were undressed, there wasn't much further they could go. Certainly not while the city authorities and the self-appointed censors were watching anyway.

To the girls it was all business. It was not a question of holding back on grounds of modesty. It was how to get the biggest hand and, of course, the biggest paycheck. We could only do so much for the stripper. We'd give her the stage, some good lighting, an expert handling the spot with gels that would set off the color of her costume. We'd help her with music, if she hadn't developed some of her own, and provide an offstage singer who would croon a chorus or two of a sentimental ballad. And then of course, there was the introduction we would give the girls when they came on: "And now we bring you the sweet, the illusive, the dainty . . ." or "the wild, the flaming, the dynamic . . ."

But the girls themselves had to supply their own wardrobe and had to have changes every week or so. This could cost them a fair amount of money, and many of them frequently sewed their own costumes. Gypsy Rose Lee was one of the top seamstresses in the business and did a lot of her own sewing.

Of course, the girls couldn't make everything, and there developed a certain number of specialists who would come around the theater to sell the "baubles, bangles, and beads" that were needed to give a costume its pizzazz. Generally speaking, the "gadget" salesmen and other purveyors came backstage since the girls had very little time to go out shopping. One man I remember—he was called only Paul—had an incredible glittering collection of G-strings and pasties—the little circlets the girls were sometimes required to paste on their nipples—had a regular circuit and was particularly favored by some of the star strippers. He handled G-strings, opera hose, a strip bra, a net bra, pasties, gloves, panels, and tassels. The only things he didn't handle were gowns and shoes, which the girls had to get elsewhere. Among the people I know he supplied were Margie Hart, Rose la Rose, Sally Rand, and Gypsy. He wasn't cheap either. A lot of the gadgets would cost up to or even more than a hundred dollars. Paul often let the girls have these items on the cuff. After all, if they couldn't work, they couldn't patronize him. He said he'd never been stiffed by a stripper. In the early days of burlesque, Paul was a good friend of both Bud Abbott and Robert Alda. He remembers Alda coming into the People's Theatre, a rather low-class joint on the Bowery, as Paul was delivering some costumes there. A rat scampered around backstage. One of the dancers fainted and Alda shook his head sadly and said to Paul, "I studied singing for years and the best booking I get is in a joint like this!"

How did the girls feel about stripping? H. M. Alexander, author of the book *Striptease,* asked one of our own girls, "Does the audience ever embarrass you?"

"Them?" asked the stripper increduously. "I should say not! I make more money, twice as much, as any of them. I'm better than they are. And that goes for actresses in the legit too. Most of them could never make the grade as strippers. They have bum bodies, bow legs and incisions."

"Didn't you ever feel self-conscious even at first?" Alexander asked her.

"Listen," said the girl, "Stripping is no work for bashful women. Besides, most strip women come up from the chorus, where they've usually had a year or so of nudity. When they get a chance to do a single they may feel nervous or get stage fright, but that's *all.*"

How did the girls feel about one another? Just like most people, except that often they spent as much as fourteen hours of their day in the theater and they got to know each other pretty well. Except for occasional squabbles, like the time Margie Hart boffed Rose la Rose in the nose, they were generally friendly. Georgia Sothern and Gypsy Rose Lee were the best of friends.

They reported for work at twelve o'clock, when everybody else was having lunch. In the afternoon they did two shows. From five to seven they were off. They did two more shows until eleven. From one to two in the morning they rehearsed. On Thursdays they stayed until three or four in the morning for dress rehearsal of the next week's show. Saturday they did a midnight show. About the only time they were off during the week was Friday and Sunday after eleven at night. So you can see they didn't get time to raise much hell. To be near work, many of them slept in burlesque hotels, like the Peerless Palace on 46th Street or the Dixie.

Waiting for the hours to pass between spots in the show, they gossiped, played poker for small stakes (sometimes with the stagehands or the comedians), bet on horses through some backstage bookie. Sometimes they would have little radios or phonographs, and we even let some of them bring their dogs in. During their spare time a lot of them would mend costumes or create new ones. Some even brought in sewing machines. Several of the girls were serious readers, and a small number actually had college degrees. Only a few of the girls dated any of the Johns who sent them notes and flowers. For one thing, they didn't have much time, and for another, they felt more at home with people in the business. Also, they would have to date people who could keep strange hours, like other people in show business, actors, cops, and the like.

Often, if they did give in and go out on a date with a customer, they were shocked or disappointed. One man kept pestering one of our girls to go out with him. Finally, he told her he'd give her a hundred bucks if she'd spend just a few hours in his company; he promised not to lay a hand on her. So, the girl, intrigued and anxious to earn the money, went. (I never heard of any of the girls actually indulging in sex for pay, but this hundred was strictly a hands-off proposition.) The girl had been warned by the others in the cast to lay off the guy. They sensed that he was some kind of a wacko, as Mayor Koch would say. But she needed the hundred. So the next Sunday night, after the show was over, she was picked up by the man's car and chauffeur. She was driven to his apartment house, a very fancy place, and taken upstairs in a private elevator. He met her at the door. As she came into the room she found it pitch black except for two lighted candles on pedestals on a raised platform at one end of the room. Between the candles was a coffin. The girl just stood there, paralyzed with fright and surprise, and as she stood there, the John went onto the platform and took all his clothes off. Then he got into the coffin. The girl, when she saw this, let out one big yell and sped out of there like a rocket never stopping to collect her hundred. One ran into all types.

Aside from the Johns and the legitimate night workers, the girls often went out with petty larceny crooks, bookmakers, numbers men, and other drifters. One stripper's boyfriend was taken for a ride and dumped into Long Island Sound.

Sometimes they married well and left the business. Sherry Britton married a wealthy manufacturer and financier. Betty Duval married the son of a wine importer. A stripper named Roxanne married and divorced the ex-heavyweight prizefighter Battling Kingfish Levinsky and managed to do pretty well on the publicity. Another, Virginia Woods, married Nick Campofreda, a wrestler. And Roselle Rowland even married a baron.

The girls stayed so close to the theater that they virtually never left it. If they needed something to eat or an errand run, the doorman Arthur was always ready. They shrieked his name, "Arthur!" and he came running with his little notebook. He wrote the girl's name at the head of the page and in ten minutes returned with arms full of marshmallow frappes and fudge sundaes or hamburgers or Chinese food.

But the star strippers were in a class by themselves. They had friends outside, often from the theatrical world and occasionally from the underworld. It was a long time before we realized, for instance, that the two plug-uglies who served as bodyguards to Gypsy in her early years were actually henchmen of Waxy Gordon and that he had appointed himself her "sponsor." This had its good points and its bad points for Gypsy, as we shall see.

CHAPTER

34

VOICE IN THE DARK: Peanuts, popcorn, rubber balloons . . .
ANOTHER VOICE: Help, someone—there's a woman here who's fainted!
FIRST VOICE: Peanuts, popcorn . . .
NEW VOICE: Fainted? Rub her wrists, rub her wrists . . .
FIRST VOICE: Rubber balloons!

ONE DAY WHEN I was sitting in my upstairs office mulling over the vicissitudes of the burlesque business and the characters in it, who should be announced but Ruth's Aunt Mae, one of the most proper and distinguished women in our family. She was the wife of Morris Raefield Cohen, a noted professor of astronomy.

"Morton," she said, "I have a problem you may be able to help me with. One of my good friends is a Mrs. Mizzy. Her son, Robert, has been courting one of the young ladies in your employ—a certain Miss Gypsy Rose Lee. I wonder if you could tell me anything about this person. Do you know anything about her?"

Did I *know* anything? Did I know *anything*? *Did* I know anything?

Gypsy was beyond question the stripper most admired in the business by the highbrows and intellectuals of the city. She had a reputation for urbanity, subtlety, wit, and grace.

I personally had never seen the Mizzy boy around the theater. If he visited her backstage, I was not aware of it. It is very possible that he met her at one of the many parties she was always attending given by people like Alexander Woolcott and that ilk. A gathering at her penthouse apartment or in the lavish house she later bought on East 63rd Street might have included Mr. and Mrs. Carl Van Doren; Deems Tayor, the composor; Marcel Vertès, the French artist; Pavel Tchelitchew, the Russian ballet set and costume designer; John and Fred of the John-Fredericks hat designing outfit; and her old pal, Georgia Sothern, just to keep things rolling.

I didn't know anything really terrible about Gypsy—just about some of the things that she had tolerated, some of the friends who had helped her on her way. If you eliminated Waxy Gordon and his four green-hatted henchmen and the fact that she showed porno movies in her dressing room and encouraged her monkeys in their obscene antics, and the fact that some of her claims to being a great reader and aficionado of the opera were nonsense, I guess she was okay. She certainly had straight teeth, if a somewhat underdeveloped bosom. She made a nice buck—I could attest to that—and she wore enough diamond jewelry to illuminate an airport runway.

I leaned back in my swivel chair, putting my hands together judiciously like one of the magistrates who was always passing judgment on our shows.

If the Mizzy boy was madly in love with Gypsy, nothing I could say would help. He would just run off with her anyway and leave behind him a miserable mother.

"I can tell you this, Aunt May," I said in measured tones, "Miss Lee is a very intelligent woman."

"Oh, Morton," Aunt May said, "is she really intelligent? Can I tell Mrs. Mizzy that she's *really* intelligent?"

"She's *really* intelligent, Aunt May, I assure you."

So Aunt May went off to report her news to Mrs. Mizzy, happy that she had been able to use her family influence to get valuable information about Mrs. Mizzy's future daughter-in-law's intellect.

Shortly after my conference with Aunt May, Gypsy eloped rather quietly and discreetly with young Robert, who was a dental supply manufacturer. Discussing him later, she told a reporter, "He was and is a nice guy."

"We were married twice," she told the *Daily News* some years later. "The first time in a small boat off Catalina. People said it was a stunt, done for the greater glory of Zanuck, my employer at the time. That's a lie!

"It was done to preserve a Hovick tradition. The Hovicks are all Norsemen and since time immemorial they have been Hovicking around just under the fringe of the North Pole. Even my name is a contraction of the phrase 'Ho Viking!'

"Anyway," she continued, "all Hovicks are married at sea. Zanuck was doubtful about that sailor's knot, and God knows I was having enough trouble being Will Haysed [the movies called her Louise Hovick, but people recognized the Rose by any other name], so Bob and I planned to go through it again.

"We had a honeymoon quarrel and called each other all the names we could think of, and we were both resourceful, especially me, with a diploma as a master cusser from all the burlesque wheels I've toured.

"It looked like curtains for that second marriage but in the midst of the confusion my dachshund bitch started to have pups. We couldn't get a vet, and Bob proved to be the kind of man you can lean on in an emergency. He did an excellent job of mid-wifery. I figured any girl like me who always travels in a cloud of animals needed that kind of man around, so we were married again."

So that's the version of her marriage that Gypsy told to the reporter and it might even be true. Although that marriage didn't exactly take, Gypsy had nothing against men in general.

In Hollywood Gypsy went on to marry an actor, William Alexander Kirkland, then a Spanish painter, Julio de Diego, and she had a secret baby by the film director Otto Preminger, a fact that has only recently come to light with the publication of the book *Gypsy & Me* by her son Erik, Otto Preminger's illegitimate child. But this was all long after her stay with us.

While working for the Minskys, she acquired enough money even without the silent partnership of Waxy Gordon to buy a house up the Hudson near Newburgh, which she called Witchwood Manor and where appropriately she stowed away her wacky mother, along with her half sister, Jean. (Incidentally, after she became really successful, she took the two monkeys out of her dressing room and farmed them out upstate with her mother.) In New York she shared her apartment from time to time with a number of the men she admired so much, including one of Bette Davis's ex-beaus.

Gypsy lost Mizzy somewhere on her Hollywood venture, which turned out to be a complete bust. Hollywood didn't seem to know what to do with her. They were terrified that her frank and charming sexuality would come across, so they changed her name back to her maiden name and made her wear costumes that covered her from her ankles to her neck. None of her pictures made a dime. Gypsy told her sister once that what she had been infatuated with about Bob Mizzy was his upbringing.

"Think, June," she said, "the same two parents all along the line. Mother, father. Just lovely people. I'm going to miss them."

From what June said, there was more drama in Gypsy's house in Malibu than there was on Zanuck's sound sets. For one thing, it was in Hollywood that Gypsy finally became totally fed up with her mother after Rose (*her* real name was Roanie, by the way, but she made everybody call her Rose for some reason) had chased Mizzy around the Malibu house with a gun.

"That episode had been part of the Hollywood saga, which includes the time Mother got dressed in worn shoes and the old coat Gypsy said they used to wear on cold nights when milking the cow back on the farm in Highland Mills. She had added a white makeup for the desired effect, then called Darryl Zanuck. He listened as she told him how weak she was from long privation and asked him for a bowl of hot soup.

"The way my sister told them," said June, who was always bitter about the fact that her mother had practically turned her back on her once Gypsy made her success, "the mother stories were all hilarious. To the press. To the outsiders. When she told them to me, however, it was a little different. 'She wouldn't let go of you, June, remember? Until you ran away.' Back then Mother had done that identical routine with a gun. Held it almost touching Bobby's (June's boy friend's) chest while she pulled at the trigger. An automatic—the safety was on. We often wondered if she understood that. Also, if the rifle she used to chase Mizzy was purposely unloaded . . ."

Gypsy had her own ideas about how to handle the crazy-mother angle. "Keep it funny, June," she told her sister. "Nobody buys a subplot like ours. Make them laugh or you lose the audience."

Whoever wrote the lines of her stories, Gypsy certainly enjoyed the most varied and fabulous career of all the strippers, if not necessarily the happiest. She went on to write two books, *Gypsy* and *The G-String Murders* (the latter was later made into a movie called *Lady of Burlesque,* starring Barbara Stanwyck in Gypsy's role and Bert Lahr), and a play, *The Naked Genius,* produced by Michael Todd, who in later years was probably the most serious and long-lasting lover but who left her for Joan Blondell and, to make matters worse, gave Joan Blondell the title role in the play that Gypsy had written, a role she had wanted to play herself.

She was a chainsmoker—three packs a day—and according to everybody who knew her, she used every form of chemical stimulation on earth, not the least of it champagne. She drove herself hard, played hard, loved hard with great passion, and died relatively young—a great and unique lady. But there was one more red-haired flaming star in burlesque who managed to carve a road of her own while sidling around backstage with a Bible in her hands and bouncing around on stage almost naked, some said with no cover over her red-thatched pubic area.

35

COMIC: (*posing as a candy butcher*): Candy! Bonbons!
STRAIGHT MAN: Do you have nuts?
COMIC: No.
STRAIGHT MAN: Do you have dates?
COMIC: If I had nuts, I'd have dates!

———————————————●———————————————

MARGIE HART, the flame-haired pixie—or the poor man's Garbo, as Walter Winchell called her—was the last of the four great strippers to get into the business. She didn't show up on the scene until 1934, when she arrived in New York all the way from Edgerton, Missouri, after polishing up her act in the burlesque hinterlands, ending up in Chicago.

There's no doubt about it. She had an exciting face and beautiful fine skin. There was a heavy sprinkling of freckles across her nose, but the audience never saw that of course. Makeup handled that problem. To me it wasn't a problem; I thought it was cute. She had a beautiful body, and I think of all the top women, she really enjoyed showing it off more than any of the others. It was a task to keep her from going completely nude, and we always lived in fear that if we didn't watch her all the time, that's just what she would do and get us thrown right out of the theater. There was a rumor around that she didn't always wear her G-string. Naturally that worried me, and I have no way of knowing whether it was true. It was enough to keep the yokels glued to their seats waiting for the slightest mistake. That sort of rumor was not exactly bad, as long as it wasn't true.

Her real name was Margaret Bridget Bryan, and she swore she was a distant cousin of William Jennings Bryan. She couldn't dance, sing, or act, but she had a vivacious manner that concealed these drawbacks. When she went on the road working on her own after the decline of burlesque, she outstripped Ann Corio and Gypsy Rose Lee by several hundred dollars a week at the box office.

Why was she so popular? A magazine writer said of her once: "She does something to the boys. Strong men grow weak with whistles and stomps, weak men are made lions again when Margie does her stuff."

Once, when she was dancing at the Werba, she had to be rescued by our house firemen after twenty-two encores.

When Margie talked to the press, you never knew whether she was making up her own lines or not, but they certainly got attention. She said that she thought that women came to see her as well as men. "They come to see my clothes," she explained waggishly, "and to make other comparisons!"

Edgerton, where she was born in 1916, was a farming village of only 452 people not far from Kansas City. She was one of nine children. Her father was an itinerant sewing-machine salesman who carted his family around as he peddled machines and dreamed of becoming a farmer someday. Margie said that her grandfather had been a prosperous farmer and slave trader in Virginia, where he had emigrated from Ireland.

"If it wasn't for the Civil War," Margie told a reporter, "I'd be sitting under a magnolia tree sipping a mint julep and weighing in slaves!"

But the bottom fell out of the slave-trading market, and Grandpappy Hart lost his plantation lands and moved West. Margie's father had a hard time making ends meet during the Depression. You had to sell a lot of sewing machines to feed nine children. One day she and a school chum named Mamie Bohenstingle left the third year of a Minneapolis parochial high school to invade the theater. They had five bucks and a letter to a Chicago booking agent. They hitchhiked to the Windy City for an audition. Mamie already had a little theatrical experience. Margie had none and no theatrical background in her family, but she certainly didn't mind leaving school. "I guess I was the dumb type," she told me once, remembering her school career. "Even at sixteen I had to draw apples to count. Besides, I was spending most of my afternoons studying the figures in Minneapolis shows."

Margie attended burlesque shows as a teenager and felt she could do as well as any of those she saw on the stage. She apparently had no sense of modesty, perhaps the result of having lived in such a big family. On the other hand, I came from a big family and it had the opposite effect.

Anyway, Mamie's introduction to the agent produced jobs for both girls. They were hired as parade girls in the rear rank of the chorus at the Rialto, a burlesque house in Chicago. It called itself the Home of Refined Burlesque. For all I know, it was. This meant that for $18 a week they acted as background, while the more experienced ladies undulated and kicked and sang as well as they could between the comic turns and the strip act.

Mamie and Margie split a $3 a week room, cooked on an electric plate, and Mamie Bohenstingle changed her name to Lolette DuVal. An excellent move in my opinion. It would be very hard to fit Bohenstingle on a marquee, and I'm not sure if it would be much of a draw.

Gossip had it that in those days Margie flung her body around somewhat freely offstage as well as on, but she denied this vigorously: "Try working five shows a day, then rehearsing until one in the morning for next week's show and showing up for rehearsal again the next day at eleven—and see how much time you've got to drink champagne out of slippers with glamour boys!"

Margie took to burlesque like a squirrel takes to nuts, and she was devastated when her father tracked her down, appeared at the theater unexpectedly, and returned her to high school. She listened to her father's lectures for two weeks and then ran away again to burlesque. It was the only job she ever had. "I promised my father," she explained, "to be a good girl. I proved you could be."

It wasn't long before Margie's remarkable talent and really fabulous body were recognized. She got a specialty to do: In the midst of the gaiety and laughter the entire cast suddenly formed a patriotic ensemble depicting the birth of Liberty. So who was standing in the background bearing a torch and wearing a crown, her red hair flaming defiantly against tyrants—every inch the Statue of Liberty—but Margie. The only difference between her and the lady in the harbor is that Margie was stripped to the waist, with blue touches to fit the red, white, and blue color scheme.

One day a gentleman, a legend in burlesque named Daddy Pickens, was so moved either by the patriotism or by Margie's commercial possibilities that he signed her up for $50 a week as an SIT—stripper in training. It was a big raise for Margie and she grabbed it. Furthermore, she had been told that Daddy Pickens knew his onions. He had a talent for developing stripper acts and had supposedly discovered Ann Corio, Gypsy Rose Lee, and Rosita Royce, an artistic young lady who divested herself of a cloak of iron-nerved pigeons roosting on her curves. Both Mamie—excuse me, Lolette—and Margie went to St. Louis to study under the master. Pickens was well aware that removing one's clothes is not just a matter of unzipping and stepping out. Margie said she spent two hard weeks merely learning poise. Hour after hour she tramped the stage of Pickens's Garrick Theatre balancing a book on her head.

After balancing the book for about 500 miles, Margie found she could ooze around the stage, operating the muscles necessary to keep the book from even vibrating. Pickens had her inserted into a rhinestone gown, and she practiced climbing in and out of it without falling.

Then one night, in 1934, Pickens put the schoolbooks aside. His star pupil was ready for her stripping premiere.

"It was a memorable occasion," she told a *Collier's* reporter "all the world of St. Louis was there—in derby hats and no white ties. In fact, they had no ties at all. And, boy"—she shudders—"was I scared!"

But the premiere was almost a flop. Margie had been practicing chanting a romantic ditty called "I'm Playing With Fire, I'm Going to Get Burned, I Don't Know What to Do!" The minute Margie stepped on the stage, she froze like a strawberry popsicle. All she could see outside the spotlight circle were dark faces gleaming wolfishly at her. The orchestra vamped and vamped, and Margie finally opened her mouth with a creaking sound. But nothing came out. Nobody had ever said that Margie was a singer, but in order to get the show moving, she had to at least recite the words. The audience began to titter. Just before they could whistle and hoot her off the stage, depriving posterity forever of one of the great stripteasers, she heard the orchestra leader prompting her hoarsely, "Peel, kid, peel!"

She fumbled for her zipper and found it. Suddenly, once the audience got a look at Margie's creamy skin and remarkable shape, everything was all right.

"The audience went off its rocker," Margie told *Collier's*. "Strong men went noisily mad. Suddenly I heard the dreaded words, 'Take it off! Take it off!' and I knew I was standing there with nothing between me and the future but a string of pearls. It was awful—but it was wonderful! I stopped the show—but I never sang another note in my life!" Thank God! Her lack of a thrilling contralto certainly never hurt her at Minsky's.

Word of Margie's sensational talents immediately spread around the burlesque wheel, and after a few months she left Daddy Pickens in St. Louis and lit hotter fires in Chicago than Mrs. O'Leary's cow. It was there that Billy got word of her, sent scouts to the hinterlands, and signed her up.

The first thing she did when she got to New York was to import her whole enormous family. She ensconced them in one of those huge rambling Upper West Side apartments in the blue mother-of-pearl bathroom-fixture district. We were paying her $750 a week at the Republic, and New Yorkers thought every bit as much of her as people did in the Midwest. About some tastes geography knows no distinction.

Margie never had the reputation for wit or cleverness that Ann Corio or Gypsy Rose Lee had. But she knew how to handle her money, and almost as soon as she got into the big time, she started purchasing annuities. When her father failed in the garage business he started out East, she made his dream come true and ultimately bought him a 120-acre farm near Lathrop, Missouri. From then on, much of the money she earned from stripping was used to stock the farm with purebred cattle, modern equipment, and college-grad hired hands, which weren't too hard to find in those days during the Depression. When she wasn't performing, she attended cattle auctions. At Christmas time she demanded cultivators and pigs from her boyfriends instead of perfume and furs. And to ensure the flow of popularity, Margie hired her own press agent, an idea she got from the other stars.

Her press agent first got her involved in some fantastic stunts. In Washington, a good burlesque town, he installed Margie in a heavy veiled outfit in the Senate gallery, and spread the story among gossip columnists that a certain senator was nuts about her—even met her at the train. He hinted to Margie that it would not do her any harm to vamp the newspapermen, with whom she had an excellent rapport in any case. They called her the "darling of the diplomatic corps."

When Margie worked in New York, her press agent started a mock feud between her and Eleanor Holm, who later went on to marry Billy Rose. Holm, who was an Olympic swimming star before she became the impresario's wife and a movie star, was accused by Margie of wearing a bathing suit with strategic padding to enhance her curves. Margie said she would show her how to take off her clothes in a strip duel for $500—the most beautiful figure take all. Holm graciously turned down the offer.

Although they were friends, Margie didn't particularly approve of Gypsy's style. "Gypsy Rose Lee's act is too subtle," she used to say. "You have to bang them in the eye in burlesque."

But she did engage in friendly competition with Gypsy Rose Lee, and when Gypsy went highbrow, Margie's press agent tried to make her compete by also reading *Schopenhauer*. Margie couldn't get past word three, but to show that she had no disdain for the intellect, she agreed to establish the "Margie Hart Scholarship for an Ambitious Burlesque Girl at Bryn Mawr." The Pennsylvania college declined her offer, but Margie was often invited to lecture at men's colleges, including Harvard.

"Harvard men," she once observed, "are gentlemen, and you can always have a long talk with a Princeton man. He's almost like a reporter. But do they teach anything but blocking and tackling at Yale?"

Like all the big stars, Margie had her special fans. Some of these even pursued her from theater to theater when she was on tour. Although she never became friendly with any of these traveling stage-door Johnnys, she recognized a lot of them by sight since they always sat up in front. One older gent always had a seat in the front row and carried a slate, on which he wrote encouraging words to her—"Great work, Margie! Keep it up!"—and other inspiring, peppy sayings. He didn't appear one day and Margie was sure he must have died. Nothing else could have kept him out of his hot front seat.

Margie was not a reader, and once, when asked about her reading habits, Margie said, "I did read *Macbeth* once, but I didn't like it—too creepy."

Whenever I ran into her backstage between shows, she would either be crocheting bedspreads and drinking gallons of coffee or playing in a marathon rummy game. She was crazy about furs, prizefights, hockey, horse racing, bowling, and especially poker, which was something of a specialty of hers. In her hotel suite I heard there were often all-night sessions at which you could find an editor, a prizefighter, a few Broadway columnists, a sprinkling of reporters, and various visiting ball players. And they didn't play strip poker either. The game was one- and two-dollar stud, and Margie seldom went home a loser. Her other hobby, dating no doubt to her farm background, was galloping around Central Park bridle paths on Sunday mornings. Unlike Gypsy, she was not much of a drinker, and smoked only nicotineless cigarettes. She seldom went to night clubs and actually disliked dancing. When it came to food, she disdained the elegant French restaurants, preferring dishes like corned beef and cabbage at Toots Shor's or Dinty Moore's or, more likely, some out-of-the-way restaurant.

I do remember that she had one great phobia. She was terrified that she would get appendicitis. In those days doctors didn't have the finesse with the scalpel that they do today, and such an operation left scars that could compete with the Grand Canyon.

"I mean," she said to me very seriously once, "a wrinkle on your face isn't as bad as one on your stomach." She remembered one friend of hers who had put off an appendix operation for three months and almost died, just so she wouldn't ruin her appearance.

She also had the professional fear that one of her zippers might get stuck. She always held a zipper rehearsal before going on just to make sure everything was sliding nicely.

"If a zipper jams," she said, "Ann Corio can do her innocent act and Rosita Royce can milk those pigeons that cover her. But what can I do?"

Of course, Gypsy didn't have this problem because she always used pins instead of zippers. All she had to worry about was that something would come unpinned ahead of time, and that might not be such a big problem after all.

We did almost lose Margie a few years after she started working for us at the Republic, when she dropped into St. Malachy's church,

the famous show business sanctuary tucked away among the hurly-
burly and dime movie houses and girlie shows. The sermon that
night happened to be against the diabolical evils of the striptease.

Margie was so impressed that she decided to give up her trade
right then and there. "But when I got outside," she told a reporter
with tears in her eyes, "I learned my father was sick. And I remembered my mother and brothers and sisters. I got realistic."

But she was so impressed with the sermon that after that she always walked around with a Bible under her arm, which became sort
of a trademark. Later on, when she was asked to go to Hollywood, as
had Gypsy, Ann Corio, and Georgia Sothern (all without success),
Margie refused, even though she had passed a screen test.

Asked once to explain her personal success, Margie said, "Maybe
it's because I'm just a wholesome, clean American girl trying to get
along." The line got a lot of press coverage, most of it cynical, but in
a certain way I always thought that that was the truth.

It reminded me of Georgia Sothern's equally frank, unplanned
remark when she was asked what she thought of while she was doing
her wild strip. She said, "Nothing. It's just a form of exercise." And
that got quite a play in the press. But I can testify that Georgia
probably was thinking of nothing, or if she was thinking of anything
it was how to manipulate us out of another few bucks on her contract.

So by 1936, we had the four top strippers in the business devoting
a lot of their time to the Minsky circuit, and we were doing better
than most people in those Depression years. There were only two
things that were preventing me from really enjoying life. One was
the constant harassment by Mayor La Guardia and Paul Moss, the
license commissioner (as well as the other buttinskies who kept trying to have our shows banned and cost us a fortune in legal costs),
the other was that low-life Weinstock and his two kids. It was clear
that a crisis was coming on both fronts.

36

SECOND BANANA: Wait a minute! Wait a minute! Don't
anybody move!
STRAIGHT MAN: What's the matter?
SECOND BANANA: I lost my wallet!
STRAIGHT MAN: Where did you lose it?
SECOND BANANA: Over there.
STRAIGHT MAN: Then why are you looking for it over
here?
SECOND BANANA: There's more light over here.

As WE INCHED into the mid-1930s, most businesses were going to hell
in a handbarrow, but burlesque was miraculously surviving despite
the endless and inventive aggravation provided by Commissioner
Moss, egged on by a growing crowd of bluenoses. While legitimate
theaters were closing by the dozens, our road shows continued to
take in money, and we would have been sitting pretty if it hadn't
been for the endless legal fees plus the big drops at the box office
whenever we were forced by the license commissioner to tone down
our shows.

Carrie Finnell, the great tassel tosser, had now become a member
of the executive board of the Burlesque Artists' Association, the performers' union formed in the wake of the pro-labor stance of the
Roosevelt regime. Observing how theaters were closing while burlesque was thriving, Carrie staunchly proclaimed, "Burlesque pro-

ducers should realize that they are the future of the American theater."

Allen Gilbert, who was producing shows for the Wilners, gave this fatherly advice to struggling actors: "Come into burlesque as either a stepping stone to better things or as a chance to tide yourself over until the break, with the right attitude and the right state of mind. . . . You are not stepping down to burlesque, you are coming over to it."

In February 1934 we celebrated the third anniversary of the Republic with the most lavish show we had ever put on, and backstage we had a fantastic dinner, including pastrami, a huge statuette of a stripper in ice, and another of a burlesque comic in chopped liver—an endless flow of goodies too mouthwatering to mention. I am proud to say that none of the cast had to be evicted for overindulgence of any sort. But certainly a few people got out of line and had to be restrained or politely advised, notably certain members of the Weinstock clan, who were increasingly becoming a thorn in the side of my brother H.K. and myself. There was simply no getting along with Weinstock, and it was becoming evident that matters were coming to a head.

I will admit that as the harassment from the city continued, Weinstock, who was usually considered the silent partner and never talked to the press, began to get so overwrought that he occasionally made public statements—some of which were not bad. Once, the New York *Times* reported at one of our hearings that Joseph Weinstock, "sobbing" and "gesticulating with dramatic force," cried out that he was doubly accursed. First he had begged the authorities to rid the sidewalks of pornographic peddlers and steerers only to be disregarded. (One alleged customer, asked if he had bought any pornographic books from these street vendors, replied, "I haven't even got a pornograph.") Anyway, Weinstock pointed out that his attempts to clear the sidewalks of these offenders had been disregarded, but just the same the city blamed him for their very presence. It was Weinstock's contention, and I agreed, that much of the pressure came from the legitimate theater-owning interests who disliked burlesque's competition. "We've been accused of everything except kidnapping the Lindbergh baby," he shouted.

So you see the words the *Times* itself used—"sobbing" and also "shouting." It was exactly this sort of emotional outburst that was eating our hearts out.

We were fighting all the time. I got a kick out of it when my brother Abe, after a hearing concerning the New Gotham Theatre, pointed out that in describing his comedy skits as indecent or obscene the city officials were simply criticizing something that had been going on in the same way and in the same style for decades and therefore could not suddenly be unacceptable. "Not one new burlesque skit has been written in the last twenty years," Abe told the license commission. And if anybody should know, it would have been him.

To even get a license to operate in the year 1935 all the managers had to sign an oath to refrain from indecency. Moss had instigated a revised departmental regulation "concerning theaters in concert." It said, in part, "No female shall be permitted on the stage in any scene, sketch or act with breasts or lower part of the torso uncovered, or so thinly covered or draped as to appear uncovered. . . .

"No vulgar, obscene or indecent language offensive to decency or propriety shall be indulged in by performers in any scene, sketch, act or play."

And so on. Obviously these rules were unenforceable and undefinable, as the courts have consistently held through all the years since then. But what did Moss care? He was on his high horse.

Weinstock, as the official spokesman of the Holly Holding Corporation, which was our corporate entity, had to sign an oath agreeing to these ridiculous demands.

So he swore a false oath. Believe me, it wouldn't be the worst thing Weinstock had ever done in his life, but we all knew at the time that there was no way we could abide by those rules and stay open.

Meanwhile, the burlesque front wasn't the only one on which the moralists had been operating.

A year before Moss's ridiculous proclamation, a book called *Ulysses* by James Joyce was hauled in front of the U.S. district court on charges of being "immoral and obscene" and therefore unfit for U.S. readers.

U.S. customs had initiated the case back in May 1932, when it seized an unexpurgated copy sent to the publisher Bennett Cerf from Paris. Cerf's lawyer, Morris L. Ernst, had made a specialty of fighting censorship cases.

The U.S. attorney, Samuel C. Coleman, insisted that there were ample grounds to consider *Ulysses* an obscene book. Judge John M. Woolsey, who was hearing the case, spent his whole vacation that summer reading *Ulysses*. Here's what he finally wrote in his decision, issued December 6, 1933: "I have read 'Ulysses' once in its entirety and I have read those passages of which the Government particularly complains several times. . . . But in 'Ulysses,' in spite of its unusual frankness, I do not detect anywhere the leer of the sensualist. I hold, therefore, that it is not pornographic. . . .

"Although it contains . . . many words usually considered dirty, I have not found anything that I consider to be dirt for dirt's sake. . . .

"If one does not wish to associate with such folk as Joyce describes, that is one's own choice."

H.K. was particularly proud of that decision because Judge Woolsey had gone to Columbia Law School, just as he had.

After a couple of more complaints from police officers and "concerned citizens," Commissioner Moss warned us that our license was in jeopardy and he finally closed us down in September 1935.

Here's the whole reason they gave for closing us down according to the testimony by a certain patrolman, Edward G. Giery:

> On June 22, 1935, at the hour of ten twenty P.M. while seated at the Republic Theater, 209 West 42nd Street, Borough of Manhattan, City of New York, I observed an act going on there— twelve girls of the act performed an Egyptian dance and in back of the twelve girls who were dancing, were six girls elevated on pedestals with their breasts completely exposed during the entire act, which lasted about seven minutes. In the next act, about ten twenty-seven P.M., a girl named Wanda Dell appeared on the stage and sang a song. . . . Encore number one, this girl dropped her dress to a point where she exposed her breasts; encore number two, she dropped her dress to her hips, exposing her body from hips to head; encore number three, she dropped her dress to the floor, exposing her whole body, except her private parts, which were covered by a string of beads, leaving the cheeks of her rectum exposed; encore number four, she walked across the stage, at that time she had a pink shawl covering her from her shoulders to the thighs, leaving one side of her body exposed. The next number, at ten forty P.M., a girl named Louise Stewart does a strip number. Encore number one, she dropped the dress to her hips exposing her body from hips to breast; on the second encore she dropped the dress to the floor, exposing her body completely ex-

cept for her private parts, which were covered by a thin string of beads. That's all I saw at the Republic."

Other policemen gave testimony about some of the comedy routines: "A comic is figuring on a pad when the female asks her friend, 'What is a baby?'; comic says: 'I got it—nine months interest on a small deposit.' All exit."

This is the sort of stuff that was supposed to send our audiences out in the streets slavering to relieve themselves at a nearby taxi-dance hall? You'd think we were holding a Roman orgy there!

But Moss had no heart. He closed us down anyway. The courts, being more sensible, let us open again while the case was being appealed.

H.K. was pleased when the National Council on Freedom from Censorship took notice of our case. We got in touch with Morris Ernst (in this case, a law graduate from *my* alma mater, NYU) and asked him to handle the case. Ernst made the point that regardless of the nature of the show, there was an important question of whether "an appointed official can arrogate to himself arbitrary power of censorship, transcending those of the Court of Appeals which has held that the Court is not a censor of plays nor does it attempt to regulate manners." The court (a blessing on its head) ruled in favor of the Minskys and pointed out that Moss had no power to revoke a theater's license for indecency unless there had been a criminal conviction. This decision was later upheld by the State Court of Appeals too.

So we were running again for a while. But how long could we keep up? We knew very well that Moss wasn't going to quit just because of a little court decision.

I had some troubles at home too. Ruth developed anemia, which had her ill for a few years; she was very slight to start with, but ultimately she got over the illness. I then decided it would be a very good thing if she decided to take on some serious work that she could occupy herself with, and I pushed her into taking an exam to become a substitute teacher. She had a friend who was doing some work at Julia Richman High School at the time, and so she started subbing in Latin and English.

As clouds began to gather over the burlesque business, I felt it wouldn't be a bad idea for her to take an exam for a permanent teaching post. I'll never forget this: 1,368 people took it and only 170 passed. She was one of them. But to show you how well known the name "Minsky" had become by this time, when she took that exam and was interviewed, it was suggested that it might be simpler for her if she changed her name from Minsky or used her maiden name to avoid any hint of scandal. But Ruth refused and went ahead anyway; in the end there was no problem.

The endless battling with the city authorities provided the newspapers with a field day. There was always a schism in the pages of the papers, with the theater section generally considering the shows amusing or praiseworthy, and the news section and editorial pages jumping on us with both feet. The more lurid the paper was, the more likely it was to attack us. One of our worst enemies was the tabloid New York *Daily Mirror,* which kept running editorials with such headlines as BURLESQUE. WHEN WILL SOMETHING BE DONE ABOUT IT? Of course, as long as they didn't close us, the publicity was all to the good, but Arthur Kobler of the *Mirror* even began running signs on the side of his delivery truck: WHEN WILL THEY CLOSE BURLESQUE? When my brother Herbert saw that, he said, echoing an old saying of my mother's, "May a trolley car grow in his stomach."

Through it all the true intelligentsia, like Mencken, gave us full support: "The great artists of the world are never Puritans, and seldom even ordinarily respectable," he wrote once in the *American Mercury.* Another time he made the statement: "If you get three Americans in one place, two will get together to reform the morals of the third."

Anyway, with all this uproar going on in the courts, Moss decided to leave us alone for a while, and to our surprise the next year our license was granted, as was everybody else's, without any trouble. Reverend Joseph A. McCaffrey issued his annual tirade on the state of morality on 42nd Street, but that was about all that year. Meanwhile, we sent a company to Hollywood with a terrific show called *Life Begins at Minsky's.* It was a sellout from the start, but apparently the Los Angeles authorities had been reading the New York papers. The show was raided, and several principals were arrested and given jail sentences, which were subsequently suspended. We put that show on the road, where it didn't have any trouble with the police, but it died like a dog.

Meanwhile, Abe, who ran a much hotter show uptown than we ever dared on Broadway, managed to get closed down again for an act that I thought, frankly, was highly imaginative and I wished I'd thought of it first. It consisted of a stripper on a trapeze taking her clothes off gradually and dropping each item to the stage. It's a shame the act only lasted about two nights before the theater was closed down.

At the time, we were talking it over in the theater and I said that I thought it was a pity about Abe being closed and that when the heat died down maybe we should think of doing that same act ourselves, if we could find a girl who could swing from her knees and strip at the same time. But Weinstock started making a big fuss all over again. Although we never got along with him ourselves, he hated Abe with a purple passion. This time his screaming and shouting display really got to me. I caught H.K.'s eyes and he nodded. We left Weinstock screaming to himself in the office, but between us we both knew that the moment had come. We could no longer work with Weinstock. It was time to go off on our own.

CHAPTER
37

CHORUS: If you love us, please don't mind
If now and then we bump and grind!
We will shimmy and we will shake
But please don't think we're on the make!

THROUGH THE SPRING of 1936 H.K. and I talked and talked about leaving Weinstock. We checked our bank balances; there was a little money there from various real-estate speculations and savings from the burlesque theaters. We had people who were willing to back us in a new venture. With the decision of the courts, Moss was temporarily quieted, and there was a chance that we could open a new theater without as much harassment as we had gotten in the past. The problem was to find a theater suitable for our needs in the Broadway area, which we were convinced was the only place to operate the sort of thing we had in mind. It would be in the tradition of Billy Minsky, who had been the first person to attract the Broadway and upper-class audience to burlesque. The Republic had all along been called Billy Minsky's Republic. There was a legal problem, however. Apparently, before he died, Billy, possibly in an attempt to give some security to his wife, Mary, had signed over the rights to his name. Or else Weinstock just stole them. Once we had resigned from the Weinstock organization, there would be no Minskys at all in his theater. I wondered if he would have the gall to still call it a Minsky theater. Whatever. We were committed to going our own way. In

May 1936 we broke our connection with Weinstock and started looking for a theater. At the same time we began to line up talent— designers and dance directors, as well as performers.

There was no question that you couldn't bring the audiences into the house with a cleaned-up type of strip that Moss and his cohorts were trying to force on us all the time. Every time we did this, the box office languished. What we had to do this time was to have some real old-fashioned lowdown burlesque but in a clean, modern theater, where women could go without feeling uncomfortable and where we expected to attract the upper-class and intellectual sets, who were just then recognizing burlesque as a great American art form. Reginald Marsh won his first acclaim as an artist for his painting of Minsky's, and *Fortune* magazine featured his pictures in a lead story on burlesque as an American theatrical phenomenon.

We searched and searched and looked at all sorts of closed-up theaters, functioning theaters, Broadway stages, movie houses, until we finally found a house on Broadway near 51st Street, that seemed ideal. We set aside $50,000 to tear out the entire interior and rebuild it as our ideal burlesque house.

We discussed and tried and threw out hundreds of ideas and worked into the night supervising the revisions through that fall. I am pleased to say that with the help of our press agents, the newspapers and magazines showed a healthy interest in our operation. To them we always stressed that this was the only and original Minsky burlesque. Certainly Weinstock had no claim to the name, and Abe was a renegade from the true Billy Minsky tradition. We decided to call the theater adjoining Philadelphia Jack O'Brien's Boxing Gym and Roseland Dance Hall, the Oriental—or to be more precise, Minsky's Oriental Theatre. In its last incarnation it had been a movie house, but now we were passing it from films to flesh. We tentatively scheduled a grand preview opening for November 26, 1936, or thereabouts. One reporter from the *World-Telegram* asked how we were going to convert the British murals that were on the wall to something with an Oriental flavor. H.K. answered the reporter with a grin, taking out the ever-present cigar from between his teeth. "We'll just leave them," he said, "and take the clothes off." The reporters kept probing us regarding our attitudes toward Abe, but we stuck to our family loyalties: "We are on the most friendly terms with Abe," I explained to the press. As to our actions since we left Weinstock's fold, I told them, "We have had a vacation and it was very refreshing. This is what burlesque needs, to get out of the rut."

"This house is going to be very different," I explained to Sutherland Detlinger of the *World-Telegram*. "Now it will be from the *Follies* to Minsky's. We're getting girls from the *Follies* and we are sending out a call for musical comedy girls. The two classes we are going to cater to are the seasoned burlesque-goers and the Park Avenue type. Maybe Gypsy Rose Lee will come back to us." (Gypsy was then working in the *Follies*.) "You know she always said she could make more money in burlesque." I explained that our plan was to have spacious lounges, air conditioning, and a Park Avenue Row. "We're going to have two hundred seats raised above the level of the rest of the orchestra for the Park Avenue crowd," I explained.

"Why not have four hundred?" H.K. suggested.

"We couldn't get that many," I said. "But we can get two hundred. We're going to have fourteen sets of earphones too, for the dowagers, so that they won't miss the comedy. And you can't get a seat in Park Avenue Row unless you wear formal attire."

There had been nothing like this in burlesque before.

While the reporter was talking to me, I had on my desk a letter from a Stamford, Connecticut, constable, who wanted four tickets to the opening on the cuff in exchange for the distributing of 200 show cards and a batch of photographs of the girls we planned to have in the show, including Julie Bryan, formerly of the *Follies,* whom we were building up as the new Gypsy Rose Lee.

We also planned to have an Oriental dancer in a glass booth in the lounge. It used to be a broadcasting booth before we took over the theater, and this seemed a good way to utilize it—to demonstrate the historic origins of burlesque in the contortions of a Little Egypt–type dancer. We planned to have two Oriental musicians serenading her, so that customers who were tired of standing around in the intermission between shows could go there and be amused. We'd also arranged with Howard Willard of the Artists' Guild to have an art gallery in the lounge, with pictures of subjects that would appeal to burlesque-goers on sale.

We also planned to keep the girls and cast happy with a roof solarium and a free lending library so they could educate themselves between shows.

"Earl Carroll used to demand that his girls stay out of the sun," I told the *World-Telegram* reporter. "The Minskys demand that their girls stay *in* the sun."

At the preview, we told the press we hoped to have "the Cream of the City, the Four Hundred and every luminary and the famous ex-Burlesquers, like Fanny Brice, Bert Lahr, Bobby Clark, with Milton Berle as Master of Ceremonies."

"The doormen and ushers are going to be dressed as Orientals," I added.

"And the executives too," H.K. said. (H.K. was so excited that he was much more forthcoming in these interviews than he had ever been before. Usually he was the silent partner. Now he was the comic chorus. I was delighted at his enthusiasm.) Of course, I'll be the first to admit that much of this was hype. We didn't always know how many of our ideas could be realized, but the more talk there was in the press, naturally, the better it was for us. *Collier's* magazine sent a reporter to see us and ran a double spread with photos timed to appear just after the opening. The *Collier's* reporter picked up on some of our best ideas:

> Messrs. H.K. and Morton Minsky were not satisfied with the traditional method of obtaining new burlesque talent and an innovation at the Oriental Theatre is a training school. Its hours will be somewhat unconventional; it will convene along toward midnight after the final show and its classes will continue until dawn. The courses will be unconventional, too. Minsky College will give lessons in dancing and singing. The most important course will be in the fine points of the strip act.
>
> "It's not easy to get strip girls," Dean Morton Minsky will tell you. "It's impossible merely to pick out some pretty chorus girl and tell her to undress. For one thing it would be indecent. For another she wouldn't hold the audience. Stripping, you see, is an art. The girl must have great personality, poise and a sense of rhythm. She must have rhythm because she takes off her clothes in time to music. She must also be able to dance a little. It helps if she can sing."
>
> The graduates of Minsky College will get jobs at the Oriental or in other houses. Dean Morton Minsky is hopeful that another Gypsy Rose Lee will be developed in good time.

If you'd like to get an idea of what we looked like, at least to one magazine writer at that time, I'll give you his impressions included in the rest of the aforementioned article:

Mr. Morton (that's what all his associates call him) is in his early thirties. He is a small man and quite dapper, with thinning black hair and eye-glasses. From his well chosen phrases and his quiet voice you might infer that he has some cultural background.

And this is what the writer Henry F. Pringle had to say about H. K. at that point:

> H. K. Minsky, who is in his middle forties, talks rather less than his younger brother, but is in full agreement with his philosophy of burlesque. He is dark, chunky in build, wears tortoise-rimmed glasses and has an air of subdued weariness about him. He takes care of the production end of the business, which may account for the weariness.

Most gratifying was the fact that our old friends at *The New Yorker* devoted considerable space to the upcoming opening of the Oriental, at the same time explaining the confusion over the diffusion of the Minsky name:

> Another burlesque theater, Minsky's Oriental by name, will open almost any minute now on Broadway, just below 52nd Street. This brings the total number of Minsky theaters in Greater New York to five, and complicates the Minsky situation almost beyond our ability to make it clear. The increasing number of Minsky places does not as you might suppose mean prosperous expansion under one management. Rather it signifies disintegration—Minsky splitting off from Minsky, non-Minskys operating by legal sleights under the Minsky name. Helluva mess, altogether.

The New Yorker went on to summarize the history of the four Minsky brothers on Second Avenue and of our subsequent move without Abe to the Republic.

> In the course of this move a Mr. Weinstock and a Mr. Hertzig entered the picture, as promoters and backers—the Minskys have always been artists rather than businessmen.
> The first schism came when Abe, the oldest of the tribe, had words with his brethren and branched out for himself. He opened Minsky's Gaiety, at Broadway and 46th Street, and Minsky's

(New) Gotham, in Harlem. The three Minskys remaining at the Republic then began calling their theater Billy Minsky's. Billy had always been the most aggressive and inventive of the brothers, and had received the most personal publicity. He died several years ago and the surviving partners bought from his widow the rights to use his name. The Republic thus acquired the sole legal right to the phrase you see on the marquee: "The Only Billy Minsky's Theatre." The rumor is that the widowed Mrs. Minsky is paid $40 a week for this privilege. The Republic management also opened another flesh pot in Brooklyn, bringing the total to four. Last spring the two Minskys remaining with Mr. Weinstock and Mr. Hertzig at the Republic got fed up and moved out. These Minskys, Herbert and Morton, are the youngest of the original four, and the only ones who went to college. They have foresightedly moved even further uptown, locating near Roseland, the Guild Theatre, and Philadelphia Jack O'Brien's Gymnasium.

All the competing Minsky houses are run on a stock-company basis, but the Oriental may, later on, book "circuit" shows—units which travel from city to city. All the girls are, naturally members of the Burlesque Artists' Association, a *very* strong union. Chorus girls get a minimum of $25 a week, strippers a minimum of $40. People who keep their ears close to the ground tell us that litigation is pretty sure to break out among the Minskys. Mr. Weinstock, having paid good money for the name of Minsky, is indignant at others using it; Abe Minsky and the Herbert-Morton clique, besides being mad at each other, are both mad at Mr. Weinstock for operating as Minsky when his name is Weinstock. The situation is further complicated by the fact that, to offset Mr. Weinstock's Mr. Hertzig, Abe Minsky has a partner named Mr. Herk while those in the show predict that Herbert and Morton, the Oriental Minskys, will have the support of a Mr. Hirst, president of an independant burlesque association. Minsky, Minsky, Minsky, Herk, Hirst, Hertzig. Trouble, trouble, trouble.

Listen, it's no trouble when *The New Yorker* starts plugging your new burlesque house. It is a lot better than a sharp stick in the eye.

So interest was mounting and mounting. We had formal engraved invitations printed up, with an idealized sketch of the sphinx at the top being adored by a fetching young lady with outstretched arms and clad in a diaphanous gown. Under the sphinx it read like this:

H. K. MINSKY & MORTON MINSKY
CORDIALLY INVITE YOU TO ATTEND
THE GALA PREMIERE
OF THEIR NEW
ORIENTAL THEATRE
BROADWAY NEAR FIFTY-FIRST STREET
ON XMAS NIGHT
FRIDAY, THE 25TH OF DECEMBER
AT 8:45 O'CLOCK
FORMAL
Two Complimentary Tickets
Will be mailed you upon receipt of enclosed Request Card

The whole thing was done with raised engraved printing and sent to prominent friends and members of the press.

Meanwhile, we had come up with even more gimmicks to class up the act. We had decided that we would have a woman named Adrienne the Psychic reading fortunes free of charge in the lounge and that we would serve free coffee and snacks, the way they did in the little art movie houses in the area.

We had hired Norman Bel Geddes, our old friend from Second Avenue, to do some of the sets and to redo some of the murals in the lounge. Although we didn't have Gypsy, she agreed to come to the opening night and break a bottle of champagne on the box office in commemoration of her origins with Minsky. We did, however, have Margie Hart to give the show a good send-off for the first few weeks, and we had the best comics in the business, Phil Silvers and Hank Henry.

There was a successful Broadway musical on the boards at the time called *Red, Hot and Blue*. We announced that we were going to call our new show *Red, Hot and Nude*, but Vinton Freedley, the producer, objected and obtained an injunction.

After we had milked all the publicity we could out of our fight with the Broadway producer, we retitled our show *Swing Baby, Swing* and sat back to anxiously await the most exciting Christmas Eve in our lives. It would be the most elegant and lavish burlesque ever produced and a tribute to our dead brother, Billy—or so we hoped.

To make sure that nobody would still be confused even after *The New Yorker* article, we put this note on the back of the opening night program:

To our Patrons:

This theater is operated by real, living Minskys (H. Kay and Morton). It was these Minsky Brothers who created for your pleasure such nationally known theaters as the National Winter Garden, long popular on the Lower East Side, immortalized in verse by such ultraintelligent poets as Hart Crane and in prose by John Dos Passos. It was these Minsky Brothers who directed and produced *Life Begins at Minskys* at the Hollywood, Cal., Playhouse in June, 1935, which created a sensation among the Hollywood sophisticates. It was these Minsky Brothers who produced and directed the glamorous shows on the Supreme Burlesque Circuit in 1934, which played in Brooklyn, Boston, Baltimore, Albany, Newark, Philadelphia. It is these Minsky Brothers who take pride in the success of their former stars, like Tom Howard, and Gypsy Rose Lee, and who now have the pleasure of personally operating this theater—MINSKY'S ORIENTAL BURLESQUE—the finest burlesque theater in America.

Underneath this was a plug for our psychic:

"ADRIENNE"
FAMOUS INTERNATIONAL PSYCHIC
SEES ALL!—KNOWS ALL!—TELLS ALL!
ASK HER ABOUT ANYTHING!
LOVE—MARRIAGE—BUSINESS—HEALTH
MISSING PERSONS—COMING EVENTS

Maybe we should have consulted Adrienne ourselves to put our minds at ease.

38

STRAIGHT MAN: Are you getting a little on the side?
COMIC: I didn't know they moved it.

———————————————•———————————————

SO THAT CHRISTMAS EVE we had all the hoopla going—the stilt walkers, the men on the street handing out publicity, ads in all of the papers, the works.

And the audiences responded. Did they come! And plenty of them showed up in black tie, as demanded on the invitations. It was a regular social event. Probably should have been reported on the society pages instead of in the show-business section of the papers.

The house seemed excited and appreciative, and all the acts got big hands from the crowd. The comments at the intermission were fantastic. "What a darling show," one Park Avenue dowager said. "I never knew burlesque could be like this!" another lady commented. "Hot stuff!" a broker who had survived the Crash added. The house was oversold, with very little papering except for Park Avenue Row, where we had in fact handed out a certain number of freebies. As far as H. K. and I were concerned, you could hardly have asked for a more exciting opening. Phil Silvers was hilarious. Margie Hart was fast, hot, and furious, and our sub for Gypsy Rose Lee was prettier and slinkier, although she didn't have Gypsy's sophistication. Gypsy did us the favor of coming over from the *Follies* (Ziegfeld's name appeared on the marquee just as Billy's did over at the Republic, although they had died within months of each other) and broke a bottle of champagne over the box office to launch the theater and get herself some always-welcome publicity.

The next day the reviews ran the gamut. Brooks Atkinson, the important reviewer in New York, titled his piece MINSKY THE MAGNIFICENT.

The *World-Telegram* was almost as enthusiastic:

GOOD SPOTS
IN MINSKY
SHOW

Only the real Brothers Minsky could have done what was done on stage of the Oriental Theater last night. A tagline that would have left the Navy Yard blushing merged into "Caro Nome" by an operatic soprano. [Herbert's touch again.] An authentic dance team capered off the stage to let a stripper set a new record for unadorned epidermis on a square inch basis. . . .

The only fact of importance to real burlesque fans is that the Minskys (H. Kay and Morton) are back in town. Whether they have been away too long only the succeeding shows will tell. Last night's was hardly a glowing triumph. Average is the word for it, but the Minskys can do better.

Our problem was that trying to walk the tightrope between the city's oppressive minions and popular taste; we had apparently leaned a little too hard in the direction of good taste. One reviewer said this:

The fan fare (much ogling and leering in a high-class way) was great and delegations poured out in boiled shirts from Broadway, Park Avenue and the haunts of the literati. But "Swing Baby, Swing" unfortunately failed to reach the usual high standard of lechery which is associated with the name of Minsky.

So what can you do? Critics or no critics the public flocked to see the show. We grossed an average of $19,000 a week—not bad for Depression times. *Variety*, as usual, tried to stab the show to death.

"LIVING"
MINSKYS DROP A DUD ON
B'WAY IN "CLASSY" BURLESQUE TRY

By Joe Bigelow

"This theater is operated by real living Minskys," reads the program and the billing for this newest stock burlesque house in New York. H. Kay and Morton Minsky opened it on Christmas Night.

The difference between a "real living Minsky" and any other kind of Minsky isn't explained. Uncle Abe Minsky, whose diggin's are down the street a piece at the Gaiety, has been doing right smart financially of late, and besides, Izzy Herk has never been known to pick a dead one. . . .

As regards the late Billy Minsky, the majority opinion in the burlesque trade is that he held a virtual monopoly on the showmanship brains of his particular branch of the Minsky clan.

Well, *Variety* was never our glass of tea. As long as we were raking in $19,000 a week with a change of shows every week, we should worry about what Mr. Bigelow had to say about us.

A couple of months after we opened we got a tremendous break when Representative Samuel Dickstein introduced a bill in Congress to restrict the entry into the United States of foreign theatrical performers. Remember, it was still Depression and there were plenty of out-of-work American actors. Dickstein invited us to come to Washington and testify about the peculiarly American nature of burlesque, particularly the striptease. This was occasioned by the attempt by one of our competitors to import one Jacqueline Joyce, the Canadian Fur-stripper. This was incredible! A chance for a million dollars' worth of publicity. Both of us appeared before the House Immigration Committee to defend the great American art. Never, we averred, would a foreigner be permitted to exhibit her flesh in striptease on the boards of Minsky's Oriental.

"The shed-your-shirt Fandango was born in America, right on the stage of a Minsky theater, and American it will remain, they vowed," the *World-Telegram* reported, and newspapers quoted us in headlines from coast to coast and abroad too. (Miss Jacqueline Joyce got a job at a nightclub called Mario's Mirador for $150 a week.)

The day after our appearance before the committee, we held a press conference in our office. There I announced the new Minsky motto: "The Stars and Strips Forever!"

"The dapper mustachioed Morton rolled [the phrase] over his tongue appreciatively," the *World-Telegram* reported.

"Hot stuff, eh?" Herbert said.

"It's patriotic and it's practical," I explained, loving every minute of it.

Herbert told the reporters, "It will be a real inspiration to our pupils. It will give them something fine to think about as they practice and practice again, wiggling out of their clothes at just the psychological moment."

I put in my two cents: "The striptease has been called vulgar. Such talk. It isn't vulgar at all. It is art. Sure it's vulgar in some places, but never in our theaters."

Now it was Herbert's turn: "A striptease artist must be tall. She's got to have poise and personality and that certain something.

"She's got to learn how to put that something into the unhooking of every garment. She's got to know how to keep in time with the music as she slithers out of her dress, peels off her brassiere, strips off her p—"

"Now, Herbert," I interrupted him.

"I was going to say 'petticoat,'" said Herbert a little stiffly.

We had a chance to talk a little more about our striptease college, of which I was the dean. I got some mileage out of that. Herbert then got back to the business in Washington and quoted the punch line he had prepared as a finale for his speech but that laughter and applause had drowned out at the House hearing.

"About this bill," Herbert said, "we have to say that foreign governments have been stripping Uncle Sam for a long time. Now it's time to strip them, and we American Minskys should take care of the stripping."

This was probably the biggest publicity coup that we had ever scored, but unfortunately all the attention and the increase in business only stirred up our enemies to new efforts. A couple of months after the congressional hearing excitement, it seemed as though brother Abe was going to get an equal publicity coup. A complaint led to a court case against his New Gotham Theatre back in August 1936 by Sumner finally came to trial on April 8, 1937, after many postponements. The newspapers were all hopped up about the story, and the courtroom "played to a packed house liberally sprinkled with women," according to one newspaper. Another reported, "The court was jammed with the typical burlesque-show audience hoping to get a peek for nothing."

The fact is that much of this "typical burlesque audience" consisted of witnesses for Abe. John Sumner got on with his usual stiff-necked and comical description of the sins he had witnessed. He told the court that he had paid $1.25 for a box and sat five feet from the stage. Minutely he described the strippers' actions. They worked in a white light. They made alluring and seductive motions with their bodies. One of them, Muriel Lloyd, he claimed, exposed her intimate person completely. People in the court giggled and the judge got angry: "If there are persons here for entertainment purposes, I'll ask them to step out."

But nobody left. This was a terrific show and for free.

After lunch the parade of witnesses continued. One of the stage electricians took the stand. Abe's lawyer interrogated the man closely.

Q. Are you a married man?
A. Yes.
Q. How long have you been married?
A. A long time.
Q. How long have you been working in burlesque theaters?
A. Since before I was married.
Q. What sort of lights do you use for a strip number?
A. The stage lights are dark blue.
Q. How about the spot?
A. Usually it matches the color of the strip woman's costume.
Q. In all the years you've worked in burlesque theaters, have you ever known a strip woman to work in a *white* light?
A. Never!
Q. Have you ever seen a strip woman expose herself completely?
A. No!

Then Maurice G. Wahl, the assistant district attorney, took over.

Q. Are you in a position to see what's going on?
A. I have to watch the principal all the time to manage the spot.

> *Q.* Have you ever seen a strip woman expose her breasts?
> *A.* Yes.
> *Q.* Her thighs?
> *A.* Yes.
> *Q.* Her buttocks?
> *A.* Yes.
> *Q.* The crevice *between* the buttocks?

The electrician became confused. He'd certainly seen that area but he didn't know how to answer the question. However, the clever DA tried to lead him into what would amount to an admission.

> *Q.* Have you ever seen a strip woman expose her *private parts*?
> *A.* No!

The audience was loving it all. The defense then called one of the ushers and had him say that his work required him to be a few feet from the stage on many occasions during the performance.

> *Q.* Have you ever seen a strip woman work in a white light?
> *A.* No.
> *Q.* Did you ever see a strip woman expose herself completely?
> *A.* Never!

Then they brought in the orchestra members, and the same questions and the same points were made. The stripper never worked in a white light, as Sumner said, and she never exposed her private parts. Next, the defense called to the stand a customer who said the same thing, and Assistant DA Wahl got on his back.

> *Q.* Where did you sit?
> *A.* In the fifth row.
> *Q.* You could have seen just as well from further back?
> *A.* Sure.
> *Q.* But you sat up close?
> *A.* Yes.
> *Q.* You wanted to get a good look?
> *A.* I like to sit down front.
> *Q.* You didn't want to miss anything?

The customer shrugged.

Q. At any time during the performance were you excited?

The guy gave him a look like "are you some kind of a moron or something?"

Then the strippers were called, and the court began to stir with excitement. They put Roxanne Sand and Jewel Sothern, Georgia's sister, on the stand. The defense attorney led them into a description of their act.

"Now show us where you put your hands," the defense counsel instructed Roxanne.

The judge got flustered at this. "Stop!" he ordered. "We're not going to have any of that *here.*"

Another girl, a stripper named Muriel Lord, also testified that she never in her life had taken off her G-string and she even denied that her performances provoked "whistling, stamping, and cheering."

Everybody denied ever working in a white light.

Next, a man of sixty was called who had attended the show every Thursday night for years. He confirmed that he had never seen a strip woman work in a white light either and that he'd never seen her expose her person completely, no matter how hard he tried.

It seemed as though Abe's team had put up a pretty good defense, and he was sure they were going to throw his case out of court. But the presiding judge, Lawrence T. Gresser (there were three judges sitting on this case!), found Sam Kraus, Abe's manager, guilty under Section 1140A of the Penal Law, the same silly regulation they'd been hitting us with all these years. At the same time, they announced that they were going to automatically revoke the Gotham's permit to operate and, worse yet, would initiate proceedings against all the other burlesque theaters, which included the Republic and the Oriental.

The next day, April 9, one morning paper carried the headline, obviously inspired by our testimony before Congress, "STRIP" TO THREE JUDGES IS NOT ART. That night, because of all the publicity, everybody in town toned down their act. We had the girls wearing heavily beaded fringes on the G-strings instead of the usual flesh-colored elastic ones. But there was standing room only. Most of the customers had never even seen a strip before. They were there because of the publicity. For ten days everybody was playing to packed houses. Of course, we had been doing pretty well even before that, but this was terrific. I even thought about sending a thank-you note to Judge Gresser. On April 18, Kraus got a $500 fine for his part in the crime. That seemed okay. We all made money out of it, and I was feeling very good toward Abe. We had been apart too long. But none of us had any idea how serious the conviction of Sam Kraus was to the whole world of burlesque.

COSTELLO: I got a new girl friend. She's from Maine.
ABBOTT: Oh? Bangor?
COSTELLO: Bang her? I just met her!

OUR SHOW HAD not even been drawing heat from Moss's office prior to Judge Gresser's announcement in court. But now it became apparent that Abe's trial was purposely held just prior to the time when all burlesque licenses came up for renewal on April 30.

I had to smile during the trial when Abe, being pushed around, opened his big mouth against License Commissioner Moss. He told them Moss hadn't accomplished one concrete thing since he had assumed office in 1934, and that was certainly an accurate statement of fact. Abe also pointed out in his parting shot that Moss was clearly prejudiced because his brother, B. S. Moss, found business very poor at his new Times Square theater, the New Criterion. It was a strong statement; it made the papers and also got Abe physically ejected from the courtroom.

The success of the Oriental and other theaters that opened in its wake seemed to stir up a whole new wave of puritanism. Churchmen of all faiths united, this time united in a common front. Jewish and Lutheran spokesmen joined the usual Catholic opposition in this assault. Rabbi Stephen S. Wise contributed this marvelous observation: "You cannot make these places decent. You might as well try to freeze hell." Patrick Cardinal Hayes's strenuous objections were echoed by the Lutheran Church and the Lord's Day Alliance. Organizations that had previously remained aloof, such as the Catholic Charities, now attacked burlesque on aesthetic grounds: "There is no element of truth in it. It has no element of goodness or of beauty, the three fundamental requisites of art in any form, whether it be literature, drama, or painting."

They even claimed that sex crimes were rampant throughout the city because of burlesque. A Reverend Brougher of Brooklyn, who had been hacking away at the Star Theatre for years, testified that a father in his neighborhood saw a burlesque show, then went home and attacked his own daughter. Three irate women swore that burlesque conditions were degrading, and their testimony seemed really appalling until it was revealed that none of them had ever been inside a burlesque theater. But the hunt was on.

Adding to the general hysteria, the district attorney of Brooklyn awoke from several years of lethargy and led three raids against the Star, Oxford, and Werba, which he now decided were "largely responsible for the sex degeneracy and sex crimes of the City."

The Oriental was going great guns with its new show every week. The box office was very happy, and the whole business seemed to have settled into a very pleasant rut of prosperity despite the bluenoses. We all felt secure that the Court decision, which chastised Moss for taking on the role of the censor, would keep the La Guardia administration off our backs for some time. In the April 16, 1937, issue of *Minsky's Oriental News*, the program for the Oriental Theatre, we took gleeful advantage of the great publicity break we had gotten from the Dickstein committee in Congress. An item on the front page ran like this:

HELLINGER DUBS EUROPE
"GREAT STRIPPER, TOO."

In "Hellinger's Hunches," Mark Hellinger's popular gossip column in the N.Y. Mirror, Mark Hellinger makes the following pertinent observation on burlesk, after the Minsky Brothers' historical appearance before the Dickstein Bill Committee:

"The Minsky Brothers have told a Congress group that they want no foreign strip tease artists invading burlesque.

"Aw, be reasonable, boys. After all, Europe has such swell

strip-tease artists. Remember the neat way in which they took the shirts off our backs during the World War?"

In the same program was an ad that gives you an idea of the prices of things in those Depression years. It was for the Gardner Bar opposite the theater: A White Horse Scotch was twenty-five cents, a Calvert's whiskey was fifteen cents, and a bonded Overholt was twenty-five cents.

Actors in Broadway shows had taken to coming to our late-night Friday and Saturday performances. Already we had entertained Gertrude Lawrence, Jackie Coogan, Margaret Sullavan, and e. e. cummings. There was an announcement in the program that on the following week we would entertain the entire cast of the Rodgers and Hart hit show *Babes in Arms*. Our show that week was titled *Honest Tease the Best Policy,* and it featured the best comics in the business: Phil Silvers, Hank Henry, and Al Golden, Jr., as well as Tommy Raft.

Commissioner Moss's hearings to renew our licenses, which were now extended only on a three-month basis, was coming up on April 30, but neither we nor the other burlesque operators were worried. After all, didn't the State Court of Appeals stand behind us?

On April 28, the day when we were all applying for renewal of our licenses, which expired on May 1, we were summoned to a public hearing at Moss's office on 105 Walker Street. According to Moss, a petition containing 1,000 signatures had been presented to Mayor La Guardia requesting this hearing. The offices were jammed with witnesses rounded up by Sumner and by a Mr. Thomas J. Scanlon, an attorney and an officer of the Knights of Columbus. It was like the last days of the Inquisition. Moss and his cohorts produced a steady stream of witnesses who described burlesque performances as inciting "not only immorality but bestiality and degeneracy."

Our old friend Reverend Brougher of the Baptist Temple in Brooklyn told the hearing that not only had burlesque shows incited fathers into attacking their own daughters, but on several occasions he had been forced to call the police of the Bergen Street Station to close brothels in the vicinity of his church. His claim was that these brothels were supported by men who visited the burlesque houses in the neighborhood. He didn't say who was supporting the millions of other brothels all over the world.

Reverend Christian F. Reisner from the Broadway Methodist Temple said that one of his parishioners, a Mrs. D. Leigh Colvin of the WCTU, had visited one of the theaters and "could not tell me the things she had seen." Two other women who also had never seen a burlesque show denounced our type of theater, saying that the posters outside were enough for them. Then another couple of guys, ministers who also had never been to a burlesque show, offered their condemnation.

Then there was some bad-mouthing by members of the Catholic Club. After hearing a few more complaints, Commissioner Moss said that "the strip-tease has been described often enough for the purposes of the record."

The next day, April 29, a Thursday, newspaper headlines reported the proceedings of the previous afternoon: CHURCHES DE-MAND END OF BURLESQUE; BURLESQUE ON THE SPOT AT HEARING; BURLESQUE BAN EXPECTED TODAY.

But the hearings continued the next day. There was a letter from Cardinal Hayes strongly urging that the commission refuse to renew our license.

Meanwhile, practically all of us were fidgeting in the last row, irritated and embarrassed by all this ridiculous testimony. We had the right to question these people, but it would have done no good. Besides, we were depending on the State Court of Appeals. Moss asked us over and over again if we had any defense, but none of us had anything to say, not even Abe. Our attorney, Jacob I. Goodstein, contended that Moss had no right to refuse us a license just because a performance did not suit him. But Moss ignored this.

There had been a series of sex crimes in the New York area just before license renewal time, and without any connecting evidence whatsoever, they were judged a logical development of the supposed moral chaos brought on by burlesque shows.

There was no doubt in my mind that one of the main reasons for Moss's vehemence in this matter was the publicity we had drawn to the area, and the fact that we Minskys had brought burlesque from the back alleys to Broadway, where the whole world could see it. As far as Moss was concerned, the die was cast; he had the political clout, and he knew that his move would be popular with his boss, La Guardia.

On May 2, Moss acted with his unprecedented, and in my opinion illegal, decision by refusing to renew the license for all fourteen existing burlesque houses and denying applications for three new licenses. In his opinion Moss stated:

> After a hearing . . . and after listening to the many witnesses representing civic and religious organizations, and reading the letters of protest from citizens and organizations that have come to my attention, I am satisfied that the proof before me clearly indicates that the type of performance, the language used, the display of nudity, are coarse, vulgar and lewd and endanger public morality and the welfare of the community and are a disgrace to the people of the City of New York.
>
> In 1934, I started to work with the burlesque people as one who understands the theatrical business. I tried to make the burlesque houses family places instead of being largely only for men. . . .
>
> The lack of imagination and the lack of showmanship as well as the general caliber of the men running burlesque is such that they do not understand that clean entertainment pays and the vulgar, cheap performances do not.

He should only have looked at our box-office receipts! Mayor La Guardia, as Moss had expected, was absolutely thrilled by the commissioner's performance. He told the papers, "This is the beginning of the end of incorporated filth." (I wish he could have lived to see that same block as it is today, with open hard-core sex acts and no pretense at theater, comedy, or humor.) "This news brings joy to my heart. . . . May God bless our Commissioner of Licenses."

If you think I'm being too hard on the Little Flower, here's what Lawrence Elliott, an admiring biographer, said in his book *Little Flower: the Life and Times of Fiorello La Guardia:*

> But he was not perfect. For it was La Guardia, the mayor who brought the City Center for performing arts and $2 opera tickets to New York, who also drove the Minsky brothers and their inimitable burlesque shows out of town. His puritanical streak, that sense of moral outrage, was so highly developed that he could make no distinction between a truly original theatrical genre, only one part of which featured the unadorned female breast, and ordinary prostitution; or between a work of literature with some four-letter words, and magazines with flagrantly lewd cover illustrations publicly displayed; or between church bingo and the

numbers racket. To him they were all the same, and he railed away at them with fine impartiality, sometimes making himself look silly.

On April 30, 1937, a time when the six Minsky burlesques in New York starred such wonderful entertainers as Phil Silvers, Red Buttons, Abbott and Costello, and Gypsy Rose Lee, when New York theater critics from A. J. Liebling to Brooks Atkinson were celebrating the genius and genuine good fun of burlesque, La Guardia refused to renew the Minsky theater licenses, banned the very use of the words *Minsky* and *burlesque* in theatrical advertising, and so put them all out of business. And throughout this favored land there are men with long memories, now well into their middle years, who have never forgiven him.

At any rate, we were all stunned by this action by Moss. About a thousand actors were put out of work, as well as an equal number of stagehands and musicians. We had thought that he'd do something a bit more drastic than before—like imposing another set of severe restrictions—but we couldn't believe that he would abolish the industry entirely. These complainants—the clergymen, the religious organizations, and the professional reformers—were prepared to testify equally against nightclubs, cabarets, and Broadway revues. Naturally, we got together and initiated a formidable barrage of stays, writs, mandamuses and superseding writs. But the newspapers had stirred up public opinion to the point where the whole atmosphere of the city was against us. All of our maneuvers failed. In Brooklyn, a grand jury voted indictments against all the theaters in that borough. In Albany, a bill was introduced authorizing, in effect, an official censor for all theatrical ventures.

Moss the big mouth attacked us personally and said that "the Minsky Brothers cannot be trusted with a license."

We blasted back, "The two of us will match our private lives against the commissioner's any day."

Our only hope was to keep the theaters open until November, when there would be an election and maybe the Little Flower would be voted out of office. In June we had a meeting with the mayor, and there was some hope that he might let us reopen by June 25. But nothing happened. On June 24 the *Herald Tribune* remarked, "The last vestiges of the once flourishing art of burlesque disappeared yesterday afternoon."

But anyway, after a couple of false starts, we were allowed to open in collaboration with Gene Buck, president of ASCAP (American Society of Composers, Authors, and Publishers), who would be a liaison between the mayor and the Department of Licenses. He was supposed to establish a new code of burlesque or, rather vaudeville, or "vaudesque" as some of the presentations were called. We burlesque operators set up an organization to perform with this ridiculous concept, knowing that we could not stick to it but hoping we could somehow last until the mayor was out. We called it the Variety Revue Theaters Association. The constitution of the association said that we were to "provide for regulation and supervision stage entertainment presented by members of the Association and to promote and uphold standards of decency with respect thereto, and to improve the artistic value of such entertainment."

What could we do? They had us up against the wall. The Department of Licenses, in order to ensure that everything would stay nice and above board, required all of us to post a $1,000 bond apiece and agree to forfeit $500 for any breach of faith. They appointed a board of censors, headed by one John F. X. Masterson, an attorney and chancellor of the Columbus Council of the Knights of Columbus, which was one of the most zealous opponents of the burlesque industry. This make Masterson practically the tsar over the entire burlesque field.

Now that the mayor's hangers-on had practically stabbed the industry to death, all of a sudden some of the newspapers spoke up on our behalf. The *World-Telegram,* in its July 14, 1937, issue, editorialized: "The text of this agreement seems to us one of the most shockingly dictatorial black-jacks we ever read. . . . It is a precedent for strangulation of almost any form of expression." And even with our signing this strangling order, the licenses we got were only good for ninety days.

All of this had brought H. K. and myself closer to Abe, and we decided that we would join forces, uniting the Minsky brothers for the first time in five years. We looked forward to the new future together, although a lot of good it would do at this point. Business was absolutely rotten. *Variety,* which had always been poking its lance at us for being filthy, lewd, and so on, now pointed out what we all knew from the beginning: "CLEAN BURLEY DOESN'T PAY—NEW YORK FINDS." Its correspondent Joe Schoenfeld commented, "It's not a vaud revival—it's just the pushing back of burlesque about ten years." Through this impossible pressure all of the Brooklyn houses with the exception of the Star, closed.

Since New York was the center of show business, the effects of Moss's decision were felt all over. "Burlesque business is terrible in all parts of the country," *The Billboard* reported in November. "Chicago, once the home of a robust burlesque theater, was now devoid of a single standard burlesque house. The elaborate Rialto Theatre, facing a revocation of its license much as we had in New York, went out of business. Even the Folly Nickelodeon, whose admission was only five cents, closed. All the scratch houses, such as the National and State Harrison, were open but struggling. In Boston the old Howard managed to hang on, still drawing from its Harvard enthusiasts, but that was about all that could be said for New England."

In New York we waited impatiently for Election Day, although all the predictions were that LaGuardia would sweep in. He did, and we knew now that we would have Moss on our hands for another four years.

Moss, however, didn't content himself with just reviling us personally; he was so infuriated about the way in which our name had become identified with burlesque theater that he said that henceforth the name "Minsky" could not appear on any theater marquee as being implicitly obscene in itself! He also said that the word "burlesque" could not appear in any theater no matter what kind of show was in it. So according to Moss, *we couldn't even use our own name* on the theater no matter *what* kind of show we put on! And we were not the only ones who could not use their name; our old nemesis, Joe Weinstock, could no longer use Billy's name on *his* theater and was reduced to calling it the Republic French Follies. But you could still see on the marquee the place where Billy Minsky's name had been.

At the French Follies, Weinstock tried a routine to conform with the new rules. He put on an act in which a girl came on almost nude. A vaudevillian named Alphonse Berg had done this number at the French Casino and the Loew's State in vaudeville, where he brought on five girls dressed only in panties (but very artistic ones, you understand) and placed them on pedestals. Monsieur Alphonse, taking care not to swing his hips so there should be no evil memory of the striptease, began draping his models, adding brassieres, and flowing

folds of gossamer cloth, which finally after many twistings and tuck-
ings became gorgeous evening gowns.

One by one the now overdraped models swept off the stage. As the
last girl, dressed as a bride, approached the wings, however, Alphonse "accidentally" stepped on her train. The whole thing came
off and the girl was back where she started.

Forget it—nothing. If the audience couldn't have the old-fashioned strip, they were not coming back. And they didn't.

Fans of traditional burlesque transferred their loyalties to the
Empire in Newark and the Hudson in Union City in New Jersey,
where burlesque still operated in more or less the old style. Soon the
fans of burlesque, lonesome for the old days, were so numerous that
special buses were scheduled from 42nd Street for the convenience of
customers of the Jersey burlesque scene.

Just before we gave up entirely, I had the idea that we might put
on an all-black show. We were the first to work with a good many
black comics in burlesque, including Pigmeat Markham, who was
the originator of the "Here Come de Judge," skit which later became so popular on television. We had also used the Berry Brothers,
Hamtree Harrington, and other black acts long before mixed theatrical performances were generally tolerated in this country. I had
the idea of getting Erskine Hawkins's band, along with a twenty-girl
chorus and the great dancing act the Berry Brothers, as well as some
of the top black comedians, including Markham, but in the general
theatrical depression that followed Moss's announcements, that particular project never came about.

And so it was that that in November, not quite a year after our
glamorous and much heralded opening, I was forced to close the
Oriental; the Apollo folded at the same time. It was the end of an
era. We were closed, broke, and out of business permanently. Burlesque was, in effect, finished in New York for good. At least that
was the way it seemed to us at the time.

The Minskys were down but not quite out though. We still had a
few plans up our sleeves to keep ourselves alive in the theater.

CHAPTER

40

SOUBRETTE: We had to shoot my dog last night.
STRAIGHT MAN: Was he mad?
SOUBRETTE: Well, he certainly didn't enjoy it!

SO THAT SEEMED to be it. After twenty-five years, in which we had risen to become the symbol of quality burlesque, we were shut down, broke, kerflooey, and not even allowed to use our own name. Moss said that it would be "contrary to good order and public decency and would be dangerous for the morals and welfare of the community." We tried all sorts of things afterward, some of them at the National Winter Garden. We ran some quality foreign films, such as the Polish-made *Yoshe Kalb*. We held benefits for the victims of the Spanish Civil War. We put together a legitimate show that we auditioned for the Shuberts, but it never got going. Brooks Atkinson ran a sardonic piece about the whole problem:

NO MORE BURLESQUE
**Lovers of Beauty Are Welcome in the Old
Booths of Wickedness**

by Brooks Atkinson

Burlesque having been banished from this City by order of the Commissioner of Licenses, a new art is aborning. The iniquitous strip tease defiler of youth has been purified. The name M-N-KY can no longer invite homeless ladies and gentlemen off the streets. Even the word "burlesque," which used impudently to blaze above the marquees in the theater district, has been consigned to the index expurgatorious. Now a citizen can promenade through town secure in the knowledge that his sensibilities will not be harassed by the wanton photographs of girls on the sidewalk bulletin boards. Ever since Commissioner Moss removed burlesque from the theater last May the whole town has taken on a more wholesome appearance. The cheeks of the people in the streets are fresher, the flesh is firmer, the eyes are brighter and men have shown a gratifying willingness to go home at night. Many people who used to idle away their time in the booths of wickedness have started to improve their minds; they feel happier under the new dispensation. Commissioner Moss is to be commended for taking decisive action before it was too late.

Thanks, Brooks. I hope nobody took you seriously and did take a walk on West 42nd Street. I did.

H.K. was very depressed by the whole thing and at loose ends. I got myself a job as a real-estate broker—after all, I had a lot of experience with my father and had dabbled in the real-estate business all through the burlesque era. For H.K. I ultimately found a job with the USO, which was just starting up then. In 1939, during the Canadian World Exposition, we went to Toronto with the idea of doing a Minsky show there. We worked out a deal with the exposition and assembled a company. We had Bobby Sanford, who had been our producer at the Oriental as the producer, and his pal Meyer Davis, the society orchestra leader, put up the money. We took the company to Toronto. The show opened with a big bang in the press, but there was no business. People had never heard of Minsky up there, and there was no burlesque. We even had Phil Silvers on stage. Phil only the year before, while working at the Oriental, had been called for to do an interview with Warner Brothers. He had grabbed one of the comics on stage, Sid Stone, who later became famous as the pitchman on the *Texaco Show,* to go up and do the restaurant skit with him. The two had never worked together, but the audition apparently worked well because Phil ultimately wound up in Hollywood. He did many theater shows, such as *High Button Shoes* and *A Funny Thing Happened on the Way to the Forum* (both of these owe a great debt to burlesque, not only in Phil's performance but also in the material used).

Anyway, we lost our shirts in Toronto, but the closing of the theaters was not really the end of burlesque in New York. A couple of very smart producers named Michael Todd and Billy Rose saw that if they took the same material and presented it as a Broadway revue, they could make a very good buck, except that it would only be available to people who could afford the price of a Broadway ticket. Mike opened the *Star and Garter,* which ran for two years of sock-o box office using all solid burlesque material. And who was the hit of this inspiration of Todd's? None other than our own Gypsy Rose Lee, who by this time had become Todd's girl friend. His next epic was a Broadway musical called *Peep Show,* based on a dozen old burlesque skits, one of which had the same title. The show featured an exotic dancer called Lillie Christine, who was a big hit at $6.60 a seat. George White hired as many burlesquers as he could for his *George White's Scandals of 1941* to ensure the show's success. In the 1940s and 1950s many of the strippers who had worked for us began appearing in high-priced nightclubs along 52nd Street, such as the Samoa, the Harem, the Lido and the Famous Door, and also in the Village on Third Street. You could hardly call this burlesque. It was just stripping with booze and at a higher price, but there is no doubt that the strippers and some of the comics who actually worked with them also got their training with us.

In March 1962 Ann Corio, possibly the shrewdest one of them all, opened the show *This Was Burlesque* off-Broadway at the Casino East Theatre, twelve blocks uptown from the site of our old National Winter Garden. Her show was simply a rehash of all the best of burlesque, and it went over fantastically. Judith Crist of the *Herald Tribune* wrote:

> The joyous thing about "This Was Burlesque" is not simply that this is what it was, kiddies—but that we finally have on hand a simple, funny revue.
>
> First we have on hand Miss Corio herself, a charming fashion-plate as Mistress of Ceremonies, who doesn't even bare her legs until the close of the first act but emerges as a tantalizing comedienne in a "White Cargo" skit in the second act. . . . burlesque (has) a Sunday School simplicity in comparison with some of our "adult" movie offerings. . . . The end result is a pleasing evening

of relaxed entertainment. And that's what we haven't had nearly enough lately.

So New Yorkers were getting to see what burlesque was like—and at off-Broadway prices. As far as I know, that show of Ann's is still on the road, and it also produced a book, coauthored by Joseph Di-Mona.

Our old friend Jim O'Connor of the New York *Journal-American*, who had been a fan of Minsky's from way back, waxed nostalgic:

> Of course burlesque is not everybody's favorite type of enter-tainment since it really lacks class or superior quality. And it may have gone out with high button shoes. Yet there are theatregoers who would like to wear high button shoes if they were fashionable again. . . .
> Last night's lively show at the Casino East Theater was called "This Was Burlesque." Laughs in the audience were long and loud. To me this *is* burlesque, with all its faults and all its fun.

Meanwhile, in all those years I was always trying to get together a show that would revive the Minsky name whether Moss liked it or not. To put it in lights again. Finally, one day, I ran into Sterling Lord the agent and told him what I was interested in. He called me back two weeks later. He said, "I've got a writer, Rowland Barber, who's interested in talking with you." Before you knew it, Rowland and I had put together a book idea. He had just finished working on *Somebody Up There Likes Me*, the Rocky Graziano story, and he may then have been working on his Groucho Marx book. Anyway, we got together and we worked out a deal. Fifty-fifty. We talked on and off for two years. I told him as much as I could remember about bur-lesque, its earlier history, and my family background. Barber also did a lot of research on his own and interviewed many people who were still alive at the time. Out of this came an excellent novel, or "fantasy" as Barber called it, entitled *The Night They Raided Minsky's*. It was published in 1960.

The book was sensational, fascinating, and funny. It also told a lot about burlesque. But essentially it was fiction. Mademoiselle Fifi, its heroine, was not a stripper, and the raid in 1925 was hardly as spec-tacular as described in Barber's book, which was a fictional account. Besides, in 1927, when the fictional raid took place, I was just growing my pin-feathers in burlesque, so my part, in actuality in those years, would have been minimal. Still I'm not complaining. Barber did a fantastic job.

I was the technical adviser on the film, which I enjoyed; mainly, however, I enjoyed the fact that the name "Minsky," which had been perhaps dim in the public mind for quite a few years, was again in the public eye. The reviews of the film were terrific. *The New Yorker* and *Cue* used words like "superb" and "excellent," and the *Times*, too. It was put together with great feeling and taste, and there was nothing in it that even Mr. Sumner or Mr. Moss could have objected to. Unfortunately, Bert Lahr died in the middle of filming, and it had to be recut and reedited. This was William Friedkin's first important directing job, and subsequently he went on to win an Academy Award for *The French Connection.*

I think Billy was a genius in the way he integrated the material. On the set he would consult me mostly for the details about my family and sometimes for audience reaction to certain routines. Joseph Weisman, who played the part of my father, had a session with me.

"What kind of man was your father?" he asked. "Was he stern? What did he look like?"

I told him, "My father was a serious man, always impeccably dressed, wore rimless glasses, and was smooth-shaven."

Weisman looked disappointed. Then he said, "Do you mind if I play him with a King George beard—very neatly trimmed?"

"Be my guest," I said, "so long as you play him with dignity." I must say he was magnificent in the part, King George whiskers notwithstanding.

In the movie Jason Robards, Jr., played Raymond Paine, the straight man, Elliott Gould played my brother, Billy, and Britt Eklund played a highly fictionalized version of Mademoiselle Fifi.

It brought tears to my eyes when I remembered what my brother Abe had said to me before he died in 1960: "Kid, you're going to be the one to see the Minsky name in lights, I know it, and I want you to make every effort." Abe would have loved it. It was more than terrific.

After the spate of excitement over the movie and book, I remained at the realty firm of Brener and Louis as vice-president, but my years of experience were not lost because I specialized in theaters. At that time movie theaters were mushrooming all over the country, in suburban shopping centers, and that was one of my big specialties. I'm still at the office every day, selling co-ops and houses and theaters, but my mind will always dwell on the glory days between 1912 and 1937, when the Minsky name symbolized everything that was great about burlesque. As I walk down the sewer that Broadway has become and the block where we opened the Republic, I can't help but think that contrary to the predictions of Mr. Moss and Mayor La Guardia, the climate of that community has gone lower and lower ever since the night they closed Minsky's and tried to take our name away from us.

BLACKOUT

Some Burlesque Sketches

Based on Shakespeare
  "Anatomy and Cleopatra"
  "Julius Teaser"

Based on Broadway shows
  "Beyond Red Tights"
  "Vanities of 1937"
  "Boy Needs Girl"
  "Folies Brasièrre"
  "A Broad at Home"

Based on great literature
  "Panties Inferno"
  "She Stripped to Conquer"

Based on Song titles
  "Tease for Two"
  "Wake Up and Give"

Based on popular speech
  "Strip, Strip, Hooray"
  "Mind Over Mattress"
  "Her Strip Abroad"

Based on the Movies
  "Wake Up and Love"

Glossary

The asbestos is down.	The comics aren't getting laughs.
Bit or schtick	Scene or sketch
Boston version	A cleaned version
Bump	Moving the hips forward with a snap accentuated by thump on the drums
Cacky	Smutty
Cover up	Conceal lapses in the lines
Detracting	One comic stooges for another
Five-percenter	Artist's representative, agent or broker, now known as ten-percenter
Flannel mouth	Straight man with false teeth
Flash	Expose any part of the body
Gadget	G-string
Guy from Dixie	A performer who is no good
Guy from hunger	See *Guy from Dixie*
Grind	What goes before a bump. It's like writing the letter O with your pelvis
In one	Working between footlights and first curtain
Jerks	The audience
Joe Morgan	The show drunk
Lecturing on the skull	The straight man talks, the comic mugs
Liverhead	A poor study; can't learn lines
Milk the audience	Begging for applause
Mountaineer	An alumnus of the Borscht Belt

Nets	Brassieres and panties
Painted on the drop	He has no lines in a skit
Pick-out number	A chorus routine in which girls are selected to do numbers as in a contest
Piece	A wig
Pitch	Candy butcher's spiel
Prim	The big voice, the prima donna
Quicky	Blackout
Quiver	Shake the bosom
Scissors	Cut the scene shorter
Shimmy	Shake all over
Skull	A doubletake or a mug
Sleeper jump	The top-floor dressing room
Slingers	The teasers
Soubrette	Fast dancer, female, usually juvenile
Street drop	Scene in from of the main curtain
Sunday school show	Warning the cops are out there
Switch	Girl's extra wig
Talking woman	A female who delivers lines in a skit, often an ex-stripper
Tit serenader	Male house singer who doubles in bits, generally a juvenile, like Robert Alda
Trailer	Chorus of music for strip girl
Yock	Big laugh from the audience

Typical Minsky Burlesque Show
as seen by the Department of Licenses

Exhibit D
CITY OF NEW YORK
Department of Licenses

In the Matter
of
POLICE DEPARTMENT and DEPARTMENT OF
LICENSES
vs.
HOLLY HOLDING CORPORATION.
premises 209 West 42nd Street.
Manhattan.

Hearing held on August 21, 1935, before Hon. Paul Moss, Commissioner of Licenses.

MR. Moss: This is a continuation of a hearing that was held on July 24, 1935. At that hearing police officers testified as to certain conditions in these theatres that day they wished to call to the attention of this Department and asked for a suspension of the license. The Department, therefore, instructed one of the inspectors of the Department to visit each of these theatres, which he did, and is now about to put into the record the conditions that he found those theatres in.

FRANK J. DONOVAN, who states he is an Inspector of the Department of Licenses, City of New York, Shield Number 68, connected with the Brooklyn Office of the Department of Licenses, first being duly sworn, testified as follows:

MR. MOSS: I want you to read the report into the record.

MR. DONOVAN (*reading from report*): As directed, I visited the Republic Theatre, located at 209 West 42nd Street, Borough of Manhattan, and beg to report as follows: This is a burlesque theatre operating under license number 3091 issued to the Holly Holding Corporation. On August 4, 1935, about 7 P.M., I purchased ticket #608582, stub of which is attached hereto, for the sum of fifty-five cents. Entered the theatre, sat in about the eighth row of the orchestra and observed a speaker offering the audience a booklet of transparent pictures given free with each purchase of a bar of Nestle's milk chocolate for the sum of ten cents. Then followed the offering of opera glasses that propel and repel and have a range of two hundred and seventy-five yards, making each seat a front-row seat. Orchestra played a selection. Curtain lifted on the artist studio scene: five show girls in statuesque positions standing in scenery frames wearing capes with breasts exposed, while twelve chorines engaged in a dance routine, followed by a female principal singing "What's the reason I'm not pleasing you"; a second female principal sings "If my heart could only talk," during the singing of which the six show girls walked from their frames holding back their capes, giving a full view of their breasts; a dance routine then followed led by another male principal, to the finish of this, the opening number. Straight man and comic next on stage; comic with a supposed "hang-over" telling about a party they attended, comic saying how the girl he was with woke up with her finger in her mouth and had no teeth and that he inquired, "Are you sure you had your finger in your mouth"; straight man and comic argue as to their ability in mathematics; straight man tells comic to put figures down as follows: "Eight balls, put your pants down, one goose and other figures"; straight man walks off, couple walk on conversing about marriage, while comic is figuring on a pad when the female asks her friend, "What is a baby?"; comic says, "I got it—nine months interest on a small deposit"; all exit. Chorine now appears in a Mexican number as Toreador while one show girl stands nude to the hips in red; they engage in a dance routine and six show girls wearing red capes, skirts and black hats with breasts exposed walk on stage; then follows a female principal in a rhumba dance, wearing skirt and breast covering, followed by a male principal singing; meanwhile the six show girls circle the stage walking with breasts exposed. Female now walks on stage and is introduced by means of a loud speaker as "Broadway's show girl—Ceil Von Dell"; she was wearing a long coat and yellow dress; she walks about in time with the music, then exits and returns minus the coat; she displays the backless dress, then shows both breasts and exits. The curtain lifts on a bedroom scene with a female wearing a pink gown while seated before a dresser when the comedian, as her husband, enters saying, "Good evening, Mrs. Open Switch," and while removing his coat, "Did you go to night school?" She: "Yes." He: "Get ready for your home work," and begins to undress. She says she wants to go out, which creates an argument; he starts to dress; they make up and speak of their early days together; how in the parlor with the lights turned low, he says, among other things, of their holding hands and how she could squeeze the knuckle, followed by his again removing his pants, which again starts an argument; he pulls on his pants while she pleads with him to stay in; they become friendly again, she saying, "Don't you remember our night?" He: "Yeah, how you got a little screwy." She: "And our trip to Niagara Falls?" He: "All you looked at was the ceiling." She: "And remember the precipice?" He: "What, the what?" She: "The precipice, the tons of water at the Horseshoe Falls?" He: "Oh, the precipice—the Horseshoe Falls, the horses were there." She: "Remember the hotel we stopped at, they gave us the bridal chamber?" He: "Yeah, you took it home for a souvenir." She: "Mother's coming to stay with us." The fight again starts, this time she dresses to leave and when ready to go he calls, "Stop," and has her remove the clothing he purchased for her, beginning with her hat until she stands in the gown, saying, "I cannot remove that, I'll be naked." He insists on its removal; she pleads if she takes it off what will she do then, when the head of another male pops from beneath the sheets and says, "Come in here, baby." End of skit. Twelve chorines come on stage wearing yellow hats and short skirts, followed by the show girls, who are introduced in [sic] the audience by means of a loud speaker as "Winnie Garrett"; "Dolores Hall"; "Patricia Harris"; "Joan"; "Connie Byron"; "Lilian Rogers"; all wearing long dresses; a dance routine completes this number. Straight man and comedian come on stage arguing: straight man asks, "How are you in arithmetic? Comic: "Fine." Straight man: "Add four and four." Comic: "Seven." Straight man: "Correct"; continuing, "How much is one from two?" Comic: "One." Straight man: "No, one from two makes three," then asks, "You're married, aren't you? You have a wife?" Answer: "Yes." "That's one, isn't it?" Answer: "Yes." Straight man: "Then you and your wife make two?" Answer: "Yes." Straight man: "Then you have a boy?" Answer: "Yes." Straight man: "Well, then, don't one from two make three?" A female wearing mourning comes on stage, crying; straight man says, "beg your pardon, lady." She: "Oh, something terrible has happened; I just came from a funeral; my husband died"; straight man repeats this to comedian, adding, "She's all alone." Comic says, "I'll talk to her"; then to her: "You have no husband, here's a couple of husbands out of work." She: "Would you like to hear my story?" meanwhile hands him her gloves; she then sings thus: "Oh, he laid on a long white table; he looked so sweet and nice," finishing with gyrations of her abdominal region. Comic repeats the question a few times, in answer to which she continues to remove her clothing piece by piece, until she finally stands wearing black net breast covering and scanties; there were wiggles and gyrations after the removal of each piece and the singing of her two lines above referred to. Straight man then says, "I'd love to see the tombstone and the grass, too"; she cries, "My poor husband died a natural death." Straight man: "No, lady, your husband didn't die a natural death." She: "Well, how did he die?" Comic: "You bumped him off"—gyrating his abdominal region; she says she's going back to her old job as charity worker; comic takes her arm, saying, "Charity begins at home"; all exit. End of this skit. Chorines come on stage with a male principal in a tap dance routine; one show girl stands in rear nude to the hips; next a female principal in a high kick specialty; chorines leave stage; male principal appears singing, "Speak to me of love," at the chorus of which six show girls walk on and at the finish of this number bare their breasts. Straight man and comedian now on stage; straight man saying he's been all around the world, in China, etc., and how he would like to take the comic to a party; comic explains he has a tuxedo, but that he has lost the front part of his shirt; straight man explains, "That's the dicky"; comic seems not to understand; then follows the removal of articles from two suitcases; just nonsense on the part of both, followed by their headline reading from two newspapers, thus: "Unclad woman escapes from hospital." Comedian: "Seventeen husbands missing." Straight man: "Man of eighty-six marries girl of sixteen." Comic: "Steady boarder wanted." Straight man: "Park commissioner orders all trees and telegraph poles cut down." Comic: "Ten thousand dogs go mad." Straight man: "Baby monkey born in Washington Zoo." Comic: "President Roosevelt blames Huey Long." End of this skit. Female principal comes on stage singing, "Hip, hip, hooray for the Eskimos," during the singing of which chorines are in the aisles and boxes tossing Eskimo pies—an ice cream confection—to the audience. Female fully dressed comes on stage singing, "I'm head over heels in love again"; at the finish of this number a male voice over loudspeaker introduces her to the audience as "Gladys Fox," who, while undulating about stage, begins her gradual disrobing; first by tossing her neckpiece in the wing, then dropping the top part of her dress, disclosing her brassiere; she then exits; loud applause brings her return before the footlights now minus the brassiere, exposing both breasts, as she slowly moves about stage, meanwhile unloosening and removing her dress by lifting the same over her head and disclosing her buttocks as her back faces the audience; she then turns about, showing a beaded arrangement at her pelvic region, her only covering other than the dress held on her arm. Straight man and comedian on stage in the scene "King Tut's Tomb"; straight man telling comic about the sphinx when comic called "Goldfarb" spies an apple at the base of the tomb; they share it and while eating it a male with a female comes on stage, he telling her, "This is the land of Egypt; that is the tomb of King Tut"; then, to the comic and straight man: "Should you swallow a seed of the apple you will instantly die." The couple then leave; comic inquires, "Where are you going?" He answers, "To the river Nile to watch the croco-diles play with their little crocks"; then a whiskered individual in white gown appears, saying, "Ha, ha, you dare eat the sacred fruit of old King Tut? You shall die. Choose the way. You will be buried one thousand feet below." Comic: "I don't care. I go home in the subway, anyway." Individ-ual: "You have twenty-four hours to live, you can have any pleasure you desire; I will give you the magic flute; play upon it. Beautiful women will appear. Remember, twenty-four hours to live." Comic: "Oh, go scrub your old woman's canary"; individual leaves, straight man plays the flute; fe-male appears wearing breast covering and purple skirt; comic says, "There's enough there for the Navy Yard." Straight man (to the female): "Who are you?" She: "Queen of the pyramids. Who are you?" He: "I'm a man." She: "What are they?" He: "Pants." She: "What are pants?" He: "Pants are something that hides concealed weapons." She: "I'm one of a thousand children" and makes as if to walk off. Straight man: "Where are you going?" She: "To my sister's tomb." Comic: "What?" She: "Tomb." Comic: "Oh." Straight man and female start to leave. Comic: "Hey, where are you going?" Straight man: "To sister's tomb to cut the grass around the edges." They leave; comic plays the flute, first saying, "I don't care if I get a goat"; he plays a tune, no one appears; he says, "I don't even get a skunk"; plays again and a female wearing breast covering and green skirt appears, asking, "Where am I?" Comic: "The good old Republic Theatre." She: "It looks so clean around here." He: "They scrubbed it out this morning." She: "What are you?" He: "A man." She: "Prove it"; he speaks of marriage and explains two can play it, only one can win; then of love and how it starts with a kiss; he starts to leave stage with her when straight man arrives and inquires, "Where are you going?" He: "I'm going to start to dig in"; all exit. Female comes on stage in long white dress; a male voice over loudspeaker at the finish of her song, "I'll Keep It New," introduces her as "Martha Lopez," who, with slow motion to slow music, begins her gradual disrobing act, first showing one breast, then both, stops long enough to raise her dress, exits; applause brings her return, both breasts exposed, stopping long enough to take off dress with her back to the audience, both buttocks showing; then faces about showing the beaded covering at her pelvic region; exits; repeated applause brings her return; now a footlight Eve, who, with wiggles of her abdominal region, and pawing of her torso, she worms her way off stage. Chorines now come on stage and circle around a pedestal on which stands a show girl nude to the hips; then a male appears, dances about the pedestal and exits; then a female does likewise; chorines finish this number in a routine dance in which the girl supposed to be in statuesque position is rolling her hips. Two comics and two straight men—just a quartette. A female with titian hair, silver-color dress, now appears singing, "And Then He Holds My Hand," at the finish of which she is introduced by a male voice over a loudspeaker as "Margie Hart," who loses no time in beginning her disrobing, first by dropping the left shoulder strap then the right; in a second she is nude to the hips, skirt hanging therefrom as she walks up and down at a fast pace; before exiting, drops the skirt, showing the spangled arrangement to match her hair at the pelvic region, her only covering as she goes off and on in answer to applause, apparently the feature stripper of this show. Chorines appear carrying suitcases while show girls stand nude to the hips in rear of stage; chorines engaged in routine tap dance on the suitcase, followed by a female principal wearing pink dress, singing, "Come On Dance, Don't Ask Me"; followed by a female in a specialty acrobatic dance and a male principal singing, "Sweet Mystery of Life"; chorines exit and return during this number wearing hats but nude to the hips; followed by all others of the company on stage, at this the finale of the show. Having seen the complete stage show, I did not wait for the showing of motion pictures which were to follow. I left the theatre about 9 P. M.

MR. MOSS: Anyone here appearing on behalf of the Republic Theatre?

VOICE: Yes.

Exhibit E.
Re Burlesque Show at the Republic Theatre, 42nd St.
August 28, 1935

SKIT

Doctor's office. Doctor at the telephone as curtain rises. Doctor's desk on right facing the stage, bed on left.

PATIENT: (man) enters saying: I am a very sick man.

DOCTOR: Well take off all your clothes and we will see what ails you.

PATIENT: That's too embarrassing.

DOCTOR: Oh, I'm used to seeing little things.

PATIENT: Little things. I've never had a complaint about it man or boy.
Patient takes off coat, trousers, and has on a long nightgown.

Doctor goes up to him and says, What you need is a good rest. Get into
bed.

Doctor puts his hands on the posterior of the patient feeling it and
squeezing it.

DOCTOR: You'll be all right—repeating it three times while feeling patient's buttocks. Patient gets into bed, pulls covers over him after doctor
leaves. A woman comes out of the left entrance on stage saying, I must have
it. I must have it, repeating this in a sing song voice and moving her stomach and buttocks advances to the side of the bed where the patient lies,
then leaves stage. Patient arises from bed, calling for the doctor, who enters
and calms patient and again repeats the act of feeling patient's buttocks,
saying, You'll be all right now, etc., repeating same. Patient says, What
were you before you were a doctor? Doctor says, I was a rear admiral. Doctor leaves, telling patient to go to bed. Patient does. Another woman enters,
crying, I must try it, etc. (repeating), moving her body back and forth, goes
up to the bed and leaves. Patient again calls doctor, who enters. Patient
tells him what happened and doctor again squeezes patient's buttocks and
patient says, Say, I'm beginning to like that, try the other side. Doctor
leaves after telling patient to go back to bed and patient says, I'm beginning to like that treatment. You get a finger wave and everything. A third
woman enters crying, holding her hands on her stomach just over her private parts, crying, while moving her stomach and buttocks backward and
forward. I just had it (repeating), going up to the bed and leaving. Doctor
again goes through the same proceedings. Then a man dressed up as a
Russian enters after patient is back in bed. The Russian makes a lot of
noise. The patient gets out of bed. The Russian takes a seltzer water bottle
from under his cloak and facing the patient squirts the contents of the bottle, aiming at the vicinity of the gown covering the private parts, which of
course wets that part of the gown. Russian leaves. Patient stands there yelling for the doctor and takes the part of the nightgown in front which is all
wet and starts to wring out the wet parts with his two hands, pulling out
the gown and twisting the gown in his hands until he has the part he is
twisting resembling the form of a penis. The doctor enters, striking the
hands of the patient away from the gown, saying, Oh you naughty boy.
Why didn't you call me first?

Another skit. Showing an artist on stage who is trying to get a married
woman to pose and another man at the side of the stage, telling what goes
on between the artist and the woman who are acting in pantomime. The
curtain in back of the studio represented on the stage rises, showing a

young woman naked, holding her both hands over her private parts, front view. The man at the side of the stage says, There is only one thing the matter with that picture—the girl's hands are too large. And later after the husband of the woman and the artist shoot each other and the woman is alone, the man at the side of the stage: I am left, let's go up to the park and I will show you how the squirrels bury their nuts.

A good many of the chorus appear during the scenes, breasts uncovered, and the four leading women, Margery Hart, Margot Lopez, Lillian Dixon, and Pat Paree, all come out at different times stripping breasts bare, till upon last appearance all nude except for covering of private part.

"Who's on First?"

The following is the origin of Abbott and Costello's "Who's on First?" The scene was played by Joey Faye and his wife, Judi.

JOEY: Oh, I'm so happy to see you. What are you doing downtown here?

JUDI: Well, I work here.

JOEY: You work around here?

JUDI: Yes, I do.

JOEY: Oh, that's wonderful because you are the only one that doesn't make me nervous. Why don't you have lunch with me some time?

JUDI: I'd love to.

JOEY: I'll tell you what I'll do. If you tell me the name of the street where you are, I'll come down in my car and I'll pick you up and we'll have lunch together.

JUDI: Sure.

JOEY: Well, tell me the name of the street you work at.

JUDI: Sure, Watt Street.

JOEY: All right, tell me the name of the street you're working on.

JUDI: Watt Street.

JOEY: Yeah, that's what I mean, tell me the name of the street you're working on.

JUDI: Watt Street.

JOEY: *I'm* asking you. Don't *you* ask me. Now, tell me the street. You don't understand. I'm asking you the name. Everything has a name. The street has a name. The city has a name. You have a name. I can't tell you what the name is, there are nice people out there. Now, what is the name of the street you work on?

JUDI: Watt. I'll spell it for you, okay? Watt. W-A-T-T. Watt Street, see?

JOEY: Oh! Watt! I thought you're making fun of me.

JUDI: Oh, come on, would I make fun of you?

JOEY: I'm sorry, will you still have lunch with me?

JUDI: Of course.

JOEY: So, you work on Watt Street. You must have a good job?

JUDI: Yes, I do.

JOEY: What are you doing on Watt Street?

JUDI: I'm dyeing.

JOEY: You look good.

JUDI: I feel good.

JOEY: Then why are you dying?

JUDI: I'm dyeing to live.

JOEY: You're starting again.

JUDI: . . . and if I can't dye I can't live. See?

JOEY: Look, let me give you a for instance.

JUDI: All right.

JOEY: Eight o'clock, I'm sick. Nine o'clock, I die.

JUDI: Oh, you can't dye.

JOEY: I can't dye? Why not?

JUDI: You don't belong to the union.

JOEY: I have to belong to a union to die?

JUDI: Oh, you want to dye as a scab? Go ahead, dye, but we won't recognize you.

JOEY: If I die, you'll recognize me.

Fifty years later Kate Smith said on her program, "And now we present two of the funniest men in America—Bud Abbott and Lou Costello."

The following is the development of the "Watt Street" skit, which became changed into the essential "Who's on First?" bit that was used in burlesque for twenty or thirty years before Abbott and Costello developed it on radio.

JOEY: Oh, excuse me. Miss, I'm a stranger hereabouts. Do you know all the people around here? I was looking for the manager.

JUDI: Oh, I'm the manager of the team.

JOEY: A lady manager?

JUDI: Sure, woman's lib, right?

JOEY: Well, tell me the names of the players so I can say hello to them.

JUDI: Well, they all have nicknames.

JOEY: The players have nicknames?

JUDI: That's right.

JOEY: Oh, you mean like Dizzy, Daffy? I have a nickname too.

JUDI: Oh, really, what is it?

JOEY: Dopey. You know the names of all the players. Tell me the names of the players.

JUDI: Okay. Who's on first; What's on second; third base, I Don't Know.

JOEY: You know the names of the players, right? All right.

JUDI: Who's on first; What's on second; third base, I Don't Know.

JOEY: You know the players, right? Maybe you don't hear too good. You know the players, right? All right. We'll take one player at a time. You got a first baseman. All right, tell me the name of the first baseman.

JUDI: Who.

JOEY: The man who plays first base.

JUDI: Who.

JOEY: The guy on first base.

JUDI: Who.

JOEY: I'm asking you, don't you ask me. I want to know what's the man's name.

JUDI: No, What's on second.

JOEY: I'm not asking who's on second. I don't know.

JUDI: Third base.

JOEY: How did we get to third base?

JUDI: Well, you just happened to mention his name.

JOEY: Well, if I happen to mention his name, who's—

JUDI: No, Who's on first.

JOEY: I don't care what the man's name is. Who's on second?

JUDI: Who's on first.

JOEY: I don't know.

JUDI: He's on third.

JOEY: We're back to third base again. You got a first baseman? Are you the manager? You paying the salary? When the first baseman comes up to your office, who gets the money?

JUDI: Every penny of it.

JOEY: If you say "Who," I'm gonna hit you right on the head now. I want to know the man's name on—

JUDI: Wait a second. Who's on first.

JOEY: I don't know. Third baseman. You gotta pitcher?

JUDI: That's right.

JOEY: Tell me the pitcher's name.

JUDI: Tomorrow!

JOEY: Let's get this straight once and for all. I'm a pretty good catcher too, right? All right, I'm the catcher. Now, suppose some guy hits the ball . . . bunts the ball. I'm gonna throw him out at first base. All right. I pick up the ball and throw it to who?

JUDI: That's the first right thing you said.

JOEY: I don't even know what the hell I'm doing anymore. And the hell with you too.

"Paid in Full"
(A Classic Burlesque Bit)

Scene takes place in an office. As the curtains part, the comedian and straight man are arguing.

COMIC: I don't care what you say, I worked for you and I want my money!

STRAIGHT MAN: Now don't get excited. I'm going to pay you.

COMIC: I know darn well you're going to pay me. I've waited a year for my money and I'm not gonna wait any longer!

STRAIGHT MAN: Well, how much do you think you've got coming?

COMIC: Well, there are three hundred and sixty-five days in the year and I get five dollars a day.

STRAIGHT MAN: In other words, you want five dollars for each day. That makes it three hundred and sixty-five times five. I'll figure out just how much you have coming to you. How many hours a day did you work?

COMIC: Every day I worked eight hours.

STRAIGHT MAN: Well, there's twenty-four hours in each day, and you worked eight hours a day, which means you worked one third of each day, which makes one third of each year you've worked. In other words, you worked one third of three hundred and sixty-five days. Now three goes into three, once—three into six, twice—and three into five goes once. That means you have one hundred and twenty-one days coming to you. Now, you didn't work on Sundays, did you?

COMIC: I should say not. I wouldn't work on Sundays.

STRAIGHT MAN: Well there are fifty-two Sundays in the year, so I will have to deduct fifty-two from one hundred and twenty-one. Which means that you have sixty-nine days coming to you.

COMIC: Yes, I know, but—

STRAIGHT MAN: Oh, yes, I almost forgot something else, we close for half day on Saturdays, do we not?

COMIC: Sure we do, but—

STRAIGHT MAN: That makes fifty-two half days or twenty-six whole days that we stayed closed. Now, deducting twenty-six from sixty-nine is . . . six from nine is three and two from six is four. That makes it exactly forty-three days you have coming to you.

COMIC: Say, wait a minute, you don't understand—

STRAIGHT MAN: Just a moment, *you* don't understand. Don't interrupt me, please. How long do you take off for lunch each day?

COMIC: One hour.

STRAIGHT MAN: That makes three hundred and sixty-five hours you took off to eat. Making it exactly fifteen days you spent eating.

COMIC: What? I ate for fifteen days?

STRAIGHT MAN: Yes, but not all at once. Just an hour at a time. Now I have to deduct fifteen days from forty-three. Five from three leaves eight and one from three leaves two. That makes it exactly twenty-eight days you have coming to you.

COMIC: Say, wait a minute—

STRAIGHT MAN: Now, where did you go on your vacation?

COMIC: Atlantic City.

STRAIGHT MAN: How much vacation do you take each year?

COMIC: I always take two weeks' vacation.

STRAIGHT MAN: Two weeks is fourteen days. Therefore I must deduct fourteen days from twenty-eight, which leaves fourteen days you have coming to you.

COMIC: You don't realize that—

STRAIGHT MAN: Just a minute, please. There are thirteen legal holidays in the year. Now, during these holidays we stay closed. Therefore I must deduct thirteen from fourteen, which leaves one day you have coming, and here's your five dollars. (*Gives comic a bill and starts to exit.*)

COMIC: Say, wait a minute.

STRAIGHT MAN: What do you want?

COMIC: (*handing bill back*): You forgot Social Security!

BLACKOUT

"The Gazeeka Box"
by Billy Minsky

Billy himself invented the "Gazeeka Box" skit, which became a standard on the burlesque circuit.

The sketch opens with the straight man reeling out a contraption that looks like a curtained phone booth. He backs it up to the upstage wall. "There it is, my friend," the straight man says to the comic, maybe Steve Mills. "The fabulous Gazeeka Box! I am willing to part with it because you *are* my best friend. I will let you have this fabulous Gazeeka Box for only one hundred dollars cash!"

> MILLS (*aside*): When did they let him out? (*To the straight man.*) "Why I wouldn't give you a hundred *cigar* bands for that old box."
>
> STRAIGHT MAN (*probably Raymond Paine*): You did not perchance hear me so good. This is *the fabulous* GAZEEKA BOX!
>
> MILLS: So let's see it gazeek.
>
> PAINE: (*making elaborate gestures in the air, passing a hand over his brow, he intones the magic words*): Abracadabra, gazeeka, gazeeka!

The curtains of the Gazeeka Box part and out of it steps a procession of gorgeous young damsels in evening dresses. Each one is more striking than the one before. And each one of them gives the straight man a kiss before she undulates off the stage.

By now Paine is so excited that he decides not to let the fabulous Gazeeka Box go for less than $200 in cash. Mills still refuses to pay it. Paine evokes another offering from the box. This time the beautiful women that step out of it, each sexier than the one before, are wearing kimonos tantalizingly slit high on the leg. They ignore Mills and only have eyes for Paine. They kiss him and he kisses them back. Mills is beginning to get excited, but when Paine raises the price again, Mills still resists. So now Paine goes into his abracadabra bit all over again. For the third time the curtains part and the girls, each one more voluptuous than the next, are wearing only the skimpiest items of lingerie, some seemingly barely pasted to their bodies. They kiss Paine and he pats them in several spots not covered by the lingerie. They giggle and wiggle off stage. By now Mills's eyes are bugging out of his head. He is sliding his feet around like a bull about to charge a toreador. He can't stand the frustration. One, two, three, four, five, he forks over five century notes to possess the fabulous Gazeeka. Paine congratulates him and walks off the stage counting his money. Mills quivering with expectation utters the magic formula, "Abracadabra, gazeeka, gazeeka!"

Out of the curtained box, limping and staggering, come a procession of crones, each older and uglier than the one before, and each of them hackling and hooting their undying love for Steve Mills. It was all visual, and it was a sure-fire crowd pleaser.

The Rest of the Candy Butcher Spiel

"Now I must tell you about this little book . . . the book that made Paris famous, the book that we had translated into black and white English and shipped to us in plain, unmarked cartons." At this point the candy butcher would hold up a small book to the audience and a boy would suddenly run down the aisle with a telegram. The butcher would tear open the telegram, scan it briefly, and his face would appear to be totally crestfallen.

"Ah, my friends, the worst has happened! This telegram is from my attorney in Paris. The bubble has burst! I can only sell these few books, my stock has been confiscated by the authorities. They are narrow-minded, bigoted people, not like you and I, men and women of the world. Ladies and gentlemen, my friends, I thank each and every one of you for your most kind and courteous attention. May God bless all of you. I regret that we will have to discontinue the sales of these books, since the authorities have no appreciation of the true art contained in this forbidden book. To give you an idea on the inside of this book you would have found about forty-two of the spiciest, forty-two of the raciest, forty-two of the peppiest, forty-two of the sexiest stories that have ever appeared in the English language. They have all been translated from the French, and in the translation they have lost none of their glamour and none of their spice. In fact, I defy anyone in the audience to read one page of any story in this book and then put it down without finishing it, because it leaves nothing to the imagination; it is written in plain English, using the same words that you yourself would use whether they're in the dictionary or not. In this limited time I cannot give you the details of all the stories, but I'll give you a rough idea by describing two of them. The first story is called 'The Madam and the Sailor.' This story contains an account of a sailor in the French Navy whose sweetheart ran one of those places in Paris where young men go for pleasure and ladies accept tips for their service. And if you think a French girl doesn't know how to give service, you're crazy. This story tells you how a sailor went away on a nine-month cruise, how he's forced to stay on the boat, and of course, during all that time he never saw a woman. When he comes back at the end of nine months you will find out how he raced upstairs to the madam's apartment, very eager and very excited. He knocked on the door and the maid answered. Then he walked into the madam's 'bood-war,' what we call a bedroom, and there was the madam just as she'd returned from the bathroom after taking a bath. [The Pitchman paused here for dramatic effect.] Well, you can imagine yourself in the place of that man. He hasn't seen a woman for nine months, remember. And he is eager as a beaver. Now, if the rest of this story wouldn't make your hair stand right up on end, either you're getting old or there's something wrong with you. Maybe you ought to go see a doctor.

"There's another story here that I remember called 'The Farmer's Daughter and the Traveling Salesman.' Of course, we all know about this, how the hotel clerk asks him to sleep with the baby. Well, that's not the story. This is an up-to-date version. Instead of the salesman going to the farm, the farmer's daughter comes to the city, meets the salesman in a hotel, and what happens is guaranteed to give you a thrill and the biggest laugh you ever had in your life.

"Also I'd like to call your attention to a photograph on page thirty-eight of a young lady who is lying down on what they call in France a 'chayze long.' This lady doesn't seem to have any clothes on, and you will notice that she has a very sad expression on her face. She looks as though she had been doing a lot of hard work, and you can imagine what kind of work that was. However, if you can't imagine it, just turn the book upside down, as I am demonstrating, place the palm of your hand over the lower part of this young lady's anatomy, and what you're going to see there will surprise you! In other words, you're going to see the sight of a lifetime. And what you see is nobody's business but your own! But unfortunately, these books have been banned by the French government, so you can imagine just what kind of material is in here."

At this point, one of the assistant candy butchers comes up and whispers in the pitchman's ear. He looks around himself in a wary way. He talks to one of the assistants in the rear of the house. "Tell me, Harry, are you sure they're no managers in the house? No? Good! All right, ladies and gentlemen. What I'm gonna do now could get me in a lot of trouble. But you all look pretty discreet to me so I'm going to risk it. On this occasion and on this occasion alone I will offer you the chance to purchase these remarkable French books hot off the docks that you'll never have a chance to see again in your lifetime. Even if you went to 'gay Paree' yourself. Now, just to make it interesting, we will include a little novelty item imported directly from Paris, France. I have in my hands what appears to be an ordinary square of black paper. But this is no ordinary square black paper. You take this paper home, you soak it in vinegar, you hold it up to the light, and you will see sights that will amaze and astound you. For all of this we are not charging a dollar, we are not charging fifty cents, but a quarter is our price. For that quarter you will get a free box of chewy, delicious bonbons absolutely free, plus this forbidden book available for this performance only and a spicy, French novelty from Paris, France. And remember, concealed in some of these boxes is a selection of bonus gifts. You buy the candy and you may receive either the watch, a twenty-dollar bill in an alligator skin wallet, the key to a Ford automobile, or a season's pass to this theater."

ACKNOWLEDGMENTS

It's been almost fifty years since we were forced to close our last major burlesque theater by edict of the administration of Mayor Fiorello La Guardia. Since then my memory may have slipped a bit on details of what took place during the Minsky era in burlesque. Milt Machlin, my writing colleague, and I have therefore taken the liberty of referring to a number of excellent books covering the era, and have also conferred with experts in the field of burlesque who were of great value in refreshing my memory of certain details, or lending the benefit of their knowledge to Mr. Machlin. Among these were Joey Faye; Dr. Joseph Lesser, of New York University; Dr. William Green, of Queens College; Sherry Britton, former stripper; Dr. Joan Pirie, also of NYU; and others.

Some of the books I used for reference were:

Alexander, H. M. *Strip Tease: The Vanished Art of Burlesque.* New York: Knight Publishers, 1977.

Allen, Ralph G. "At My Mother's Knee (and Other Low Joints). In *Popular Entertainment,* edited by Myron Matlaw. Westport, Conn.: Greenport Publishing.

Barber, Rowland. *The Night They Raided Minsky's.* New York: Simon and Schuster, 1960.

Corio, Ann, with Joe DiMona. *This Was Burlesque.* New York: Grosset and Dunlap, 1968.

Green, Abel, and Joe Laurie Jr. *Show Biz: From Vaude to Video.* New York: Holt, 1951.

Green, William. "Strippers and Coochers." in *Western Popular Theatre*. London: Methuen and Co. Ltd, 1977.

Havoc, June. *More Havoc*. New York: Harper and Row, 1980.

Lee, Gypsy Rose. *Gypsy*. New York: Harper, 1957.

Sobel, Bernard. *Burleycue*. New York: Farrar Reinhart, 1931.

Zeidman, Irving. *The American Burlesque Show*. New York: Hawthorne, 1967.